FRAMING SUKKOT

Jason Baird Jackson, *editor*

FRAMING SUKKOT
Tradition and Transformation in Jewish Vernacular Architecture

Gabrielle Anna Berlinger

Indiana University Press, in cooperation with the
Mathers Museum of World Cultures, Indiana University

This book is a publication of

Indiana University Press
Office of Scholarly Publishing
Herman B Wells Library 350
1320 East 10th Street
Bloomington, Indiana 47405 USA

iupress.indiana.edu

© 2017 by Gabrielle Anna Berlinger
A free digital edition of this book is available at IUScholarWorks:
http://hdl.handle.net/2022/21232.

All rights reserved

No part of this book may be reproduced or utilized in any form or by any means, electronic or mechanical, including photocopying and recording, or by any information storage and retrieval system, without permission in writing from the publisher. The Association of American University Presses' Resolution on Permissions constitutes the only exception to this prohibition.

The paper used in this publication meets the minimum requirements of the American National Standard for Information Sciences—Permanence of Paper for Printed Library Materials, ANSI Z39.48-1992.

Manufactured in the United States of America

Library of Congress Cataloging-in-Publication Data

Names: Berlinger, Gabrielle A., author.
Title: Framing sukkot : tradition and transformation in Jewish vernacular architecture / Gabrielle Anna Berlinger.
Description: Bloomington, Indiana : Indiana University Press, [2017] | Series: Material vernaculars | Includes bibliographical references and index.
Identifiers: LCCN 2017041133 (print) | LCCN 2017036944 (ebook) | ISBN 9780253031839 (e-book) | ISBN 9780253031815 (cloth : alk. paper) | ISBN 9780253031822 (pbk. : alk. paper)
Subjects: LCSH: Sukkah—Buildings, structures, etc.
Classification: LCC BM695.S8 (print) | LCC BM695.S8 B47 2017 (ebook) | DDC 296.4/33—dc23
LC record available at https://lccn.loc.gov/2017041133

1 2 3 4 5   23 22 21 20 19 18

All photographs are by the author.

Contents

Acknowledgments	*ix*
Note on Language Use	*xiii*
Introduction	1
"A New Generation Is Living in Tents..."	1
Into the Field	3
An Ephemeral, Ritual Architecture	6
A Transient Shelter on a Journey Home	7
A Permanent Place	9
A Folklorist's Approach	10
Guiding Questions	11
Evolving Methods and Meanings: Vernacular Architecture Studies	12
Ritual and Festival Studies	14
Jewish Folklore	18
Theory in Practice	19
Mapping the Book	20
1 Translating Text: *Sukkot* in Bloomington, Indiana	27
In Text	27
In Architecture	31
In Ritual Performance	33
Bloomington Vignettes	36
Key Infrastructures	37
Bakol Geller	39
Yonit Kosovske	43
Mediating Tradition	46
2 Shchunat Hatikva, Tel Aviv: A Geography of Difference	49
Drawing Borders of Distinction	50
North and South	52

	Ashkenazi and Mizrahi	60
	Israeli and Foreign	65
3	Within Shchunat Hatikva: Values and Spaces	79
	Shuk Hatikva	79
	Bnei Yehuda	83
	Houses of Worship and Sites of Belonging	88
4	*Sukkot* in Shchunat Hatikva	107
	Sukkot in Practice	107
	Place and Protection	111
	Gratitude and Grace	125
	Relativism and Labor	139
5	*Sukkot* in Jaffa and Jerusalem	152
	Dreams and Love	153
	Family and Equality	166
6	The Right to House and Home	178
	Building Sukkot in the Park	184
	The Last Night	186
	"Without Aravah, Nothing Is Equal"	187
	Occupy Sukkot	192
7	Transcending Architecture: *Sukkot* in Brooklyn, New York	195
	Joseph Piekarski	197
	Rabbi Chaim Halberstam	198
	Mayer Preger	201
	Rabbi Ephraim Piekarski	203
	Conclusion	209
	Objects and their Reach	209
	Equality	211
	Ephemerality	212
	The Right to House and Home	213
	Memory and Modernity	215

Appendix: Materials Chart and Sukkot Floor Plans	*221*
Bibliography	*237*
Index	*243*

Acknowledgments

Like building a sukkah, writing this book has brought together friends and family, newcomers and neighbors, to create a space for sharing. I am grateful to so many who helped build and dwell in this space with me.

In graduate school, I received my first guiding lights from my dissertation advisors. Henry Glassie has been my model of an ethical folklorist and compassionate scholar, offering endless support and vision. Michael D. Foster and Judah M. Cohen showed me how intellectually curious scholars could pursue their work with artistry and integrity. For Jason Baird Jackson, my advisor and friend from the first day of my graduate studies, few words can convey my immense gratitude. He has been my steadfast supporter and motivator, inspiring me with his hard work, commitment, and ideals. I owe each of these mentors a great debt for cultivating the highest standards of committed research, writing, and collaboration, and for continually encouraging me with their personal wisdom and kindness. Many other faculty and staff members in the Department of Folklore and Ethnomusicology and in the Jewish Studies Program at Indiana University, Bloomington, offered valuable support to me over the years as well, and to each one I am deeply grateful.

Continuing this project during my Andrew W. Mellon Postdoctoral Fellowship at the Bard Graduate Center and as Assistant Professor of American Studies and Folklore and Babette S. and Bernard J. Tanenbaum Fellow in Jewish History and Culture at the University of North Carolina at Chapel Hill, has been immeasurably enriched by the support of colleagues and students. In particular, Bernie Herman, Marcie Cohen Ferris and Bill Ferris, Patricia Sawin, and Glenn Hinson have welcomed me into a North Carolina folklore community with warmth and generosity, and the UNC American Studies and Jewish Studies faculties have energized me with their curiosity and commitment to interdisciplinary exchange.

I am also thankful for the funding that has enabled me to study, research, and write. My doctoral studies were funded by the Jacob K. Javits Fellowship Program of the US Department of Education and by Grants-in-Aid of Research from the Robert A. and Sandra S. Borns Jewish Studies Program at Indiana University. Hebrew language study and preliminary field research were funded through a Foreign Language and Area Studies Grant from the Center for the Study of Global Change at Indiana University and the US Department of Education, and a Pre-Dissertation Travel Grant from the Office of the Vice President for International Affairs at Indiana University. My dissertation writing was further supported by a College of Arts and Sciences Dissertation Completion Year Fellowship from Indiana University. All of these resources allowed me to undertake, pursue, and complete this research.

Beyond the university, the individuals who became my community of scholars and friends during my fieldwork in Indiana, Israel, and New York deserve my greatest appreciation. Without their open doors and open hearts, their interest in and patience with my questions, and their willingness to share their life experiences and beliefs with me, my research would not have been possible. To these individuals and so many others whom I cannot all name here, you give this project its spirit, meaning, and reason for being. Thank you, Pnina, Adi, Neta, Amir, Itay, and Asaf Cohen; Dror and Smadar, Suad (Tikva), Sharon and Yair, Doron and Fani, and Ronen Kahalani; Simon Tobi; Yoram, Yonah, and Gila Meshumar; Uriel, David and Edna Zada; Zina and David Borochov; Shmuel, the pomegranate juicer in the *shuk*; Eliyahu and Batya Saig; Simcha and Chaim Maimon; Nisim Boaron; Yosef and Naomi Meshulam; Dina and Yitzhak Emunah; Amnon Hezkiah; Shaul and Sivan Moyal; Drori Yehoshua; Baruch, Meital, and Israel Rada; Lea Chekol; Dana and Itzik Amsalem; Pazit and Zehorit Adani; and all the women in the Beit Dani Community Center Senior Program who treated me like a granddaughter, feeding and blessing me daily; Bakol Geller; Yonit Kosovske; Rabbi Chaim Halberstam; Mayer Preger; Joseph Piekarski; and Rabbi Ephraim Piekarski. For the honesty, wisdom, kindness, and friendship that all of these individuals shared with me, I am deeply indebted.

Colleagues and friends inspired and supported me through every stage of this project. To Selina Morales and Aaron Spector, Maria Kennedy, Chris and Anna Mulé, Thomas Grant Richardson and Carrie Hertz, Rachel González-Martin, Jen Boles, Erin and Mike Lee, Devi Mays, Devorah Shubowitz, Zilia Estrada, Suzanne Godby Ingalsbe, Hsin-wen Hsu, Teri Klassen, Allison Distler, Paul Colbert, and Ed O'Brien, you made Bloomington a home for me and helped me write this chapter of life. In New York, Kay Turner, Steve Zeitlin, Amanda Dargan, Miles Robert Parker, and Wendy Weiss shared an appreciation for the beauty and humor of everyday life amidst and despite New York's madness, and I will always be grateful. My colleagues and friends in Israel were also invaluable contributors to my growth, learning, and quality of life during my fieldwork. Karen Ross, Fiona Wright, Maya Shapiro, Lisa Feinberge, Sonia Smith, Mary Loitsker, Vicki Idzinski, and Tal Shamur, thank you for listening, empathizing, and challenging me in the field. Last of all, I thank my cousin Roni Arbel who, on a whim on the last day of Sukkot in 2009, dropped me off at the curb on Etsel Street in Shchunat Hatikva when I asked him where I might photograph sukkot in Tel Aviv. Without knowing it, he gave the next years of my life meaning and direction.

Gary Dunham, Janice Frisch, and the staff at Indiana University Press deserve great appreciation for believing in this project and supporting its publication with the highest level of collaboration and professional expertise. I am indebted to them for their wise advice and patience. I also thank the two readers who provided valuable comments on the manuscript.

This book honors my great-grandparents Hanna and Naphtali, Frieda and Shmuel, Bryna and Itzhak, and Shayndel and Menachem who built sukkot in Germany, Romania, Hungary, and Palestine. My family and close ones at home have always been my foundation. Vicki and Mike Grove, JD and Bruce, Silvan and Jasper, you have each buoyed me with your enthusiasm and interest in my research, and you have inspired me with your ability to live so close to the earth and to your core values with simultaneous sincerity and wit. My parents and sister have allowed me to push their curiosity, generosity, and love to the limit as I have relied on them for intellectual exchange, emotional support, and comic relief over these ten years of research and writing. My mother and father have offered unending kindness, encouragement, and patience as the most thoughtful readers and keenest editors. They have read this manuscript more times than I can count. I love you and could not have found my way without you. To Michael Grove, you have brought light, art, and love into your houses and into my life. I dedicate this book to you and our little Alice Frieda.

Note on Language Use

One of the most challenging, yet rewarding, features of this research project was navigating multiple language situations during my fieldwork in South Tel Aviv. Although I spoke, read, and wrote Hebrew conversationally when I set out into the field, I planned to conduct my interviews in English and alternate between the two languages in everyday exchanges as needed. Unexpectedly, most of the Jewish residents of Shchunat Hatikva, the main site of this ethnographic work, did not speak enough English to converse at length with me, and most of their grown children, first- and second-generation Israelis who did speak English fluently, had moved out of the neighborhood. The remaining older residents spoke a variety of Arabic dialects, having emigrated largely from countries across the Middle East and North Africa, and had learned Hebrew as a second language after settling in Israel. At home with family or friends, they often communicated in their mother tongues, but Hebrew was the language that they spoke in public and in which I communicated with them. Thus, by necessity, my Hebrew fluency increased rapidly from the first day of my fieldwork. Fortunately, many people in the community sympathized with my early struggle to improve my Hebrew and took me under their wings, helping to translate complex exchanges as well as they could. The partnerships we formed through this process were an unexpected and meaningful boon to my fieldwork experience, helping to integrate me into the community and gain trust through mutual dependency.

While writing this ethnography, I relied upon professional translators and native speakers of Hebrew to assist me in the precise translation of formal interviews as well as informal recordings made throughout my sixteen months of fieldwork. When transliteration as well as translation of Hebrew words was needed, I drew upon the American National Standards Institute (ANSI) transliteration of Hebrew as the guide by which to ensure consistency. All italicized words are transliterated from Hebrew unless otherwise noted.

Regarding names, I have used a variety of ways of referring to those whom I quote in this book. Following standard academic practice, I cite scholars by their full name first, and then by last name only in every subsequent instance. Most often, I refer not to academic scholars but to those with whom I lived and worked during my fieldwork research—the sukkah builders and users who informed this research and my collaborators on the ground. Although I introduce them initially by their full names, I then refer to them by first name only, in contrast to my references to scholars. These individuals became friends in the course of my research and calling them by last name only would inaccurately represent the

xiii

relationships we formed as well as the way that family, friends, neighbors, and I addressed them in everyday life. When individuals outside the community, particularly those with official positions such as rabbis, enter the research, I refer to them as they were addressed by community members; for example, Rabbi Amsalem, rather than Chaim Amsalem or Amsalem. In no way are the people whom I refer to by first name only of less distinction than those referred to by last name only, and in no way is the information that they provided me with of less value. Indeed, the friends that I made during my research and the knowledge that they shared with me are the heart of this book, and the meaning of this work comes from them.

FRAMING SUKKOT

Introduction

"A New Generation Is Living in Tents . . ."

In the fall of 2011, as the Jewish holiday of *Sukkot* approached, I would often bike to *Gan Hatikva* (Garden of Hope), a small park in South Tel Aviv, Israel, where members of the surrounding neighborhood had erected a protest encampment as part of the civil demonstrations that had erupted earlier that summer. On July 14, 2011, following the Arab Spring and just ahead of the Occupy Movement in the United States, Israeli undergraduate film student Daphni Leef had pitched a tent on the café-lined Rothschild Boulevard in central Tel Aviv and slept in it to protest the increasing rent of her apartment. In the following days, students inspired by Leef's action joined her demonstration against Israel's escalating costs of living. Their protest set off a national response as disparate communities across the country suddenly seized the moment to proclaim their numerous frustrations about Israeli society. Foremost among their concerns was the ongoing government corruption that had perpetuated structures of social inequality that disproportionately affected their quality of life. These daily injustices had often been neglected while threats to national security commanded the nation's attention and resources, but Israel's disaffected citizens had now stepped into the spotlight. Members of different social classes and ethnic communities joined together to challenge economic inequality, public housing shortages, and fundamental social inequality. As the months passed and the demonstrations continued, outdoor protest encampments took root and spread across the country.

Biking to Gan Hatikva in the morning or the late afternoon to check on the state of the camp became my daily routine during these months. I sat with protesters drinking cups of *café shachor* (black coffee) prepared in the outdoor "kitchen"—a small trailer with a refrigerator, wooden table, camping burners, and an electric water heater—and attended planning meetings to discover who had been confronted by police or municipal authorities overnight. As I sipped my coffee, I would listen to the stories of the day: the camp's electricity had gone out again, rain had flooded half the tents the previous night, the encampment had split into two adversarial groups because of disagreements over representation. Though internal conflicts over leadership in the park's community were increasing, the group remained a united force when confronting the larger city beyond.

One afternoon, as the encampment's leaders gathered with megaphones to organize a march, a woman's voice rang out in song from the center of the crowd:

We have no money	אין לנו כסף
We have no home	אין לנו בית
There is a new generation living in tents	יש דור חדש שגר באוהלים
Without gas, without water	בלי גז, בלי מים
Only heaven and mercy come to us from above	רק השמים ודחמים אלינו ממרום

Other protesters soon joined her, their voices projecting strong familiarity with the words and melody, which, unknown to me, had been sung a generation ago. In the early 1990s, singer George Bar had released "Children of Tents," the song from which this chorus was taken. It was a response to the state's failing system of public housing, against which residents of South Tel Aviv were protesting back then, as they were on this day. The working-class women and men who had adopted this song as their anthem two decades earlier to draw attention to their neglected living conditions had raised children who had inherited the same conditions and struggle. On this Tuesday evening, many of those children, who were now single mothers and homeless residents, recounted that story for me. "I remember my aunt living in a tent in this park twenty years ago. Every twenty years it happens," one woman told me before the group began to march, conveying her sense of the inescapable nature of the situation. "I'm doing this because I hope my children won't be living in tents twenty years from now."

For nearly six months, these low-income residents of South Tel Aviv inhabited nylon tents and makeshift wooden huts that they had erected in the park of Gan Hatikva. The middle-class college students who had fomented the summer's demonstrations had remained in their tents on Rothschild Boulevard only through September, when the academic year began. However, the city had granted the residents of South Tel Aviv permission to remain in their tents beyond September since these low-income and homeless families, many with young children, had fewer options for relocation. For this segment of the protesting public, the encampment had become their permanent shelter. As evidence of this stark reality, some protesters had built temporary shacks in the park out of scrap lumber and recycled pieces of plywood, some even wrote their names on the outside of their scavenged doors to create a new sense of community. These shacks stood side by side with the tents, together affirming the need for support. By the time the weeklong Jewish holiday of Sukkot arrived in early October, the encampment was not only filled with protest tents and huts, but also with *sukkot*, the holiday's temporary ritual architectures that are symbolic of domestic space.[1] For the one week of Sukkot that year, temporary ritual architectures flanked the temporary protest huts, demanding recognition for both the fragility of physical shelter and the strength of its builders.

Although I had chosen to research the holiday of Sukkot because of the literal and symbolic meanings of the holiday's ritual actions—primarily, the construction and use of a temporary dwelling—as political demonstrations in Tel Aviv persisted throughout the summer and fall of 2011, I found myself examining the protest movement in ways that paralleled my analysis of the Sukkot ritual. Both events were distinguished by social relationships that were forming and dissolving throughout their performance, and both were characterized by evocative narratives and imagery that reached beyond the present moment into past and future circumstances. Most striking, however, was the shared use of temporary, vernacular architecture as a tool of communication, political power, and a declaration of values and belief. The biblical narrative of Sukkot commemorates the search for both a physical shelter and a conceptual home on the Israelites' journey across the Sinai Desert toward the Promised Land. The struggle for fair housing rights in low-income communities like South Tel Aviv is a contemporary expression of the same yearning. This is the ongoing quest that animated the ancient holiday and the present-day protest: the search for housing and the longing for home. This book explores how the construction, use, and interpretation of the sukkah in contemporary life shed light on the relationship between individuals and their sense of place in local and remote Jewish communities, as well as how they envision "home" in near and distant contexts.

Into the Field

During the heat of that summer of 2011, I was nearing the end of one year in the field, having established myself in a low-income, multiethnic, multicultural neighborhood of South Tel Aviv, Israel, to study contemporary Sukkot observance. I had planned to document two cycles of the weeklong holiday's ritual practice, and in between those celebrations of 2010 and 2011, I would participate in the life of the neighborhood as fully as I could. A broader understanding of the residents' daily customs, work routines, social activities, cultural events, and religious practices would enable me to contextualize their weeklong Sukkot observance.

The holiday of Sukkot has been celebrated by Jews around the world for one week each fall for over three thousand years. The timing of this holiday with the harvest season is not a coincidence for Sukkot is known in Hebrew as *chag ha-asif*, or "Festival of Ingathering," a name that evokes an agricultural peak and abundant harvest. Alternatively called *chag ha-sukkot*, however, or "Festival of Tabernacles," this holiday also commemorates a seminal historical narrative: the forty-year period during which the Israelites searched for the Promised Land after the exodus from Egypt. Within this historical framing, Sukkot recalls a period of longing and life without permanent shelter. The festival marks a journey toward home and homeland, presents a relationship between people, nature, and the divine, and asserts a reconceptualized notion of "community" in the face of prevailing uncertainty.

I was initially drawn to Sukkot for the variety, creativity, and meaning of the central ritual action of its observance: the construction and decoration of a temporary ritual architecture called the *sukkah* (booth, tabernacle) that is erected outside one's home—in driveways, courtyards, and streets; and even on lawns, sidewalks, terraces, roofs, and fire escapes. The construction and the decoration of this structure, which stands only for the duration of the holiday week, may be understood as a material expression of the builders' and users' social, cultural, and physical environments, as well as of their religious observance. By documenting contemporary Sukkot ritual practice in a dense and diverse working-class neighborhood of South Tel Aviv, I sought to discover patterns within material variety and the social meanings that those patterns created.

By the end of the first cycle of the holiday in September 2010, I had taken over one thousand photographs and recorded dozens of audio files—the sound of hammers banging on wood planks during the days of construction, the strict orders of sukkah builders about erecting a wooden frame or constructing a brush roof, and informal conversations of family members about cherished Sukkot traditions. But as the second cycle of the holiday approached in 2011, unexpected sociopolitical events developed in Israel that compelled the public to reenvision Sukkot in a dramatic new way. Beyond the cultural and religious expressions I had recorded the previous year, during the holiday week of 2011, I documented unprecedented demonstrations against social and economic inequality in Israel that coincided with worldwide national and international demonstrations known as the Occupy Movement. Participants in the Israeli protests seamlessly incorporated the messages of the protest movement into the material and spiritual practice of Sukkot, adding a striking new interpretation of the ancient narrative of the holiday. Drawing upon shared Jewish history, the past illuminated the fractured Jewish present.

This ethnography began as a folkloristic study of contemporary Sukkot observance in a multiethnic neighborhood of South Tel Aviv. I documented the construction, decoration, and use of the sukkot structures I visited, contextualized by the lived experiences, individual interpretations, and beliefs of their builders and users. I considered the multiple dimensions of thought and landscape in which builders and users created the ritual architecture, how they used materials for their construction and ornamentation, and how they communicated the meaning of the structure's separate parts and entirety during the Sukkot holiday.[2] Furthermore, I situated the temporary ritual activities of the week within the ongoing life patterns of the builders and users throughout the year in order to frame the ritual moment with surrounding layers of meaningful experience. Expanding this folkloristic study, the protests in Israel further revealed that Sukkot ritual practice may offer a creative response to both historic experience and current circumstance. Holiday observance provided "equipment for living"—resources that allowed for a reevaluation of the past and present in order to envision an idealized future.[3]

I discovered these resources not only in Israel. From 2007 through 2015, prior to and following my sixteen months of research in Israel, I documented Sukkot observance in Bloomington, Indiana, and Brooklyn, New York, bracketing the diversity I observed in Israel with these two contrasting communities and deepening the meaning I found within the patterns of this material tradition. In the dispersed and largely assimilated Jewish community of Bloomington, a Midwestern American town, and in the densely populated Orthodox Jewish community of urban Brooklyn, the interpretations of sukkah builders and users expanded beyond the holiday observance I encountered in contemporary Israel and enlarged my understanding of the role of this ritual in Jewish life.

What purpose does an ancient ritual of placemaking serve in the lives of twenty-first century Jews who are born and live throughout the world, speak different languages, and identify with their Jewishness and national and local cultures in radically divergent ways? How do such different individuals interpret the holiday's historic and agricultural narratives that recall an annual harvest, a forty-year journey in the wilderness, and a search for a home? How does their creative material construction mediate between past, present, and future, self and society, and reality and hope? The individuals whom you meet in this book practice Sukkot rituals with intention, determination, and artistry. Their traditions are rooted in an historic holy text, nurtured through material creation, and renewed through their personal interpretation of a shared practice. Thus, Jewish text, material culture, and interpretive discourse are linked in the ritual tradition of Sukkot, this book foregrounding the material culture of this religious practice, the individual within its festival performance, and the narrative expression of its architectural act. Each participating family in this book imparts a message through the distinctive creation and use of their ritual structure that reaches beyond the boundaries of the holiday week: a message about social values, community cohesion, or hope—one that anchors them in the past and projects them into the future despite an unstable present. These individuals build and use their sukkot each year to locate their place on a journey toward a "home" that is no longer a physical destination but a metaphor and ideal.

In a period of constant migration, immigration, and displacement around the world, how do people envision the dream of home? How do people experience a feeling of home in their actual places of residence? The sukkah presents a temporary architectural construction that is symbolic of the domestic space in structure, ornamentation, and use. Its structure, in particular, symbolizes home in three powerful ways: as an ephemeral, ritual architecture; as a transient shelter during journeys of migration and immigration; and as a permanent place. Although seemingly dissimilar, these three evocations of the sukkah's structure coexist simultaneously to lend the sukkah its range of richly nuanced meanings and relevance across the world today.

An Ephemeral, Ritual Architecture

The concept of the sukkah as an ephemeral, ritual architecture seems to contrast with the notion of a home space or a permanent architecture. Religious law requires that the structure be temporary, leading scholars to interpret the space within the sukkah as liminal, a place where binaries coexist and conflicting circumstances arise where elsewhere they may not. For architect and cultural scholar Miriam Lipis, sukkot are "hybrid places of belonging" that allow for "the tendency of those in a diaspora to look backward, creating ties to a distant place through memories" (2011, 107). At the same time, however, she notes the "liberatory powers of diaspora," where individuals are released from "a monolithic connection to a single place" (107). The sukkah can be simultaneously located in a shared imagination and disparate actualities, she says: "The architecture of the ritual houses creates a space where divergent places can meet, the local and Jerusalem, the real and the mythical, the text and the territory, home and diaspora" (107). Her insight into the potential of this "hybrid" space to evoke multiple time periods and places at once corresponds with a development in Jewish Studies and, more broadly, cultural studies toward space- and place-based studies.[4] As the world globalizes through expanding technology and increasing migration, we attempt to understand the changing relationships between individuals and physical places and how those changes affect perceptions of belonging to communities, societies, and nations. Because of its multiple, concurrent meanings, the sukkah can be seen as a microcosm of this evolving sense of place, a place where contrasting perceptions meet and collide.

Others claim that the ritual construction of the sukkah challenges the ancient idea of Jerusalem as the center of the Jewish religious world by viewing it as a place-making practice that strengthens networks of Jewish centers around the world. Barbara E. Mann describes the current Jewish world as "post-*makom*," post-"space" or post-"place"—a world in which Jewish spatial practices are "widening circles of engagement" rather than pendulum swings between exile and homeland (2012, 154). The *eruv* (a ritual enclosure that expands the private domain to public spaces) and the sukkah are two key examples of this phenomenon as domestic space is extended through the construction, transposition, or multiplication of ritual space (3, 154). Similarly, Galit Hasan-Rokem considers the biblical prescription of Sukkot observance, together with the historical and symbolic evocations of the structure and the environmental and cultural adaptations that observers have integrated into their ritual practices, to be elements of a process that disrupts the dichotomy between movement and placement in Jewish culture (2012, 164).

All these scholars perceive the power of the sukkah's ritual nature to remap Jewish geography through its liminal, place-making potential. Through its material construction and use, the sukkah integrates past experience and hope for the future into present conditions, splitting former binaries into prisms of possibility. These possibilities embedded in the ritual construction attest to the mobility of the Jewish people and the adaptability of Jewish practice, and they deconstruct the single, concentric model of the Jewish world with Israel at its center. My interest in the sukkah as an ephemeral, ritual architecture is not intended to contest the notion of Israel as a homeland from which a diaspora remains displaced; rather, given the space of material and spiritual possibility created through sukkah construction and ritual performance, I seek to understand how tensions that are otherwise suppressed may be expressed—how interactions of individuals in the liminal space of the sukkah create reconciliation between lived experience and imagined possibility. Mann asserts that the biblical desert in the story of Sukkot is not actually a landscape of punishment and deprivation in opposition to a Promised Land, as it is commonly imagined to be, but rather, "a psychologically rich site, one characterized by conflicting desires and the tension between promise and delivery, between present conditions and future possibilities" (2012, 83). She views the desert as an ambiguous space, one of potential. Similarly, the sukkah, which originated in that setting, is an ambiguous place of tension and action that bridges individual practice and social performance, religion and politics, private and public space, reflection and action, and doubts and dreams.

A Transient Shelter on a Journey Home

Within its historical frame, the biblical narrative of Sukkot recounts a decades-long journey across the Sinai Desert in search of the Promised Land. The annual observance of Sukkot offers recurring opportunities to reinterpret this biblical journey in the context of contemporary life. Conceptually, observers seek to define how the holiday's themes of transience and permanence, materiality and spirituality, and wilderness and domestication illuminate their own values and ways of life. In fact, many sukkah builders and users have faced times of immigration or migration in their lives. All of the Jews in Bloomington, Indiana, whom I researched had relocated to this small Midwestern town from larger East Coast and West Coast cities for educational or job opportunities. The Jews in South Tel Aviv who became my friends and research partners came to Israel from Middle Eastern, North African, and Central Asian countries in the decades following the founding of the State of Israel in 1948; and the Orthodox Lubavitcher Jews in New York trace their community's journey to Brooklyn back to their spiritual leader's emigration from Russia after World War II. The geographic and emotional separation from their native homelands, common to all the Jews in this book because of their own, their parents', or their grandparents' dislocation, imbues their Sukkot holiday practice with personal and powerful notions of home.

Current-day Sukkot observance in the United States and Israel illustrates how individuals convey the personal and collective histories, circumstances, values, and beliefs that shape their notions of home through the construction of material environments. However, people locate meaning in different elements of the sukkah's physical form: its frame, decoration, roof covering, or the totality of its architecture. The varied meanings attached to these different material elements reveal the great range of interpretation that this Jewish ritual practice evokes. This variety appeals to a critical approach to the study of "vernacular religion," defined by Leonard Primiano as "religion as it is lived: as human beings encounter, understand, interpret, and practice it" (1995, 51). Rather than relying upon the often-hierarchical and reductive categories of "folk," "unofficial," or "popular" religion to describe religious practice, Primiano integrates the perspectives of folklore and religious studies to emphasize the intimacy, the artistry, and the agency that characterize individual belief systems. These values center this study of Sukkot from the perspective of vernacular religion.

The chapters that follow present contrasting conceptions of home that are linked to associations of nation, ethnicity, equality, and the divine. These ideals emerge from the sukkah builders' and users' personal and shared experiences of home, and they are communicated through their individual ritual constructions. Across the varied interpretations of this symbolic home, however, three facets of the sukkah builders' and users' lives are linked in a dynamic relationship: their physical place in the world, the material expression of their beliefs and experiences, and their particular dream. Across geographies and cultures, we witness how the creative shaping and interpretation of our material surroundings allow us to transcend them as we individually and collectively search for home. As Philosopher Gaston Bachelard has observed, "the house shelters daydreaming, the house protects the dreamer, the house allows one to dream in peace" (1958, 6). In the context of Sukkot, the dream is the vision of "home" that each sukkah builder nurtures through her or his practice—an ideal state of consciousness in which the integration of thoughts, memories, and hopes is realized.

A Permanent Place

Finally, the sukkah may be considered a permanent place in two distinct respects—spiritual and political. A Jewish resident of South Tel Aviv who emigrated from Iran to Israel in the 1950s and has lived there for decades told me that "in the Talmud, it is written that the sukkah is a metaphor for what is eternal." The dining room in which we were sitting at the time was the temporary structure, he explained, while the sukkah's fabric sheets that were waving in the wind on his terrace created the everlasting refuge. Uprooted from the land in which he was born, and then again from each stop along the journey to his current place of residence, he found security and faith in the spiritual home embodied by the sukkah's structure. The sukkah is a constant, recurring, unfailing place of homecoming.

From a political perspective, the sukkah may also be viewed as an enduring structure when, in particular circumstances, builders transform it from a transitory architecture into a permanent shelter. In South Tel Aviv during the housing demonstrations of 2011, the protesting community in Gan Hatikva built a community sukkah in the park. On the final night of the holiday, they invited a political figure, Rabbi Chaim Amsalem, to meet with them. Gathered inside the sukkah, they first discussed the ethical principles of the holiday, the rabbi interpreting the symbolism and ritual actions of Sukkot. The group then turned to the current living conditions of the community. Homeless and low-income residents who had been camping in the park demanding public housing reform for three months feared the oncoming winter and were in need of permanent shelter, which the wooden structures of the sukkot had provided them during the holiday week. They asked Rabbi Amsalem if they could transform their park sukkot into permanent shelters at the close of the holiday rather than dismantle them as required by Jewish law. Recognizing the personal plea, political statement, and spiritual longing that were all implied in the question, the rabbi responded with an answer that expressed his awareness of their plight and the legitimacy of their request: the sukkah is the house and the home for which we are still searching, and yes, the ritual structure could be simply altered to become an ordinary shelter. As the biblical narrative of impermanent shelter converged with the reality of impermanent shelter in the residents' lives, the sukkah became a ritual means to a sociopolitical end for these homeless individuals.

Sukkot is a timeless holiday. It is an annual event dependably recurring each fall that has been observed by Jews around the world for thousands of years. This particular study of Sukkot unexpectedly coincided with the worldwide socioeconomic instability across the world in the latter half of the first decade of the 2000s that culminated in simultaneous international uprisings: the Arab Spring of 2010; the Spanish "Indignant" Protest Movement of 2011; the subprime mortgage crisis in the United States, which gave way to the Occupy Movement in 2011; and most relevant to my research, the Israeli social protests of 2011. At that particular moment, when homeowners were being evicted into the streets and vast economic inequalities were being exposed, the meaning of this holiday gained a powerful, resonant relevance.

Central themes within the Sukkot narrative, such as the search for shelter and home and the impermanence of the material world, resonated with current housing crises and highlighted a clear relationship between the holiday and the ongoing political, social, and economic upheavals. The flexible nature of traditional practices like those of Sukkot were also realized. By annually reconstructing sukkot to commemorate the Israelites' shelters as they journeyed through the desert, we awaken questions about our present journeys across the deserts of our time.

A Folklorist's Approach

I ground this study upon several key folkloristic principles regarding social and cultural expression. The most essential of these tenets is that all people are creative communicators in their everyday lives. Through different modes of expression, such as religious beliefs and practices, visual arts, storytelling, dance, dress and body adornment, cooking, building traditions, and more, individuals convey their experiences and worldviews to others. These forms of creative expression that give shape to our everyday lives may be likened to genres, each with its own structural design and repertoire of material. Folklorists acknowledge that within each repertoire, certain performances stand out as "virtuosic"—exceptional examples of a form of creative expression that communicate meaning with particular consequence. These are the performances from which folklorists may learn most explicitly about the relationships between the individual and society, the "self" and "other," text and context, form and function, and repetition and innovation. Analyzing the dynamics of these relationships, the tension within them offers insights into why and how we live as we do.

I elected to study Sukkot observance to explore these relationships in two ways: first, to examine how the vernacular construction, decoration, and use of an architecture function as modes of expression and reflection; and, second, to discover how individuals transform everyday, ordinary spaces into temporary, extraordinary spaces for intensified ritual performance. In addition, approaching the study of this Jewish ritual performance from the angle of creative material expression, use, and interpretation, I sought to learn how observers of the holiday define their own and others' social networks locally, nationally, and internationally as part of the complex processes of migration and social adjustment. I observed Sukkot practice across three different social and geographic settings in order to include both American and Israeli Jews as well as majority and minority populations, peoples living in contexts of economic comfort and disadvantage, and circumstances of social inclusion and exclusion. Examining the details of the aesthetic performances that sukkah construction, decoration, and use require, I discovered how the creation of a symbolic home anchors individuals in their current circumstances and enables them to envision their futures, regardless of the differences in socioeconomic status or religious affiliation within these settings.

Guiding Questions

Three critical research questions guided me into the field to pursue this research project by relating it to larger questions of human adaptability and belonging. The first of these questions concerned how individuals design and construct their sukkot today, which located this project in vernacular architecture studies, a subfield within folklore studies.[5] I studied the materials and methods of sukkah construction to identify the physical and metaphysical resources with which individuals build meaningful structures in their lives. In doing this, I sought to understand how people create places in which they feel they belong, most fundamentally exemplified by the space they call "home."

My second question addressed the experience of social belonging. Perceptions of belonging may be based on religious custom and belief, or they may be shaped by political, economic, cultural, social, or individual life experiences. I was interested in the ways in which notions of "self" and "other" are negotiated and expressed in the intensified space of the sukkah, and how Sukkot ritual practice communicates these individual and shared perceptions.

My third question was the broadest, probing the most individually significant purpose of Sukkot observance in contemporary life. What specific elements of sukkah ritual construction and use do builders and users find meaningful and why? Beyond religious obligation or cultural custom, how does the annual reconstruction of this ritual architecture serve them each year? My first question about the physical sukkah required photographic and architectural documentation; my second question about social belonging necessitated observation and discussion of social relations inside and outside the sukkah; this third question about the significance that ritual participation conferred required sukkah builders and users to share their personal interpretations of their particular practice. Their responses drew upon their life histories and broader, personal conceptions of Jewish religion and culture, as well as on information that contextualized their worldviews, such as local political and socioeconomic circumstances. Documenting these individual perspectives was thus an ongoing, open-ended process in which their views became increasingly layered over time.

The answers to these core questions address conversations in the fields of vernacular architecture, ritual and festival, and Jewish folklore to which this work speaks. With respect to vernacular architecture studies, this ethnographic approach to studying the built environment aligns with the work of other, more recent folklorists who emphasize the value of oral testimony and interpretation by the builders and users of the structures, rather than relying upon the study of the physical artifact alone.[7] Within the field of ritual and festival studies, the question of social belonging through individual performance is highlighted in this work, rather than belonging through collective experience. Departing from the common approach to studying ritual and festival events through group participation, emphasizing the individual and her or his relationship to this practice uncovers distinct and complex worldviews, beliefs, and customs that shape perceptions of belonging. Finally, to the field of Jewish folklore, focusing on the builders' and users' interpretations of their Sukkot observance offers new frameworks for and examples of Jewish ritual performance in the twenty-first century.[8] This structural approach to the study of the sukkah's form, and performance-centered approach to the study of its function, contrast with studies of Jewish religious expression that center on the analysis of Jewish texts. It is an in-depth ethnographic study of contemporary Sukkot observance that brings material culture and individual, interpreted performance to the fore as a way of understanding Jewish histories and contemporary cultures. Anyone questioning how people integrate and make meaning from the disparate elements of their past, present, and future through daily expressions of their creative agency will be enlightened by meeting the individuals in this book.

Evolving Methods and Meanings: Vernacular Architecture Studies

The timeframe for the physical construction of a sukkah extends for four days from dusk at the close of *Yom Kippur* (Day of Atonement) to dusk on the first evening of Sukkot, allowing for a gradual building process. Because most sukkah builders dismantle their sukkot soon after the holiday ends, I was only guaranteed the seven festival days during which to observe, photograph, measure, and sketch sukkot in their complete form. My documentation of these sukkot includes exterior and interior photographs, descriptions of the materials used for construction, decoration, roofing, and furniture, measurements of the sukkot's dimensions, sketches of floor plans, and observations of the placement of the sukkot in relation to permanent features of the surrounding environment.

Documentation of the sukkah demonstrated to me the flexibility and subjective nature of meaning that vernacular architecture possesses. Vernacular architecture may be defined as "both a *type of architecture* and an *approach to architectural studies* that emphasizes the intimate relationship between everyday objects and culture, between ordinary buildings and people" (Carter and Cromley 2005, 7)—a statement that emphasizes process as much as product. I considered the builders of the sukkot that I visited to be vernacular architects—individuals who learned to construct their ritual dwellings through informally acquired methods of construction. Consistently, the builders of sukkot—friends and strangers—generously invited me inside their sukkot to document the structures. As they watched me take out my measuring tape to record the length, width, and height of their sukkah's frame in line with standard vernacular architectural methods, they would smile and say it was unnecessary to measure the dimensions. The size of their sukkah, they said, depended on the physical space available for building and on how many people they expected to host, which could vary each year. The significance of the sukkah's size was not measured by its numerical dimensions but by its capacity for hospitality. Its ability to fulfill its purpose, to allow its builders and users to host and be hosted, was the single most determining factor in judging its size. Often, when I sat inside a sukkah with its builders and users, they would tell me that they planned to build an even bigger and better one the following year. The most compelling motivation for the desire to increase its size was the wish to invite more guests.[9]

Despite the builders' bemused smiles, over the course of two holiday cycles I recorded the lengths, widths, and heights of sukkah frames for structural comparison. I soon comprehended, however, the limited meaning of a sukkah's dimensions when not expanded by an understanding of the space inside and the narrative discourse of its builders and users. Although I had modeled my method of documentation on established standards of vernacular architecture study, the builders and users of the sukkot that I studied imbued the materials and methods of their construction with meaning drawn from shared or individual social, cultural, and religious values. The significance of a ritual construction like the sukkah cannot be fully explained through material analysis of its frame structure or roof weaving, or the temporary nature of its existence, but through an understanding of the intentions with which the builders construct it and the users act within it. Toward this end, I focused on the dynamic interaction between architecture, architect, and user.

Since the 1970s, performance-centered studies of expressive culture have proliferated in the field of folklore, but vernacular architecture studies that use performance as a theoretical lens have been less prevalent, especially those that focus specifically on ritual architecture.[10] In 1975, Henry Glassie broadened the field of vernacular architecture studies through his commitment to examining both the process by which form is derived and the rules that govern material creation—which, "like those in a grammar, are unconscious" (Glassie 1975, 21).[11] Since then, scholars have stretched the boundaries of research on built and natural environments with studies of gardens and yards, spatial memory and experience, the transformation from the rural to urban environment, and the role of oral testimony in architectural study.[12] With this in mind, this ethnographic and performance-centered study of the sukkah emphasizes the varied possibilities of an architecture's meaning and definition when analysis of the physical structure is enhanced by the interpretations of its builders and users. The contemporary construction, decoration, and use of the sukkah contributes to the widening scope of the field of vernacular architecture with the goal of encouraging a dynamic inquiry into a ritual architecture in current and recurrent use. Challenging the sole categorizations of the sukkah as "Useful and Functional," "Temporary and Transportable," and "Jewish" within the international survey of traditional architectures in the *Encyclopedia of Vernacular Architecture of the World* (1997), the sukkah builders and users whom I interviewed diversely characterized their structures according to varied social, cultural, economic, and religious qualities.[13] My purpose is to indicate the limitations of the objective classification of a structure whose significance is embedded in the experience and worldview of its builder and user, and to add greater nuance, from an international perspective, to the concept of the sukkah as vernacular architecture.

Ritual and Festival Studies

As a holiday of the biblical calendar, Sukkot contains elements of both festival and ritual events. Observing the holiday demands social performance through which features of the festival form, such as group heritage and identity, are enacted. Observance of the holiday as an embodied social contract, a feature of the ritual form, obligates participants to perform socially by accepting or rejecting religious laws, customs, and values.[14] Beverly Stoeltje has explained that the separation of the festival and ritual genres resulted from attempts by modern religions to eliminate native religions, relegating indigenous systems to "festival" or "fiesta" while "official" religious events were designated "rituals" (1992, 262). Although these two forms of expression were once unified, she clarifies their discrete functions in modern times: "festival" may be viewed as an exploration and experimentation of meaning while "ritual" is an attempt to control it.

Festival exploration and ritual control are both expressed in Sukkot observance through the holiday's central tenets, the notions of hospitality and social belonging. The practice of hospitality lies at the heart of Sukkot observance, manifested in the custom of welcoming outsiders into one's sukkah for food, drink, and rest during the week of the festival. Observers of this custom frequently cite the biblical story of Abraham welcoming three strangers into his tent (Genesis 18) as the model for their generosity. In return for his gesture of kindness, Abraham's unexpected guests reveal to him that his wife will soon bear with a longed-for child. Hospitality to strangers, it is believed, opens a door to unknown providence. As one sukkah builder in South Tel Aviv explained, "God loves hospitality. Abraham our Father searched for guests to host, for God said, 'First you will respect hospitality, then you will respect me.' God loves a person who welcomes guests into his home." The commandment to be hospitable drives social behavior during the week of Sukkot, affirming and questioning the roles of friend and stranger. As a liminal, ritual structure defined by its "moment in and out of time," the sukkah creates a space of intensified inclusivity, suspending ordinary boundaries and beliefs about belonging until the holiday ends (Turner 1969, 96). The imperative to welcome the stranger into the symbolic home temporarily erases the division between outsider and insider and confirms the experience of belonging.

The implications of the Sukkot ritual of hospitality unfolded in significant ways during this research, particularly when considered in the context of the Jewish Diaspora. Historically, the term *Jewish Diaspora* refers to the global dispersion of Jewish people following the Babylonian captivity (sixth century BCE) and the Roman destruction of the Temple (70 CE)—historical events that have engendered a "Jewish self-understanding of collective peoplehood in exile" (Jackson 2006, 18–19). This consciousness was evident in the Sukkot ritual performance that I observed among the sparse Jewish population of a small, Midwestern American city, the dense Orthodox Jewish community in a large East Coast American city, and the multicultural community of Jewish immigrants in a major Israeli city. In these contrasting social environments, discussions about builders' and users' choices regarding sukkah construction and decoration revealed the interrelated local, national, and international networks with which they felt affiliated as members of a dispersed people. An American Jew in the Midwest decorated her sukkah with an Israeli flag to express her connection to Israel and with a treasured Wedgewood plate passed down in her family for generations. Bukharan Jews who emigrated from Uzbekistan to Israel hung a picture of an Uzbeki politician whom they still support alongside fresh Israeli pomegranates and dates, two of the "Seven Species" found in the land of Israel in the Bible. Northeastern American Jews pinned laminated drawings of the Western Wall in Jerusalem on the sides of their sukkah while tinsel decorations and strings of Christmas lights, purchased in a local craft store, dangled above them. Such material interventions in the space of the sukkah express these Jews' multiple identifications and sites of belonging.

The diverse materiality within the custom of sukkah decoration provides vivid examples of "insider"–"outsider" identifications that weave together near and distant landscapes and peoples. As Jason Baird Jackson explains, "the artistic, expressive, and customary practices of globally dispersed populations—which often take on the privileged and self-conscious status of 'heritage'—are central to the establishment and maintenance of a diasporic identity" (2006, 19).

The material traditions of sukkah construction and decoration illustrate how this expression of Jewish "heritage" helps to define an identity in which a sense of belonging is achieved through a nuanced, individual orientation of the self to the "other."[15]

The ritual act of hospitality within the sukkah's space nurtures a second kind of meditation on "self" and "other" that speaks to a broader social awareness. Commenting on the week of Sukkot, when observers move out of their permanent homes to dwell outdoors in impermanent, interim shelters, one sukkah builder, Drori Yeoshua, explained to me the significance of the sukkah's outdoor placement: "The sukkah is a space of meeting. It's supposed to be a way to be together, in solidarity and partnership, before the arrival," he said, referring to the journey to the Promised Land in the biblical narrative. The neutral space of the outdoor sukkah is a place to pause and join together in coexistence, a moment to cross social and physical boundaries. Each year, the ritual of hosting and being hosted in the sukkah prompts this man to contemplate his personal boundaries and open his home and heart to unfamiliarity and difference. "It's not the idea of *v'ahavta l'reaacha camocha* (Love your neighbor as yourself), which is important in and of itself," he said, "but how do people on a long journey in the desert arrive in a new land and all live together? How do people of different cultures come together to create one society?" The ritual sukkah has the power to bridge differences by temporarily creating a time and space for reflection on how to live with each other in fairness and in peace. Interpreting the space of the sukkah as a biblical moment of potential that preceded the Israelites' arrival in the Promised Land, this builder reflected deeply upon how to create a just and equal society today.

The ritual hospitality that distinguishes social behavior during the week of Sukkot from that of the rest of the year was also highlighted during the sociopolitical events that unfolded in South Tel Aviv during the period of my research. For sixteen months between 2010 and 2011, I conducted fieldwork in Shchunat Hatikva, which in Hebrew means "Neighborhood of Hope," a low-income neighborhood of South Tel Aviv, Israel. Shchunat Hatikva is a multiethnic quarter of the city that received waves of Jewish immigrants from Yemen as early as the 1930s, and subsequent waves of Iraqi and Iranian Jews by the 1950s. Today, the neighborhood is also home to Jews from a variety of Middle Eastern, North African, and Central Asian countries including Syria, Egypt, Libya, Morocco, and Uzbekistan. Carrying with it a history of violence and crime that ended decades ago, this rehabilitated working-class neighborhood still struggles to free itself from a stigmatized image in the eyes of the greater city.

In 2005, an influx of non-Jewish foreigners began settling in South Tel Aviv. Eritrean and Sudanese asylum seekers, fleeing violence and hardship in their home countries, sought refuge in Israel and were placed in low-income neighborhoods across the country such as Shchunat Hatikva. The population crossing into Israel reached its peak during the period of my research, and by 2013, the number of Eritrean and Sudanese asylum seekers living within Israel's borders had exceeded sixty thousand. These new populations occupy an undefined place in Israeli society. Allowed to enter the country in search of sanctuary and a better life, they nonetheless have unrecognized status, are denied work permits, and subsist on insufficient aid. The public outcry by the Jewish community of Shchunat Hatikva regarding the incoming asylum seekers resulted from the danger they perceived to the safety, stability, and identity of their neighborhood. As reports of increased crime in the area circulated and concerns for its Jewish identity grew, the community blamed the Israeli government for placing thousands of desperate individuals in the nation's poorest areas. The absorption of large numbers of non-Jews with different social, cultural, religious, and linguistic traditions seemed to them to threaten the Jewish character of their neighborhood and its way of life. This reaction provided me with insights into not only how veteran Jewish residents viewed the newcomers to their neighborhood, but how they viewed themselves and more privileged Israelis, as well as the government—all of which contribute to their sense of "self and "other" that informs their religious, social, and cultural practices.

Although I conducted my research interviews with a focus on Sukkot ritual belief and practice, conversations inevitably expanded to include a range of broader concerns, experiences, and histories. I was not alone in recognizing the likeness between the situation of the asylum-seeker population and the story of Sukkot. When veteran residents explained how they interpreted the Israelites' journey through the Sinai Desert, several individuals connected the narrative of Sukkot to the plight of the tens of thousands of Eritrean and Sudanese asylum seekers who were crossing Egypt into Israel in search of safety and opportunity.[16] They noted this parallel between historic and present events with empathy for the homeless foreigner but also with reserve. They perceived the tension between the ritual obligation to welcome the stranger into one's home, and the fear of doing so. Two contrasting yet comparable journeys toward home now coexisted in a single place, provoking profound questions of social belonging—the first of a Jewish population historically treated as "other" in Israel, ritually reliving the dislocation of the ancient Israelites; and the second, of a non-Jewish population, currently treated as "other" in Israel, displaced from their homelands and seeking refuge.

The first eight months I spent in Shchunat Hatikva were framed by this backlash against the thousands of asylum seekers settling in South Tel Aviv. How does a community reconcile the conflict between an ethical and spiritual commitment to inclusion reinforced by an historic experience of otherness, and the need to compete for diminishing resources, intensified by the fear of losing one's cultural and religious identity?

At its core, Sukkot holds the yearning for belonging and acceptance of others as equals. By examining the ritual of hospitality within the festival space and time of Sukkot, we learn how individuals both in the "Diaspora" and "the Promised Land" enact their particular ways of belonging through physical construction, material decoration, social performance, and personal interpretation of the sukkah. Learning to read these markers of social belonging reveals how the ritual nature of this annual observance enables participants to continually reevaluate and reorient themselves to others in a shared society.

Jewish Folklore

This book crosses temporal and disciplinary boundaries in its analysis of Jewish material culture in order to understand current-day Jewish experience, practice, and social values.[17] Compared with the range of studies from historical, anthropological, sociological, or religious perspectives, folkloristic studies of Jewish social and cultural practices are surprisingly few in number, particularly from the vantage point of material culture.[18] Academic, religious, secular, and popular scholars have published analyses of Sukkot customs and laws based on close readings of religious texts such as the Torah, Mishnah, and Talmud; and historical, sociopolitical, and disciplinary histories of Sukkot explain how the phenomenon of Sukkot observance developed in the United States, Europe, and Israel.[19] However, examinations of Sukkot observance in the modern day that explain its current perpetuation and forms of expression are less common (Ben-Amos 1990; Kirshenblatt-Gimblett 1990).[20]

In order to learn about the diversity of Jewish ritual performance in the twenty-first century, I sought out perspectives from the practitioners themselves, sukkah builders' and users' interpretations of their own ritual practice, that reveal the nuances of how individual and shared experiences come together to shape cultural performance. Barbara Kirshenblatt-Gimblett has examined how the folklore of immigrants—individuals who straddle cultural borders—illustrates the role of expressive culture in the construction and presentation of the self.[21] "When does an individual foreground his identity as Jewish, by what means, and to what ends?" she asks; "What is the cultural content of this social differentiation? What is the display of Jewishness counterposed to? Who are the relevant others?" (1987, 87). Kirshenblatt-Gimblett helps lay the foundation for examining the folklore of Jews as socially generated creative expression that, within larger socioeconomic and cultural contexts, becomes a tool of mediation and empowerment.[22] Engaging this performance-centered approach, I examined how Sukkot observance is a means of self-expression, a way to place oneself in relation to surrounding people and places. I investigated the philosophical, psychological, and affective dimensions of sukkah construction, contextualized by broader worldviews and histories, to relate the ritual experience to the greater human experience.

Often, when discussing their Sukkot observance, individuals alluded to biblical stories and beliefs about Jewish customs that reached beyond the boundaries of the holiday. They most often attributed moral tales and attitudes to texts from the Torah, the teachings of revered Talmudic scholars and rabbis, or to common knowledge.[23] They spoke out of a collective awareness of accepted truths founded on shared experience and wisdom. Their narratives about Sukkot observance and the contexts in which they practiced illuminate worldviews rooted in particular life experiences, each narrative broadening awareness of the role that ritual plays in the production and presentation of self. This is a study, therefore, that not only foregrounds material culture as a lens through which to learn about Jewish cultural expression, but which highlights individual agency within Jewish cultural expression through a focus on intentional narrative choices and social performance.

Theory in Practice

A vignette of one family's sukkah in Shchunat Hatikva during Sukkot of 2011 will elucidate how the perspectives of material culture, ritual studies, and Jewish folklore offer insights into the purpose and function of Sukkot observance and the holiday's broader themes, such as social belonging and the notion of "home." Dina and Yitzhak Emunah, respectively of Yemenite and Iranian descent, build their sukkah in the narrow, enclosed area in front of their house. The materials they use to decorate their sukkah root them in their Yemenite and Iranian heritage, as does the social life of their neighborhood. A wool rug that depicts animals in the Bible hangs on an interior wall by the sukkah's entrance—a weaving from Iran that the couple received from Yitzhak's mother. This rug is traditionally presented to a newly married couple to hang in their home as a blessing and symbol of happiness. Dina and Yitzhak hang the brightly colored rug in their sukkah each year to renew that wish and to connect them to their family history. A gathered bunch of eucalyptus branches also dangles from an inside wall, reminding the couple of the sukkot of their youth—sukkot whose walls and roof covering their parents wove entirely of eucalyptus branches, as generations in their families had done in both Yemen and Iran. The fragrance of the eucalyptus enveloped them completely when they entered those sukkot, they said, which they likened to a spiritual experience.

Dina and Yitzhak also decorate their sukkah with materials that connect them to their immediate community. Pomegranates wrapped in silver foil and pinned to one of the sukkah's tarp walls are one such example. On each of the seven days of the holiday, Dina visits different sukkot at the homes of her friends and neighbors and, on each of these days, she receives a pomegranate from a different host, totaling seven by the week's end. Upon returning home with each newly acquired fruit, she wraps it in tinfoil to preserve it and hangs it from the wall of her own sukkah. At the close of the holiday week, Dina takes the seven pomegranates, juices them together, and distributes cups of the pomegranate juice to women in the community whom she knows to be having trouble becoming pregnant. They drink the blessed pomegranate juice, produced from the generosity of other members of their community, and, Dina says, receive the good wishes of those individuals—as many wishes as the pomegranate has seeds.

With different objects that symbolize his beliefs, Yitzhak also connects to his community. Across from the bed on which he sleeps in the sukkah, and on the surrounding green tarp walls, he hangs photographs of the rabbis he reveres and whose teachings he studies, rabbis from both Ashkenazi and Sephardic traditions. He points out the photographs of Baba Sali, the Lubavitcher Rebbe Menachem Schneerson, and Rambam, among others, who together represent spiritual followings from Morocco, Yemen, Iraq, Egypt, Russia, and the United States. Yitzhak explains to me that these images inspire him, his family, and his guests when they gaze upon them, as they sit in the sukkah. The images communicate the social values and beliefs that he holds close and represent the spiritual communities of which he is a part, communities that span geographic, ethnic, and cultural borders. "If you ask me, 'To whom or what do you belong?'" Yitzhak says, "I'll say, 'I don't belong to anyone' . . . Here we are, a united ingathering of exiles, so I have no problem hanging all the pictures that I have at home together."

The interior decoration of Dina and Yitzhak's sukkah displays material indications and evocations of the social and spiritual networks to which the couple belongs. While documentation of the materials and methods of construction convey information about local environmental resources and socioeconomic conditions, the interior design and the builders' narratives about their design reveal social relations and cultural values. To focus one's gaze on the interior of such a structure is to peer into a mirror of the builder's or user's mind, heart, and spirit.

Mapping the Book

This introduction has offered three areas of research within folklore studies to which this book is relevant: vernacular architecture studies, ritual and festival studies, and Jewish folklore. More broadly, however, one will find that this book investigates the relationships between text and context, mobility and settlement,

Fig. 0.1. Dina and Yitzak Emunah sit with family on the bed inside their sukkah. Wrapped pomegranates decorate the left wall, and images of venerated leaders hang above the bed. Shchunat Hatikva, Israel. 2011.

ephemerality and permanence, and imitation and innovation, demonstrating how these concepts are intertwined in the observance of Sukkot. It demonstrates how sukkah builders and users translate a single, static, holy text into dynamic and creative expressions of the self; how they evaluate and orient themselves to their larger social and physical environments through interpretation of this practice; how they communicate their histories, present conditions, and imagined futures through their ritual constructions, decorative displays, and interpretations; and how they connect with contemporary local and distant networks and adjust their social position within them through this vernacular practice that has been reenacted in Jewish communities across the world for thousands of years.

Chapter 1 offers background on the holiday of Sukkot drawn from religious and historical narratives. Biblical, textual sources of Sukkot observance enable us to understand how people interpret written prescriptions through philosophical and material creative expression. A set of vignettes of Sukkot observance in Bloomington, Indiana, then provides the basic tools of analysis necessary to understand the dynamics of Sukkot performance that unfold in the main site of my fieldwork, in Israel, which forms the foundation of this study. Chapter 2 moves across the world to this site of extended ethnographic fieldwork, Shchunat

Hatikva in South Tel Aviv, Israel, during the years 2010 and 2011. From the perspective of outsiders to the neighborhood, this chapter examines the geographic and political boundaries of difference by which those who live beyond the neighborhood's borders characterize it. Chapter 3 presents the neighborhood from within through the social dynamics that take place inside Shchunat Hatikva's borders and the neighborhood spaces in which residents connect through collective experiences and values. Chapter 4 examines the Sukkot ritual practices and interpretations of three families living in Shchunat Hatikva, families of mixed Yemenite, Iraqi, and Iranian descent. Chapter 5 then examines the Sukkot ritual practices of one family of Moroccan/Syrian descent living in Jaffa and one family of Kurdish descent living in Jerusalem. These two cases expand the study beyond Shchunat Hatikva to provide a comparative perspective, while still focusing on the Sukkot ritual practices of Israeli Jews of Middle Eastern and North African descent. Chapter 6 returns to the coincidental occurrence of the international civil uprisings of 2010 and 2011 with which this introduction began. Relating the worldwide economic crisis of 2008 and the following years to an annual ritual experience of homelessness illustrates how the tensions between permanence and impermanence, materiality and spirituality, and inclusion and exclusion, were dramatized through public protests against social inequality during the Sukkot holiday. The simultaneous occurrence of the religious and socioeconomic events emphasized the universality of the themes and rites of this traditional practice. Chapter 7 brings us back to the United States with vignettes of Sukkot ritual practice and interpretation in the Hasidic Lubavitch community of Crown Heights, Brooklyn. Highlighting more recent examples of Sukkot practice from 2014 and 2015, these voices add to the diversity of the cases already visited by extending the range of practice to Orthodox Ashkenazi Judaism, and notably by presenting a particular custom of sukkah construction that refrains from decorative practice. This brief case from New York parallels the book's opening case from Indiana, both serving to enrich the comparative analysis of Sukkot expression that is synthesized in the conclusion. The conclusion presents five principles of Sukkot observance that thread together the ritual expressions of the individuals in this book.

This book affirms the powerful role of ritual in the formation and fragmentation of community. It addresses both particular and general questions about how human beings reconcile their needs with their conditions of existence through creative expression, or as Henry Glassie describes the dynamic, the interplay of will and circumstance. It provides an original, in-depth ethnography of the contemporary Sukkot ritual practices of Jews of Middle Eastern, North African, Central Asian origin in Israel, and European origin in the United States; and, it addresses the worldwide demand for fair housing in recent socioeconomic demonstrations around the world, in the universal search for "home." In a world unsettled by economic instability and social change, a tradition founded on these two aspirations, one practical and one existential, inspires hope, creates possibility, and promises shelter.

Notes

1. *Sukkot* has several meanings. When capitalized, it represents the name of the annual Jewish festival. Uncapitalized, as in its second usage in this sentence, *sukkot* is the plural form of *sukkah*, the temporary ritual shelter or "booth" constructed during the holiday of Sukkot.

2. Recent scholarship in material culture studies has directed attention to an object's full life cycle from the conception of its creation through its afterlife. This approach tracks an object across the many contexts of its use, assessing its variable value according to the multiple ways that people relate to it. Toward this end, Arjun Appadurai examines "the social life of things" (1988), and Henry Glassie describes a methodology by which to study material culture: "Envision contexts as a series of occasions belonging to three master classes—creation, communication, and consumption—that cumulatively recapitulate the life history of the artifact" (1999, 48).

3. Kenneth Burke. (1973) 2015. *The Philosophy of Literary Form: Studies in Symbolic Action*, 296–297. Berkeley: University of California Press. Burke proposes the notion of "literature as equipment for living" to suggest that such forms of human cultural expression are created by ongoing social circumstances.

4. In "Reimagining Home, Rethinking Sukkah: Rabbinic Discourse and Its Contemporary Implications" (2010), Marjorie Lehman also adopts a space-based approach to her analysis of the sukkah, but with particular attention to the implications of rabbinic discourse about the sukkah's space in gender roles and relations.

5. Definitions of "vernacular architecture" have changed over time with the shifting skills and goals of researchers. Folklorist Simon Bronner reaches to back to the term's Latin roots to describe its realm of study: "*Vernaculus*, or 'native,' these buildings tell what is indigenous, common and shared in a community or region . . . Vernacular identifies buildings as social representations and links them to coherent cultural systems of values and beliefs" (2006, 24). Art historian Suzanne Preston Blier considers vernacular architecture within a larger cultural context, as "a farrago of building traditions that lie outside canonical largely Western building exemplars created generally by formally trained architects" (2006, 230). Henry Glassie interprets the term by placing it in relation to "architecture that is more often studied," viewing it in a broader sociopolitical framework. Vernacular architecture "marks the transition from the unknown to the known: we call buildings 'vernacular' because they embody values alien to those cherished in the academy," writes Glassie (2000, 20).

6. Henry Glassie's structural analysis of folk housing in middle Virginia (1975) and international study of vernacular architecture (2000) demonstrate how a semiotic structural approach to the study of buildings may be enriched with historical and social data that importantly includes builders and users in their own landscapes and histories. "Culture is pattern in mind, the ability to make things like sentences or houses," he writes, investigating "how a house is thought" beyond only "how a house is made" (1975, 17, 21). Glassie identifies the limits of studying objects in isolation of their creators, importantly emphasizing how the ethnographic study of how individuals relate to their material objects could produce more meaningful analysis than that of a text alone. Other leading scholars who have similarly foregrounded

oral history and ethnographic methodology in vernacular architecture study include Michael Ann Williams, Gerald Pocius, Joseph Sciorra, and Rebecca Ginsburg, among others.

7. By "Jewish folklore" I mean folkloristic study of Judaism-based topics. I do not imply that Jewish researchers conduct this study or that the research has "Jewish" qualities beyond the subject itself. I use this phrase because it is concise.

8. The *Shulchan Aruch*, the most widely accepted compilation of Jewish law, was composed by Yosef Karo in 1563 in Safed (northern Israel today). It decrees details of sukkah construction with restrictions on the minimum height, the minimum area, and the maximum height of the sukkah; however, there is no restriction on the maximum area of the sukkah. The size of the sukkah's area (rather than its height) is that to which individuals referred when they told me that they wanted to make their sukkah larger, for the sukkah's increased area enabled its greater capacity to host individuals inside. It is not that the sukkah builders with whom I spoke considered the sukkah's height insignificant; however, they did not evaluate the size of the sukkah for me according to Jewish law. Instead, they appreciated it for the size and quality of social space that they were able to create.

9. Exemplary studies include: Henry Glassie 1982; 1993; 2006; John Michael Vlach 1981; Michael Ann Williams 1991; Gerald Pocius 1991; Amy Kitchener 1994; Simon Bronner 2006. Of particular relevance to this study are three recent publications: Thomas Carter's *Building Zion: The Material World of Mormon Settlement* (2015) investigates the architecture and cultural landscape of early settlers in Utah's Sanpete County, illuminating the relationship between Mormonism and material culture; Joseph Sciorra's *Built with Faith: Italian American Imagination and Catholic Material Culture in New York City* (2015) examines the Italian American Catholic devotional art and architecture that populates community-based sacred spaces in New York's urban neighborhoods; and Rebecca Ginsburg's *At Home with Apartheid: The Hidden Landscapes of Domestic Service in Johannesburg* (2011) interrogates the social and racial landscapes of suburban South Africa during apartheid through attention to domestic workers' home spaces. This book dialogues with each of these innovative material culture studies in their focus on the intersection of religious faith and the built environment, and the use of oral narrative in vernacular architecture study.

10. In Glassie's later work, he directed the attention of vernacular architectural scholars to the insides of homes instead of only the outsides of houses. He argued for the examination of design and use of interior spaces to expand architectural histories with the contributions of women as well as of men in the creation of house and home. As active vernacular architecture scholars in the United States today, many of Glassie's students have led this more recent effort. Dell Upton and John Michael Vlach, two among them, coedited a significant collection of essays, *Common Places: Readings in American Vernacular Architecture* (1986), in which scholars addressed elements of construction, function, history, design, and intention in American vernacular architecture as craft and as study. The essays, by scholars spanning decades of vernacular architecture study from Fred B. Kniffen (1936) to Thomas Hubka (2004), offer an overview of the field as it took shape in the United States.

11. Westmacott 1992; Bahloul 1996; Williams 1991; Heath 2001.

12. Cross-cultural comparisons in the encyclopedia reveal similarities between one kind of architecture and another, or perhaps more accurately, differences between them. The sukkah is not referenced in the encyclopedia's entries on timber frame construction, where structures in New Guinea, the Philippines, Australia, and Africa are highlighted; decorated dwellings, which includes structures in the British Isles, Turkey, Congo, and Mauritania; or symbolic spaces, with examples from Indonesia, India, and Japan—all descriptive features of the sukkah. Neither does the text connect the sukkah with like structures cross-culturally

within the United States—for example, a Yuchi (a Native North American people of the Southeastern United States) summer dwelling that contains a meaningful evocation of the sukkah's structure. With arbor frames constructed from lumber and plastic tarps, and a flat roof of green boughs or willows, the Yuchi structure temporarily shelters cooking, eating, and gathering that takes place during the annual Green Corn Ceremony, making it a structure of ceremonial form and function closely related to that of the sukkah, yet the reader is not guided to relate them (Jackson 1997). Although the encyclopedia is rich in indexing and in its comparison of individual material components and methods of construction, the sukkah as a vernacular architectural form is restricted to the categories of useful/functional, temporary/transportable, and Jewish.

13. Theories of ritual by such influential scholars as Arnold Van Gennep, Émile Durkheim, Claude Levi-Strauss, Victor Turner, and Mary Douglas must be acknowledged for their foundational development of this field of study; however, I aim here to examine more thoroughly the work of more recent folklorists and anthropologists who have built upon their base.

14. While I here pursued the relevance of the notion of belonging in the context of Sukkot in the Jewish Diaspora and in Israel, scholars have importantly challenged the historical binary of periphery and center in a discussion of the Jewish Diaspora. Galit Hasan-Rokem, for example, identifies the sukkah as that which mediates between mobility and stability, a model of a religious material practice that has "undermined the dominant idea of a concentric Jewish universe" (2012, 3).

15. This parallel in experience and narrative between the Israelites' exodus from Egypt and journey across the Sinai Desert, and the Eritrean and Sudanese migrants' escape from their home countries and subsequent journey across the Sinai Desert, has been explicitly noted in Israeli news media. The primary context for the comparison, however, is the holiday of Passover, rather than Sukkot. Media attention to this parallel was spurred by an annual event called the "Refugee Seder." This Passover meal is hosted by the African Refugee Development Center (ARDC) on the first night of Passover in Levinsky Park in South Tel Aviv, the public park that became an unofficial public "home space" for migrants after being bussed there from the Israeli-Egyptian border. See, Frucht, Leora Eren. "For African migrants in Tel Aviv, Exodus is more than distant memory," *Haaretz* (March 24, 2013). Last accessed April 4, 2013. http://www.haaretz.com/news/features/for-african-migrants-in-tel-aviv-exodus-is-more-than-distant-memory.premium-1.511522.

16. Babylonian Talmud, Bava Metzia 71a.

17. Many studies of Jewish material culture and ritual practice outside the context of this holiday have served as influential theoretical analyses. These include the work of Barbara Myerhoff (1980); Barbara Kirshenblatt-Gimblett (1982; 1985; 2007), Jenna Weissman Joselit (1990; 1994), Joëlle Bahloul (1996), and Vanessa Ochs (1999; 2007).

18. Although I do not here address pre-State cultural studies of Jewish creative expression, the important research that emerged in this early period from Jewish ethnologists and musicologists valuably contributes to the broader history of Jewish folkloristics. Among these influential scholars were A. Z. Idelsohn, Moses Gaster, and Robert Lachmann, but for a thorough bibliography of such foundational scholarship, see Baron (1940).

19. Jeffrey L. Rubinstein, for example, has examined the meaning and practice of the festival of Sukkot in the Second Temple and Rabbinic periods (1995) and considered the sukkah in various theological and philosophical frameworks (1994). Others have offered overviews of the holiday's history and practice (Fabricant 1958), provided analytical introductions to its narratives and themes (Goodman 1988), or foregrounded emerging trends in Sukkot observance, such as environmental and universally spiritual overtones (Bernstein 1998; Migram 2004).

20. Among the folklorists who have examined Sukkot, Simon Bronner valuably analyzes the sukkah as a vernacular building tradition in the early part of the twenty-first century, viewing the ritual construction as an expression of individual and communal identity (2006). Dana Hercbergs has analyzed the "geographies of play" that are manifested in the transitional space of the sukkah (2010), and Galit Hasan-Rokem has perceived the sukkah to be a site where itinerancy and locality intersect (2012). Rooted deeply in biblical narrative, Hasan-Rokem's analysis brings together Jewish text and material culture through a spatially oriented interpretation of ritual.

21. Central to this discussion is sociologist Erving Goffman's theory of the presentation of self, which posits that face-to-face interaction is like theatrical performance. In these social exchanges, people frame themselves in particular ways to position themselves in a desired social role or express a certain identity (Goffman 1959).

22. Although I do not discuss the fundamental works of foundational anthropologists Raphael Patai, Ruth Benedict, Margaret Mead, or Barbara Myerhoff, they each contributed crucially to the development of the field of Jewish ethnology and ethnography. More recently, the work of Israeli folklorist Haya Bar-Itzhak complements Kirshenblatt-Gimblett's theory by defining, in the Israeli context, folkloric expression as "not only an expression of the chaos experienced by any group when it settles down in a new place," but also as "a means to turn this chaos into cosmos, using cultural implements from the past and adapting them to the new reality" (2005, 69). Bar-Itzhak examines immigrant folk narratives as one form of creative expression that enables immigrants in Israel today to strengthen their socioeconomic security.

23. Although mainstream religious authorities (groups such as Shas or Chabad) have a constant presence in neighborhoods of South Tel Aviv through public outreach (community events) and varied types of media (pamphlets, posters, radio, television), individuals with whom I spoke about their Sukkot practice rarely cited these authorities as the source of their knowledge.

1 Translating Text: *Sukkot* in Bloomington, Indiana

EACH INNOVATION IN the construction and interpretation of the sukkah evokes a history of adaptation of Jewish tradition. In 70 AD, the destruction of the central sacred site of the faith, the Second Temple, demanded an adaptation to changing conditions of life, which resulted in the transformation of Temple worship into written religious law. The evolution of performance into text sustained Jews in their scattered settings. The later development of distinctive, individual practice based upon written law helped to ensure the survival of Jewish religion and culture. The creative diversity found in the ritual construction and use of the sukkah today is a vibrant example of how the dynamic process of tradition adjusts to shifting circumstances. As folklorist Simon Bronner explains, tradition "demands attention to form . . . [and] fidelity to cultural continuity, while inviting alteration and extension for social needs" (2006, 26). Tradition links the past with the present and future through its inherently flexible nature.[1]

The wide-ranging manifestations of the sukkah in this study illustrate the dynamic expressions of tradition. Though they were built with attention to form and fidelity to cultural continuity, they demonstrate the alteration and extension elicited by the particular socio-economic conditions in which they were constructed. Architectural historian Mitchell Schwarzer sees the adaptation of Jewish religious law to personal expression as "faith humanized." In his view, individual interpretation of official texts is the positive affirmation of Jewish law rather than a challenge to its authority (2001, 484). Through centuries of individually interpreted architectural practice, sukkot are annually reconstructed and Jewish identities redefined.

In Text

Sukkot, otherwise known as the Feast of Ingathering, the Feast of Tabernacles, and the Festival of Booths, is one of three Jewish pilgrimage festivals decreed in the Hebrew Bible (*Torah*). The last of the three holidays, Sukkot follows on the heels of the Days of Awe—*Rosh Hashanah* (the Jewish New Year) and *Yom Kippur* (the Day of Atonement)—as a joyous seven-day celebration of the Israelites' survival in the Sinai Desert after the exodus from Egypt. As historical narratives accumulated over time, the holiday also gained an agricultural character through its alignment with the harvest, the Sukkot practice of ritual booth construction recalling the shelters that farmers commonly built in fields during the fall so they could store their fruit harvest overnight and avoid daily travel back and forth from home.

The timing of the two other pilgrimage festivals, *Passover* and *Shavuot*, also corresponded with the agricultural calendar in this ancient period. Passover coincided with the barley harvest and Shavuot with the wheat harvest. Sukkot, decreed to begin on the fifteenth day of *Tishrei*, the seventh month of the year (Leviticus 23:39), was thus one of three annual celebratory pilgrimages to Jerusalem during which individuals would make offerings at the Temple in thanks for the fruits of their harvest. Advancing with Jewish history, however, these holidays acquired additional meanings linked to historical events. Passover, therefore, primarily recalls the exodus from Egypt, Shavuot honors God's giving of the Torah to the people of Israel at Mount Sinai, and Sukkot commemorates the Israelites' forty-year journey across the Sinai Desert in search of the Promised Land. Today, the ritual booths built during Sukkot primarily represent the temporary desert dwellings in which the Israelites sought shelter during the period of their displacement in the wilderness (Lipis 2011).

In the third book of the Torah, Leviticus, chapter twenty-three, verses forty-two and forty-three prescribe the observance of Sukkot: "You shall dwell in booths for seven days. All native Israelites shall dwell in booths, that your generations may know that I made the people of Israel dwell in booths when I brought them out of the land of Egypt" (English Standard Version). Given the conciseness of the commandment, scholars, religious and secular leaders, and laypersons throughout postbiblical history have extrapolated further prescriptions from the verse for ritual practice. The most prominent elaborations are documented in Judaism's central texts, the *Mishnah* and the *Gemara*, which together comprise the *Talmud*.

The Mishnah is a codification of the Jewish oral law that Moses is said to have received from God at Mount Sinai together with the written law of the Torah. Around 200 CE, the revered *Rav Yehuda HaNasi* (Rabbi Judah the Prince) compiled the text, based on generations of discussions and study by sages (Goodman 1973, 22). The Mishnah is arranged by subject matter into six *sedarim*, or "orders," one of which is entitled *Moed*, or "Festival." This order, which contains the legal requirements of different festival practices, is itself organized into twelve tractates, the sixth of which is called "Succah," which is also further divided into two chapters of its own. The first of these chapters details laws pertaining to the physical construction of the ritual shelter—the dimensions and material composition of the walls, acceptable sources for the sukkah's roof covering (*schach*), and rules of construction. The second chapter reviews uses of the space contained within the sukkah—a study of the breadth and depth of meaning in the commandment, "to dwell." The voices that codified, and are codified in, the oral laws of the Mishnah dissect the Torah's decree into manifold possibilities for ritual action. This dissection is a process of delicate distinction, determining how to read an historical text in the context of current circumstance. The oral and written laws of Sukkot observance may therefore be understood as expressions of negotiation between individuals' religious, social, and physical worlds.

For centuries, rabbis in Palestine and Babylonia, the two historic centers of Jewish study, debated the technical, legal, and ethical obligations of the Mishnah's text. The Gemara, containing this rabbinic interpretation, was the product of this analysis. Deconstructing and reconstructing the religious prescriptions with even more explicit philosophical inquiry and narrative analysis, the Gemara was produced nearly three hundred years after codification of the Mishnah. Together, the Mishnah and Gemara became known as the Talmud, distinct versions of which were constructed in both Palestine and Babylonia. Although commonly referred to in the singular as "The Talmud," the two versions are distinguished in several ways—the single reference simply denotes that one version is understood to be the common reference. The two versions, known by their places of origin as the *Talmud Yerushalmi* and the *Talmud Bavli*, were compiled in different time periods, in different locations, and by separate schools of scholars. The Talmud Yerushalmi (the Jerusalem Talmud, later known as the Palestinian Talmud or Talmud of the Land of Israel) was composed between the fourth and fifth centuries CE in what is today northern Israel. It was written in a western Aramaic dialect and remains incomplete and erratically composed. The more frequently referenced version is the Talmud Bavli, composed in Babylonia (current day Iraq) in approximately 500 CE in a different Aramaic dialect, and is more comprehensive in its documentation of generations of rabbinical exegesis. Although not every Mishnaic tractate has a complementary Talmudic interpretation, Tractate Succah fortunately elicits analysis in both the Yerushalmi and the Bavli versions. The two versions reveal narrative and linguistic differences that illuminate differences in the cultural and social contexts in which they were each produced. Perhaps inspired by the multiple voices and interpretive variation that characterize these texts, Jews today create meaning from these texts by framing them within the contexts of contemporary life.

While they are the central texts of the Jewish religion, the Torah and the Talmud do not contain the entirety of early religious interpretation of Sukkot. Galit Hasan-Rokem notes that later books of the Hebrew Bible describe the actual celebrations of the three pilgrimage holidays, specifically referencing Sukkot in

1 Kings 8:2, Ezra 3:4, Nehemiah 8:16–19, Zechariah 14:16–19, 2 Chronicles 8:13, and classic rabbinic literature written from 250 CE to 750 CE that includes the Mishnah and its supplementary work known as the *Tosefta* (2012, 159). In these secondary texts, Hasan-Rokem recognizes a wide range of "concrete and imaginative variations and contradictions" regarding the technical factors of sukkah construction—the materials, the height, and the specific conditions of eating and sleeping in the sukkah. The "concrete" variations and contradictions may include the maximum possible height of a sukkah or if it may be constructed under a tree (Sukkah 1:1–2). "Imaginative" variations and contradictions concern such questions as whether one may construct a sukkah on the back of a camel or on the deck of a ship (Sukkah 2:3). Constant scrutiny of Jewish texts to redefine or enlarge Jewish performance reveals a continuing search for meaning through material practice. The synchronized development of Jewish textual interpretation and Jewish religious performance throughout history has its roots in these early textual practices.[2]

Understanding the relationships and interactions among Jewish history, Jewish text, and Jewish practice helps clarify the transition that Sukkot makes from biblical prescription to ritual performance. As noted earlier, reflecting on the relationship between Jewish architectural history and Judaism's central texts, Mitchell Schwarzer argues that the destruction of the Second Temple in AD 70 spurred religious discourse that attempted a metaphoric rebuilding of the Temple in text. The Mishnah's sixty-five tractates of technical interpretation of Jewish life translate the Temple's "singular geography of holiness into a flexible set of microgeographies by which individual Jewish communities could structure their lives" (Schwarzer 2001, 477). In response to the loss of a single center of faith, multiple conceptual centers were gained through the construction of the Mishnah. Miriam Lipis similarly observes the causal relationship between Jewish history and Jewish texts by noting that "as Judaism developed from a temple-based to a book-based religion, the text became a meeting place between God and the people as the Temple had once been" (2011, 96). A physical place of worship was transmuted into a conceptual space as Jewish texts came to mediate between the Temple and the Jews, between one authority and many. Both a process and a product of adaptation, these Jewish texts pluralized the sanctified centers and altered the spatial element of Jewish religious and cultural practices. The construction of the sukkah, a spatial ritual practice that evokes the Israelites' uprooted existence and reroots Jews in different actual and abstract lands, endures, in part, through its continual adaptation of the material elements across geographies and time periods. This historic splintering helps to explain the simultaneous consistency and diversity of Sukkot ritual practice today. The narrative of a single permanent temple broken up into a disparate number of portable sanctuaries nurtures Jewish cultural and religious thought and behavior in communities across the world.

In Architecture

With few legal requirements and myriad symbolic meanings, the ritual of Sukkot enables individuals to connect with a common Jewish historical consciousness through the structure's physical and conceptual construction. From an historical perspective, the sukkah evokes a period of displacement in Jewish life and the search for home and homeland. Religiously, it symbolizes the "Clouds of Glory" with which God surrounded the Israelites to protect them in the wilderness (Rubenstein 1994). Ecologically, it acknowledges the relationship between the Jewish people and the natural world and embodies an idealization of a simpler existence. Culturally, it challenges the value and permanence of the material surroundings that human beings increasingly consume and upon which they increasingly rely. And, individually, each sukkah acknowledges a Jewish tradition and defines the builder's self through personal, creative expression.

The fundamental requirements of sukkah construction that conjure these meanings are few. In accord with Jewish *halakha* (religious law), the sukkah must have at least two full walls that are connected to each other, and a third wall that is at least one *tefach* (handbreadth) wide; and the *schach* (roof covering) must be constructed out of organic material that is removed from the earth. As described in the section above, elaborations on and interpretations of these two laws of construction fill the Sukkot tractates in the Talmud and in later rabbinic writings. Examples of these rabbinic prescriptions declare that the schach must provide more shade than sun inside the sukkah on a bright day; that nothing, such as a tree, may cover the sukkah and act as a second roof; and that one must be able to see the stars in the sky through the weaving of the roof. Innumerable debates about requirements over the years are due to interpreters' differing social and spiritual goals for the experience of dwelling in the space of the sukkah.

The schach is the defining feature of the sukkah as its material determines whether it is pure, regardless of the rest of the construction. The requirement of the walls pertains to number and size, not material, and therefore the materials used to construct the frame and walls have varied over time without compromising the structure's holiness and religious integrity. An example of this variability in the sukkah's frame and wall composition is today's increasingly popular prefabricated "sukkah kit" that provides metal frames and nylon walls intended to be reused annually, replacing formerly widespread handmade constructions of wood, brush, and cloth. A second example is a construction method traditionally employed in Yemen, among other countries (examples of this construction exist in Israel today as well) where a room of one's permanent house is constructed so that it may be transformed into a sukkah once a year by removing a precut piece of its roofing. During the week of Sukkot, this piece of roofing is removed and replaced with schach, permitting the observance of Sukkot within the space it shelters below. Such diversity in the sukkah's form demonstrates the creative incorporation of local resources and emerging practices into the construction of the ritual shelter, while remaining faithful to the religious requirement of the schach to ensure the sukkah's sanctity.

Though decoration of the sukkah is not prescribed in Biblical verse, for many, it has become as meaningful a part of the material ritual as the construction of the frame. While not specifically referring to Sukkot, Exodus 15:2—"This is my God and I will adorn Him"—is credited with motivating the desire to beautify the ritual structure. Talmudic interpretation of this verse has nurtured the development of the Jewish principle of *hiddur mitzvah*, or the aesthetic enhancement of a mitzvah. This belief, regarding the fulfillment of any Jewish commandment, holds that the aesthetic embellishment of any expression of devotion enhances the act by appealing more strongly to the senses. Beautifying the sukkah is therefore viewed as honoring God as well as the commandment. One example of the commitment to *hiddur mitzvah* is the extravagant amount of money that very pious Jews spend to acquire the highest quality and most perfectly formed *etrog* (ritually required fruit) that can be found for use in prayer during Sukkot—at a cost that often reaches far beyond their financial means. While less observant individuals question the logic of such an expenditure, those who assume this financial burden take pride in their ability and willingness to glorify God through the utmost aesthetic expression of devotion.

Causing less financial but greater social impact, a great diversity of decorative practices inside the sukkah also demonstrates a commitment to aesthetics. Adorning the sukkah's interior space is a popular family practice, and it has been likened to decorating the Christmas tree for its positive social and educational effects. Children may make drawings and paper-cut hangings that feature imagery of the harvest or the Bible in school and at home in the weeks before the holiday begins, and adults often choose items of personal meaning from their homes to display in their sukkot. The sukkah's decoration, like the structure's construction, communicates elements of the local environment—for example, hanging local fresh fruit or special textiles made in the region. In addition to such diverse creative expression, individuals may display painted murals or illustrated hangings that feature images of imagined and actual locations in which the sukkah builders place themselves through this practice, such as Jerusalem or the Temple. In the personalized decoration of their sukkah, individuals transform the ritual structure into a place of individual expression and social belonging.

In Ritual Performance

In addition to the construction of the sukkah, certain rituals that take place during the holiday week lend meaning to the holiday's observance. Among them, *arba'at haminim* (Four Species), *ushpizin* (guests), and *simhat beit ha-sho'evah* (Rejoicing at the Place of Water Drawing) are the most established ceremonial performances. The ritual of arba'at haminim originates in Leviticus, where it is written, "And you shall take on the first day the fruit of splendid trees, branches of palm trees and boughs of leafy trees and willows of the brook, and you shall rejoice before the Lord your God seven days" (23:40 [ESV]). The four plants referenced in the text are the *etrog* (fruit of the citron tree), *lulav* (closed frond of the date palm tree), *hadas* (branch of the Myrtle tree), and *aravah* (branch of the Willow tree). To be used as a single ritual bundle for prayer, the lulav, hadas, and aravah must be bound together in the proper order, and then held together with the etrog in both hands. With the Four Species pointing away from one's body, a prayer of thanksgiving (*Hallel*) is made and the bundle is waved in six directions—east, west, north, south, as well as up and down—signifying God's omnipresence. This ritual may be performed in either the sukkah or the synagogue every day of Sukkot, usually in the morning.

Different rabbinic interpretations of these four plants have been suggested over the centuries. A common notion metaphorically compares the biological character of each plant with a particular "type" of Jew in the world. The etrog, for example, has both taste and smell, representing those who both study Torah and perform good deeds. The lulav has taste but no smell—those who study Torah but do not perform good deeds; the hadas has smell but no taste—those who do not study Torah but do perform good deeds; and the aravah has neither taste nor smell—those who neither study Torah nor perform good deeds. Bound together, these four plants are meant to symbolize the entire Jewish nation.

Another interpretation likens each ritual plant to a part of the human body according to shared physical attributes. The round etrog symbolizes the heart, the straight lulav is the spine, the almond-shaped leaves of the hadas are the eyes, and the long, thin leaves of the aravah are the lips. According to this interpretation, when bound together, the four plants symbolize a whole person: the heart, the most valuable organ, giving power to the body and nurturing compassion; the spine supporting the upright body; the eyes enabling sight and enlightenment; and the lips allowing for expression, particularly prayer. Together, these four plants, like these four parts of the body, comprise an entire expression of self.

These explanations are the most commonly cited, but the Four Species have inspired a collection of other interpretations that unite the earthly realm with

Fig. 1.1. A young boy assembles the ritual bundle used for prayer during Sukkot. This ritual object, called the Four Species, is made by tying together *aravah*, *hadas*, *etrog*, and *lulav*. Shchunat Hatikva, Israel. 2011.

the divine. More recent analysis has even related the Fours Species to concepts of the diaspora and exile in Jewish history and cultural consciousness. Galit Hasan-Rokem, for example, associates the sites of production of the four plants and their routes of trade with Jewish rootedness in Israel and global migration. She notes that "these branches and fruit do not usually grow in Europe— the symbolical objects are like the Jews, conceptually if not always realistically from 'somewhere else'—and have thus required a lively trade with the Jews of the Holy Land" (2012, 167–8). These ritual plants, products of the earth and symbolic of human qualities, are an evocative symbol of practical and spiritual relationships among Jews, between Jews and non-Jews, and between Jews and God.

The ritual of ushpizin, or welcoming guests into one's sukkah, is a second custom of particular meaning to Sukkot. This custom dates back to the late medieval period and is first mentioned in the *Zohar*, the mystical commentary on the Torah otherwise known as the *Kabbalah*, of thirteenth-century Spanish origin. There it is written, "When a person is seated in his *Sukkah*, Abraham and six distinguished visitors partake of his company" (Zohar 5103, b). Traditionally, the seven guests are Abraham, Isaac, Jacob, Joseph, Moses, Aaron, and David, one guest invoked each night of Sukkot and celebrated both for honorable character traits and corresponding spiritual attributes, such as loving-kindness, power, beauty, victory, truth, splendor, and sovereignty. Through the evening, biblical stories may be told and songs may be sung about the evening's guest of honor. During the sixteenth-century revival of Jewish mysticism under Rabbi Itzhaq Luria in Tsfat, a center of kabbalistic thought in the Galilee region of northern Israel, the ushpizin ritual gained popularity.[3] Though this custom is still practiced today, alternative guests of honor have now also been included to diversify the customary patriarchal group. Primarily, biblical matriarchs (*ushpizot*) are now included, observers ritually inviting and honoring Sarah, Rivka, Leah, Rachel, Miriam, Avigail and Esther throughout the holiday week.

While the invocation of these biblical guests is performed through spoken prayer before the evening meal in the sukkah, ongoing material expressions of hospitality toward these guests are performed as well. Posters and cloth hangings displaying images of the seven Biblical guests and their paper-cut names adorn interior walls of many sukkot today, reflecting the increase in commercial production of decorations for the sukkah. Prefabricated sukkah packages even feature nylon walls that already have the names of guests printed directly on the cloth, as part of the structure. In addition, a custom more typically observed by Jews of Sephardic and Mizrahi heritage is the placement of an extra chair in the sukkah for the ushpizin or ushpizot. This chair is often left empty but for a ceremonial cloth draped over it and holy Jewish texts placed on or near its seat. During my fieldwork, I observed this custom in the placement of a child-sized wooden chair in the corner of a sukkah of a family of Iranian descent, a full-sized wooden chair in the corner of a sukkah of a family of mixed Syrian and Moroccan descent, and a full-sized plastic chair attached to the top corner of the sukkah's wall, nearly touching the roof, in the structure of a family of mixed Libyan and Tunisian descent.

While this particular custom of inviting Biblical guests is rooted in Jewish mystical writing, a broader custom of hospitality drawn from the Hebrew Bible also characterizes Sukkot observance. The hosting of friends and strangers in one's sukkah recalls the Biblical story of Abraham being visited by three strangers in his tent. In return for Abraham's kind gestures of hospitality, the unexpected guests reveal that his wife Sarah will soon bear a longed-for son (Genesis 18). Sukkah builders and users often recounted this story to me as the model for their general practice of hospitality, particularly during Sukkot.

The last of the ritual performances specific to Sukkot, simhat beit ha-sho'evah, is a "Water Drawing Ceremony." This ritual takes place during the intermediate days of the holiday week to commemorate the daily water libations that were offered at the Temple during Sukkot in supplication of God's blessing for rainfall in the coming year. Relating to the agricultural context of the festival, this ceremony was also characterized by joyous performances of music, song, and dance that filled the streets of Jerusalem each evening as torches were lit and pilgrims feasted in celebration. In the most observant neighborhoods of Jerusalem today, such as *Mea Shearim*, this ritual continues in the form of music and dance in the synagogues and study halls that last late into the night, crowds of men throbbing in unison in concentric dance circles that fill the rooms, wall to wall. Only men partake in the singing and dancing in these contemporary ritual performances in accordance with religious restrictions on women's dancing and singing in public. Observant women in these communities either remain outside the synagogues and study halls with children, or watch the men's festivities on large screens erected away from the center of activity.

During my fieldwork, many sukkah builders and users did not attend this ceremony, yet made sure to quote a line from the Talmud for me that, to them, conveyed the importance of recalling the Water Drawing Ceremony and the important role of rejoicing in holiday observance: "He who has not seen the rejoicing at the place of the water drawing has never seen rejoicing in his life" (Sukkah 51a). While a majority of Jews today around the world commonly build sukkot, pray with the Four Species, and host and are hosted by others throughout the week of Sukkot, they no longer perform the Water Drawing Ceremony. However, it is still considered essential to Sukkot observance to experience joy, a central element of holiday practice.

Generations of religious, academic, and legal scholars have filled texts with interpretations of Jewish ritual practice, which remain the foundations for observance today, whether practitioners abide by the spirit or the letter of their prescriptions. Rather than review the acknowledged analyses of Sukkot found in holy and rabbinic texts, this book examines the transformation of those texts into structures of material, belief, and performance. This chapter has introduced the first part of this three-part study that links in dynamic relation religious text, material expressions, and interpretive discourse. Tracing these expressions in relation to each other, the book explores how an annual Jewish ritual enables people to reevaluate and reorient themselves to their individuality and common heritage as Jews, in changing times and transitional places.

Bloomington Vignettes

My fieldwork journey began in the fall of 2007 in the Midwestern university town of Bloomington, Indiana. The following vignettes of Sukkot observance in Bloomington illustrate the defining elements of performance that informed my later fieldwork in the main site of my research, in Israel. Amid Indiana's farmlands, forests, and foothills, I documented the ritual structures that seventeen Jewish families living in Bloomington built during the holiday of Sukkot.

I examined their material constructions and aesthetic designs, as well as the meanings that their builders and users invested in them. Without professional training, these vernacular architects had informally learned how to erect these structures, and had formalized their processes through practice.

Henry Glassie likens architecture to any other realization of human desire. In the construction of a building, he writes, "Plans blend memories with a reading of the immediate situation," and intention collides with condition to create "images of will and wit" (2000, 18). In my study of these sukkot, I sought to understand how individual intentions met the collective conditions of Jewish life in Bloomington, Indiana. I questioned how the minority status of Jews in this Midwestern university town influenced individual practice; and, how the mediating space that each builder constructed in the space of the sukkah defined her or his Jewish identity through personal interpretation of the Biblical commandment.[4]

Key Infrastructures

Bloomington's social and institutional structures contextualize Jewish expression in two ways. First, its social structure reveals the dynamics of a Jewish minority living within a non-Jewish majority population. In this minority ethnic community, cultural and religious identity and practice are conditioned by small group size and a distinct sense of otherness and difference. While I recognized the physical forms and metaphysical functions of these sukkot as reflections of their creators' unique life experiences, understanding the broader social environment in which these sukkot were created added important context to my analysis.

The year before this fieldwork began, in 2006, Indiana's Jewish population numbered 17,420, three-tenths of one percent of the entire state population (6,271,973).[5] Bloomington is the sixth-largest city in Indiana, located in the south-central part of the state with its own population of nearly 83,000.[6] More than half of that population is made up of students who attend Indiana University in Bloomington, setting the median age of its residents at a relatively low number but creating a plurality of races, religions, and cultures within the university's international population.[7]

Bloomington's Jewish demographic may be divided into two parts: students and non-students. Jewish enrollment at Indiana University is marked at about four thousand of its thirty thousand undergraduate students, and nine hundred of its nine thousand graduate students.[8] While this seems a sizable ratio compared to the state's total proportion of Jews to non-Jews, there is only one Jewish congregation beyond the university campus, the Beth Shalom Congregation, built in 1971 and formerly known as the University Jewish Community and then the Bloomington Jewish Community.[9] That year, the synagogue had forty-three families and no rabbi, but two hundred people showed up for the first High Holiday services. Before this formal founding of the congregation, since the 1950s, its members had been meeting in individuals' homes and at the university Hillel building. Claiming approximately two hundred member households today, Beth Shalom is officially designated a "small" congregation according to the Union for Reform Judaism, of which it is a member.[10]

Despite the implications of small group size, being a minority Jewish community living within largely non-Jewish Midwestern America does not sufficiently contextualize this study; small Jewish communities exist in small towns all across America. That Bloomington is a small *university* town in Midwestern America, however, adds a second level of telling background—the institutional structure that particularizes this study. Indiana University, situated in the heart of downtown Bloomington, draws people from all over the world with its educational and career opportunities. These cosmopolitan residents become university-affiliated members of the Bloomington community. Most of this community is transitory, most having resettled here from larger urban centers for short-term or indeterminate amounts of time, and as students, teachers, and researchers, often with spouses, partners, and children.

Experiencing this kind of abrupt resettlement, individuals must decide whether to adapt to the prevailing culture or maintain familiar ways in this new environment. Significantly, several of the Jews whom I interviewed said that they had begun the ritual of building a sukkah with their move to Bloomington and might end it with their departure, decisions contingent upon the number of Jews in the community in which they lived. These families had not found it necessary to build a sukkah when they lived in cities densely populated with Jews, but in the largely non-Jewish community of Bloomington, they felt impelled to define their Jewish identity through tradition.

In the seventeen Bloomington sukkot that I documented, the extent of decoration varied widely from plain tarp walls and bare brush roofs to poster-filled interiors with evocative handmade objects hanging from the roof. Objects of adornment included strings of lights, laminated photographs and paintings, tinsel, chimes, and real and plastic fruits and vegetables (gourds, dried ears of corn, pomegranates, and grapes). Sukkah-builders purchased their decorations in stores, selected objects from their personal home collections, and crafted adornments with their children. One woman bought silk flowers from what she referred to as the "Christmas tree aisle" in Hobby Lobby, while another man described the interior of his sukkah as lit by "Christmas lights," in spite of the intentionally selected blue and white colors (colors of the Israeli flag). Although not created specifically for Sukkot, these items were reimagined by the sukkah builders through recontextualization in this Jewish ritual space. For Bloomington's sukkah builders and users, both "explicit" and "implicit" Jewish objects were used in ritual decoration, transcending their intended function to become icons, indexes, and symbols of particular Jewish experiences and identities.[11] An iconic poster of the Sinai Desert illustrated the literal context of the Sukkot narrative, while a dried ear of corn indexed the harvest that Sukkot celebrates, and an Israeli flag symbolized the Jewish State, and thus, the Jewish people. Builders of sukkot arranged consumer, family, and Jewish objects in personally meaningful assemblages as expressions of the self.

Bakol Geller

Bakol Geller is a teacher and actress who grew up in Canada and lived in Israel before moving to Bloomington. She is married to Shmuel Geller, an Indiana University research associate and international consultant, and they have one teenage son. Although Bakol attended Hebrew school in Toronto through grade twelve, she experienced little formal ritual practice growing up and learned to speak only a handful of Hebrew words. She does not have many memories of childhood sukkot, but she does recall the vegetable-decorated sukkah that her community synagogue built, which she is quick to dismiss as a model for the one that she now builds. "I never wanted to hang red peppers. I didn't want a Canadian sukkah," she says, remembering fresh vegetables and fruits as the only objects of adornment in the sukkot of her youth. In Bloomington, Bakol attended both Jewish Renewal and Conservative services at the Beth Shalom Synagogue, moving between various categories of affiliation as they fit her preferences of practice, which she describes as "eclectic Judaism."

Bakol's house is one of many similarly designed houses that line the curving paths that cut through Bloomington's residential enclaves. Using the back wall of her house as one wall, Bakol's sukkah faces a clear-blue swimming pool. Given the desert setting that the sukkah is meant to evoke, Bakol finds this placement so amusing that she has nicknamed the structure her "Hollywood Beach Sukkah" and justifies its location by its convenience (being near the kitchen) and privacy. Asked if she would consider building the sukkah on her front lawn instead of the back, Bakol said that she would feel "self-conscious" about doing so, not because of its visual presence but because her neighbors would hear her family when they sat inside for meals. Bakol noted that when she lived in Israel, "there were three [sukkot] in the parking lot by our apartment and everybody could hear one another, but here, I'd feel self-conscious about having it in the front."

The frame of Bakol's sukkah is constructed with lumber and metal brackets, its walls made of hanging green tarps, and its roof covered with brush. These materials (excluding the brush), though mundane when separated, are stored together in her garage all year as "the sukkah," and not used for any other purpose. In her ritual construction, Bakol adheres to halakhic (religious required)

Fig. 1.2. Bakol Geller stands in front of her sukkah. Bloomington, Indiana. 2007.

standards, explaining her strict ritual observance as a way of connecting with "something bigger" than her own particular life experiences. "It's very real to me that even when I'm gone, something I belong to will go on, [something] that was always here and that will always be here," she says, referring to the tradition of sukkah construction—"the roof space and three walls." She follows this tradition as a means by which to "step into the stream" of Jewish practice that she feels is a central part of her identity.

Bakol's Jewish identity is defined in part by adhering to Jewish tradition, but also by connecting with Israel through ritual. "I know [this ritual] is part of the Jewish religious practice but so much of that for me is tied to being in Israel," she said. Being "*chutz laAretz*," or living outside of Israel, she builds the sukkah to connect to Israel, and ultimately to her Jewish self. "In Israel we lived more simply, in smaller quarters. Since I've been here, I've accumulated more things," she said, seeing the simplicity of her circumstances in Israel and of the sukkah as pointing to the same ideal: a simpler life. "I like the idea of [the sukkah] as a reminder that our refuge isn't in the material . . . That what's going to happen and what's not going to happen doesn't depend on how thick the walls are. Being outside and being in nature . . . it's a reminder of simplicity," she said.

Fig. 1.3. Bakol Geller builds her sukkah by the pool behind her house. Bloomington, Indiana. 2007.

Beyond her halakhic construction, Bakol finds and makes meaning in the building process through the display of decorative objects that she places inside the structure. Her personalized array of ornaments includes pictures cut from old Jewish calendars (laminated at Kinko's), Israeli flags, and family heirlooms that she brings from her home. She describes her selection process as random but meaningful, choosing materials that evoke memories of her family and of Jewish culture: "I just walk around the house, picking up things to hang. I choose them for color; I choose them for noise. It always seemed like a desert thing, a Jewish thing, to have a tambourine . . . I always hang Israeli flags here because that's part of what is being Jewish in America . . . And when my mother died, I didn't take much but *shabbos* [Yiddish: 'Sabbath'] candles and this little Wedgewood plate, which is by my shabbos table."[12] To explain her method of decorating, Bakol says, "I bring objects that are symbolic of my identity." She relates the creative freedom with which she adapts Jewish ritual to her interpretation of religious law: "There are things we have been told to do but the reason that I can do them is because I make them my own," she said. "That's very important for me in terms of my observance or my identification as a Jewish person."

Although decoration of the sukkah is not a prescribed part of holiday observance, Bakol finds meaning in the objects she assembles, as much as in the

42 | *Framing Sukkot*

Fig. 1.4. Bakol Geller decorates the interior of her sukkah with laminated pages from Jewish calendars, Israeli flags, and family heirlooms that evoke memories of her family and historic Jewish experience. Bloomington, Indiana. 2007.

traditional building of the structure. An undecorated sukkah, she told me, would be "a sukkah that hasn't been finished." Exploring the meaning behind material arrangements on women's private, domestic altars, folklorist Kay Turner characterizes the altar assemblages as having "an *aesthetic of relationship*" (1999, 95). This aesthetic is dynamic and based on "images and objects that have no immediate affinity [but] are nonetheless yoked together to forge new, interrelated meanings" (98). Bakol's relationship to Jewish culture is based on the material compositions that represent both shared Jewish laws and history, and her individual Jewish identity. While she connects to a stable, authoritative practice through the sukkah's construction, she relishes the space for individual interpretation in ornamenting the sukkah. Bakol's sukkah unites the authority of the religious text (the frame's construction) with that of her own text (her interior decoration), the identity of the Jewish people and her own.

Yonit Kosovske

Yonit Kosovske, a harpsichord musician and teacher and mother of three, was raised in a Reform Jewish household in South Carolina. Before settling in Bloomington over twenty years ago, she lived in Berkeley, California; Boston, Massachusetts; and abroad in Spain and Israel. Regardless of the landscapes across which she has traveled and the new communities that she has joined, Yonit has relied on her Sukkot ritual observance to ground her in her Jewish identity. "I was more aware of my minority status in South Carolina and am more aware here in Indiana than when I had a sukkah in Berkeley, Boston, or Israel," said Yonit. In Bloomington, she attends both Jewish Renewal and Conservative services at the synagogue, and identifies as an "artsy-urban hippy chick" rather than an affiliate of a single denomination.

In her Jewish observance, Yonit seeks a connection between Judaism and the environment. On Rosh Hashanah (Jewish New Year), she goes camping with friends and family "to bring the divine energy that's outside into our hectic lives and into Judaism, and not just have it be something in the synagogue." Yonit emphasizes the union of natural and spiritual elements in her personal practice because she feels that Jews have lost a connection with the land, "especially outside of Israel where the holidays don't necessarily match up with the seasons of agriculture." More than the Jewish people, however, Jewish synagogues neglect environmental issues, says Yonit: "We're very much into human conditions but somehow we separate saving the trees from ourselves."

The sukkah that Yonit and her husband, Wolodymyr (Vlad) Smishkewych, built in 2007 stood at the back of their house, its vine-covered wooden frame a stable arbor all year long. They built the structure out of a scrap lumber frame, red cotton sheets from the Goodwill thrift store, and greenery collected from their yard, laced on top as a roof covering. Yonit and Vlad sought recycled materials to build their first sukkah in Bloomington years earlier not only because they were financially constrained graduate students, but also to create a makeshift rather than manufactured feeling—"like you're in the desert; rustic and raw but pretty." Their materials are unconventionally reused to shape this ritual space, but their method of building conforms to traditional Jewish law. Yonit can easily

Fig. 1.5. Yonit Kosovske stands with her child in the entrance to her sukkah, themed that year after the novel *The Red Tent* by Anita Diamant. Bloomington, Indiana. 2007.

recite for me the prescriptive rules that guide her construction: "It should have three sides and not be permanent, high enough to stand in and wide enough for one person to sit in, and have a ceiling that allows open holes to see the stars." Her building may be founded on the religious laws of construction, but Yonit elaborates on the design with changing ideas about the form.

Although the family constructs it together, Yonit conceptualizes the sukkah's ritual and symbolic space before its construction, and for her, the holiday of Sukkot "has always been a woman's holiday." She imagines the sukkah to be "womb-like, like a sacred space," and all the more so when she first became a mother. She calls the structure a "temporary holding place for life," evocative of the cycles of life. A space that Yonit associates with meditation, nature, and womanhood, her sukkah is adorned with colorful scarves and tasseled sarongs, "Indian jingly mobiles," laminated artwork, and gourds. Yonit gathers these textiles, objects, and pictures along her travels, in art stores, from her home, and from her children.

Although creative collection and decorative design of the sukkah's interior is not specific to Yonit among the sukkah builders in Bloomington, she is unique

Translating Text: Sukkot in Bloomington, Indiana | 45

Fig. 1.6. An evening in the sukkah with Yonit Kosovske and her child. Bloomington, Indiana. 2007.

in imagining a theme for her sukkah of 2007 upon which to base her ritual. "The Red Tent" is the theme she chose for that year, adapted from the title of a novel of biblical fiction by Anita Diamant in which Dinah (daughter of Jacob and a midwife) narrates her story from a first-person and typically neglected female perspective (according to standard translations of the Bible). The "red tent" of the novel refers to the place where, according to ancient law, women must seek refuge to menstruate and give birth, and where they receive support from the women in their lives—their mothers, sisters, and aunts. This was the first year that Yonit chose a theme for her sukkah building and ritual practice, feeling compelled to do so after "having a vision of having a real red tent in my backyard and telling people they could come, just sit, and do whatever they wanted in it." Her interpretation of the holiday and of her personal experiences of "pregnancy, women, the moon, and the idea of the red tent" coalesced in this creation, draped in scarlet cloth and infused with maternal spirit. The "aesthetic of relationship" that Turner observed in women's home altars is created through the assemblage of objects and images that act as "gauges of belief, memory, emotion, experience, and transformation," and which "refer to the immeasurable worth of actual relationships and their effect on the altar-makers" (Turner 1999, 109). Yonit approaches her sukkah in this way by creating a setting through material

Fig. 1.7. The interior of Yonit Kosovske's sukkah is decorated with fabrics collected on her travels and pictures that her children drew. Bloomington, Indiana. 2007.

collection and design that awakens spirituality and encourages women to gather and affirm their female experience.

Yonit's sukkah construction and the ritual performance that it nurtured (which included "a women's ushpizin," or ritual gathering of mothers) were born of her interpretation of Judaism as an ecologically aware practice, of Sukkot as a maternally resident holiday, and of her own life experience as a Jewish woman. Yonit's sukkah mediates between a closed past and an open future: her construction adheres to an already-scripted observance of what has been, but her decoration is informed by an imagined experience of what may be.

Mediating Tradition

In these two vignettes from Bloomington, Indiana, Bakol and Yonit construct their sukkot according to what they understand to be the requirements of religious law, but they conceptualize Jewish identity personally through individual interpretations of the sukkah's structure, space, and use. Bakol asserts her sense of place in Jewish history most explicitly through the ritual building. She accesses a common Jewish experience by following the rules of construction, claiming the space through personalized decoration. Bakol builds her sukkah to recognize the Jewish people and affirm her Jewish self within it.

Although Yonit follows the halakhic rules of sukkah construction, her holiday observance is motivated by an appreciation of the natural world and its ability to strengthen spiritual awareness and human relationships. "The building is physical," she said, "but it brings us closer to nature and the divine and the spiritual world." Her holiday observance is grounded in a religious structure but she interprets it through her connection with the environment, her experience as a woman, and her family, infusing her Jewish practice with personal meaning.

Both women locate themselves in historic, ethnic, religious, cultural, and family tradition through their participation in this ritual, redefining a Jewish past, reasserting a Jewish present, and imagining a Jewish future. They build impermanent shelters to affirm and protect enduring identities.

Notes

1. I align my concept of tradition with those of folklorists Henry Glassie and Richard Bauman. For Glassie, tradition is a temporal concept. It is a means of deriving the future from the past; a "volitional, temporal action" and process by which culture exists; a "swing term between culture and history," which designates folklore as the "mediating agent" between the fields of anthropology and history, contributing to a more successful cultural history (2003, 181, 192). Bauman views tradition as "the element of historical continuity or social inheritance in culture, or the social process by which such continuity is achieved." Tradition is the referent of a particular people's, culture's, society's, or group's collective identity (2001, 15819). Bauman further notes that, "[the process of traditionalization]—under the rubric of tradition, heritage, patrimony, custom, or the like—is a prominent resource in the service of nationalism" (15823). This observation makes explicit how the politics of identity are embedded in the notion of tradition.

2. A commercial indicator of the successful continuation of Jewish textual interpretation lies in the growing industry of Jewish publication. Artscroll Library/Mesorah Publications, based in Brooklyn, New York, is one of the largest Judaica publishing houses in the English-speaking world. From an Orthodox Jewish perspective, Artscroll Library/Mesorah Publications issues translations of religious texts, rabbinic commentaries, and a variety of "nonreligious" genres, including a popular cookbook series, *Kosher by Design*. While their publishing house has been the source of some controversy concerning issues of ideological agenda and authoritative legitimacy, they continue to prolifically publish and internationally distribute Jewish texts in multiple languages in both print and digital form. For more on Artscroll Library/Mesorah Publications and controversy over the ethics of their translation, see Jeremy Stolow, *Orthodox by Design: Judaism, Print Politics, and the ArtScroll Revolution* (University of California Press, 2010).

3. Hasan-Rokem identifies earlier historical experiences that may have shaped the place of this ritual in cultural consciousness as well: "The historical circumstances of the notion of inviting guests into the *Sukkah* also reinforce the concept of Jews as guests, which has been investigated by Kader Konuk as a cultural memory of their welcome in the Ottoman Empire in the wake of their expulsion from Spain in the late fifteenth century" (2012, 174).

4. I use the term "identity" as folklorist Roger D. Abrahams (2003) has defined it: a "cultural, social, and spiritual wholeness." In the study of expressive culture, writes Abrahams,

identity may be viewed as the "voluntary associations" and "badges of both individuality and group membership" that are made manifest in expressive culture (203). Of note, however, Henry Glassie challenges the prevalent use of "identity" in folklore studies. Acknowledging sociocultural and historical contexts that encourage more precise definition of such terms, he comments that "identity is a latent dimension of creative life that is made manifest by stress, in particular during the struggles of minorities within nations or the struggles of nations against imperialist invasion, whether military or economic" (1994, 240). In place of "identity," Glassie asserts that the concepts of tradition, communication, performance, art, history, and culture all convey well the "interplay of the individual and the collective in the personal," which lies at the heart of folklore study (139). I appreciate this observation and use "identity" in this chapter in the context and acknowledgement of the minority status of Jews in Bloomington.

5. Statistics cited on the Jewish Virtual Library website, accessed May 20, 2016, http://www.jewishvirtuallibrary.org/jsource/states/IN.html, and originally printed in Sheskin and Dashefsky 2006.

6. The US Census Bureau lists Bloomington, Indiana's population at 83,322 as of 2014. US Census Bureau website, accessed May 20, 2016: http://www.census.gov/quickfacts/table/PST045215/1805860.

7. According to a Bloomington Indiana Tourism Center website, "the county's median age (28.1 years) is much younger than that of the state as a whole (35.5), with a high proportion of residents in the eighteen-to-twenty-four age group" due to its university draw. Bloomington Indiana Tourism Center website, accessed May 20, 2016: http://www.visitbloomington.com/about us/community/information/.

8. Indiana University Hillel website, accessed May 20, 2016: http://www.hillel.org/college-guide/list/record/indiana-university.

9. Although Beth Shalom is the only synagogue in Bloomington, the Lubavitch Chabad House/Jewish Student Center, established almost thirty years ago near the Indiana University campus, holds regular Sabbath and holiday services and community events for Bloomington's Jewish student population.

10. Beth Shalom Congregation website, accessed May 20, 2016: http://www.bethshalom-bjc.org.

11. Vanessa L. Ochs defines two categories of Jewish home objects: "explicit" and "implicit"—both "folk oriented" as they privilege Jewish practice and account for personal meaning, which other classification systems often neglect to do in their adherence to traditional Jewish law and ritual observance. Explicit objects, such as a *mezuzah* or *Shabbat* candlesticks, define boundaries that "create a demarcated Jewish world" in the home or secular environments and help establish Jewish identities. Implicit Jewish objects, by contrast, such as family photograph shrines or shelves of books, "embody, create, and express *kedushah* [Hebrew: 'holiness'] by their presence, but do so subtly and indirectly," gaining new meaning and function in a Jewish context (Ochs 2007, 101–102, 106). Implicit objects act as indicators of both Jewish identity and assimilation into a larger home culture using non-Jewish goods in Jewish ways, and enabling Jews to turn new lands into homelands.

12. Bakol's association of the tambourine with the desert and Israel may be traced to "The Song of Moses" in the story of Exodus. In this passage, the Israelites cross the Red Sea to safety while the Pharaoh, his chariots, and his horsemen drown in its waters. It is written, "The people of Israel walked on dry ground in the midst of the sea. Then Miriam the prophetess, the sister of Aaron, took a tambourine in her hand, and all the women went out after her with tambourines and dancing" (Exodus 15:19–20 [ESV]).

2 Shchunat Hatikva, Tel Aviv: A Geography of Difference

In the middle of July of 2010, I arrived in a neighborhood of South Tel Aviv, Israel, called Shchunat Hatikva, or "Neighborhood of Hope." I chose this area for my in-depth ethnography of Sukkot observance because I wanted to examine the ritual practices of Jews from a variety of ethnic and cultural backgrounds, and this quarter is known to be one of the densest and most diverse. More generally, I based myself in Israel because it was a conceptual, if not actual, foundation for the Jewish ritual practice that I had observed in Indiana, and it was the destination of the Israelites in the biblical story of Sukkot. The narrative of the holiday describes the relationship between a people and their Promised Land; I wanted to trace the many journeys and identify the different "Promised Lands" of Jews today. I would not only research how Jews outside of Israel were relating to local and distant communities through Sukkot observance, but also how Jews within Israel, the biblical "Promised Land," formed relationships with their local and distant communities. Thus, I arrived in Shchunat Hatikva (colloquially referred to as Hatikva) in the hot summer of 2010 to pursue fieldwork for sixteen months, aiming to document two cycles of the weeklong Sukkot holiday. During the first cycle in September of 2010, I would devote the seven festival days to documenting as many ritual structures as possible and follow up with individual interviews in the months that followed. During the second cycle, in October of 2011, I would spend extended time with the families whom I had already befriended the previous year, having now received personal invitations to share holiday meals with them in their sukkot.

After each of the holiday weeks in 2010 and 2011, I used the months that followed to conduct open-ended conversations with builders, decorators, and users of these sukkot about their life histories, ritual practices, and worldviews. Additionally, in 2011, I had the opportunity to spend time in Hatikva's public park, Gan Hatikva, where homeless and disadvantaged residents of the neighborhood were camping out in protest as part of the country's widespread social demonstrations. In this park, next to the tent encampments in which they had been living for three months, Hatikva's lowest-income residents built wooden sukkot in

Fig. 2.1. A typical street in Shchunat Hatikva, lined with two- and three-story residences. Tel Aviv, Israel. 2010.

observance of the holiday. I photographed these sukkot in the park and participated in the social gatherings inside to document this unexpected new context for Sukkot ritual practice.

This chapter examines the Hatikva neighborhood through its relationship to the geography and communities of greater Tel Aviv that lie beyond its borders. The following chapter presents Hatikva through the relationships that its residents have with each other, within its own borders. Contextualizing the Sukkot observance that I documented, these introductions to the history and social life of the city's southern corner frame its residents' current religious beliefs and ritual practices with a description of their everyday life and worldviews beyond the duration of the holiday.

Drawing Borders of Distinction

While lying within the official borders of the Tel Aviv-Jaffa municipality, this southern quarter of the city has a distinct identity shaped by a conflicted history of neglect and uncertain present circumstances. Officially, the neighborhood of Shchunat Hatikva is not sectioned off from Tel Aviv proper; however, in all unofficial respects, this neighborhood is contained within clearly defined borders.

Shchunat Hatikva is a working-class quarter of Southeast Tel Aviv-Jaffa. It has long been known as a mixed ethnic neighborhood that was settled by Jews from Yemen as early as the 1930s, with waves of Iraqi and Iranian Jews arriving in the 1950s. Today, this neighborhood is home to Jews who have immigrated from Syria, Egypt, Morocco, Libya, and Uzbekistan, as well as from Yemen, Iraq, and Iran. The social and ceremonial lives of Hatikva's Jews are rooted in the Arab nations from which they emigrated, in their common Jewish heritage, and in their current position in Israeli society. In recent decades, Hatikva has also become home to foreign, non-Jewish migrants who have settled in this lower-income area to find a means of survival. As different populations have migrated into and out of Hatikva since the earliest Jewish immigrants settled among its orchards, its social history has been continually marked by patterns of change.

In 2010, just months before I moved to Israel begin my fieldwork, an article in *Haaretz*, a main Israeli newspaper, reported municipal efforts to increase tourism in this overlooked quarter of the city. The article began, "Hatikva means 'the hope,' but to many people South Tel Aviv's Hatikva Quarter is a symbol of anything but: a site of poverty, crime and violence on the unfashionable side of Tel Aviv" (Kosharek 2010). Hatikva's stigmatized image has persisted in Israeli consciousness until today and has frayed the social fabric of the neighborhood since its establishment. It continues to unravel its threads by perpetuating a lack of appreciation of the social and cultural value of life within its borders.

My encounters with Israelis outside of Shchunat Hatikva throughout the period of my fieldwork reinforced the disreputable image of the neighborhood that "outsiders" perceive. In more positive moments, friends and acquaintances would admire how "authentic" the people, culture, beliefs, and food were in Hatikva.[1] At other times, they would call my fieldwork "hard-core," describing Hatikva to be full of dangerous and desperate individuals who bemoan their problems from sunrise to sunset, waiting for government handouts. I heard these comments from friends and strangers who lived outside the neighborhood, north of Hatikva, and who presumed that the neighborhood's marred past had evolved into a deprived and demoralized present. Many who had never visited South Tel Aviv shared these impressions with me, then eagerly following their remarks with a request to meet later in the week for a tour of Hatikva's most "authentic" eateries serving foods that they yearned for from their homes in other parts of the city. The requests were innocent and sincere, but they emphasized to me the essentialized image of Hatikva within the consciousness of the population beyond its borders.

The spatial and social distance between Hatikva and greater Tel Aviv can be explained by three conceptual and actual dichotomies: North and South (or Upper and Lower Class), Ashkenazi and Mizrahi, and Israeli and Foreign. Ethnic, racial, cultural, and class differences have defined Hatikva's history, and these three dichotomies have defined its sense of self. Here, they serve as a structural frame for a narrative of the neighborhood's social history.

North and South

Shchunat Hatikva lies in the south of the city, east of the Ayalon Highway, Israel's main north–south expressway. The significance of Hatikva's location in the southeast section of Tel Aviv's cityscape reaches back to a time before the Ayalon Highway even existed, when Hatikva's children still played in the *wadi* (streambed) that the highway would later replace. Until the highway's construction in 1982, the Ayalon River flowed in its place across the country, seeping into the life of neighborhoods such as Shchunat Hatikva. Children splashed in its refreshing waterbed in the hot summer months and took cover at home when the river deluged neighborhood streets during winter storms. Hatikva, lying to the east of this natural division, is not only physically removed from the rest of the city, but is conceptually removed as well. During my early weeks of fieldwork, when I searched in bookstores across the country for a map of Tel Aviv to navigate Hatikva's streets, I was unable to find a single city map that included this southeast quarter in its rendering. Drawings of Tel Aviv's expanse commonly depicted its eastern border at the vertical line of the Ayalon Highway—Hatikva's streets trailing off the sheet, or, if I was lucky, onto a small back corner of the page.

The symbolism of the Ayalon Highway physically sectioning Hatikva off from the rest of Tel Aviv is reinforced by an even more meaningful geographic feature: the Tel Aviv-Jaffa border, to Hatikva's south. This second border to the neighborhood reveals the further significance of Hatikva's location on the periphery of both Tel Aviv to its north and Jaffa to its south. Although Tel Aviv and Jaffa merged into one municipality in 1950, until then, a contested and shifting border separated these two cities and the populations that occupied them—or, at least, the majority of the populations. Shchunat Hatikva, lying in the borderland between Tel Aviv and Jaffa, was only officially annexed into Tel Aviv after the war in 1948—two years before the cities merged. Thus, from Tel Aviv's founding in 1909 until 1948, Hatikva and other southern neighborhoods in the Tel Aviv-Jaffa borderland area hovered in ambiguity, existing between "Hebrew Tel Aviv" and "Arab Jaffa." In this in-between space, Arabs and Jews lived together among fields of *sabras* (cactus fruit) and citrus orchards, an area characterized by Middle Eastern ethnicities and municipal neglect.

In his social analysis of Tel Aviv's urban planning, Nathan Marom describes the city's expansion in the early 1920s to highlight its preferential development:

> New upscale neighborhoods (such as the "Heart of Tel Aviv") consolidated at the center, while unplanned territories of tents, shacks and

self-constructed houses appeared on the periphery of the city's built-up area, absorbing many newly arrived immigrants. As Tel Aviv continued to expand northward according to the outline of the 1925 plan prepared by Patrick Geddes, its shanty neighborhoods were constrained to the south of the city, particularly to the ethnically-mixed areas on both sides of the porous Tel Aviv-Jaffa boundary. Within a few years, spatial distinction between the planned north and the spontaneous urbanism of the south, between the "city" and its "slums," had emerged. (2009, 15)

This urban development, fueled the city's social stratification as municipal officials, turned their attention to the north and their backs on the south. The shanty neighborhoods on both sides of the Tel Aviv-Jaffa border of which Marom writes are further described by Deborah S. Bernstein as both the "periphery" and "frontier zone" for the unique socializing and marginalization that characterized this slighted territory. Bernstein describes how the shifting, permeable borderline demarcated the separation between Tel Aviv's Jews and Jaffa's Arabs during the British Mandate period (1920–1948), "an area of contact, crossing, and mixing . . . an area that manifested many of the contradictory aspects of borders—division and permeability, a focus of attention and at the same time a peripheral and marginal section of the urban entity" (2012, 117).

The southern neighborhoods' peripheral status within Tel Aviv was in part physical and in part conceptual. Their physical exclusion was due to the municipal neglect of social and physical infrastructures in the city's south: "The roads were not paved, nor was there an adequate drainage system to channel the strong winter rains causing floods, damage to property, injuries to children and elderly folk, and subsequently diseases and failing health. Similarly, the lack of an up-to-date sewage system, which could be found in the rest of Tel-Aviv, created extremely unsanitary and unhygienic conditions" (Bernstein 2012, 128). As a result of this physical neglect, or perhaps because of it, the marginal identity of these neighborhoods was confirmed in the consciousness of greater Tel Aviv: "These neighborhoods were perceived as marginal both from within and from without: residents of these neighborhoods saw themselves as excluded from the rest of the city, while residents of the city-center saw them as peripheral, both socio-culturally and in terms of infrastructure" (132).[2]

The social exclusion felt from within and without the southern neighborhoods is a local condition that architect Sharon Rotbard attributes to national and international dynamics. Rotbard views the social divisions in Tel Aviv as a product of the city's planning; furthermore, he criticizes the role that urban development plays in Israel's nationalistic agenda. His work questions the dominant narrative of Tel Aviv's architectural history, according to which German Jewish architects designed its over four thousand Bauhaus buildings after escaping the threat of

Nazi Germany. The exceptional concentration of Bauhaus structures that these architects created in Tel Aviv as a result earned the city a UNESCO designation of "World Cultural Heritage site" in 2003, an international mark of distinction that yielded a new label for Tel Aviv—the "White City." Rotbard, however, does not consider this label a source of pride, for in its wake, it threw into relief an unrecognized "Black City" in Tel Aviv's south. In contrast to UNESCO's "White City," Rotbard's "Black City" is the site of displaced and forgotten citizens, Tel Aviv's marginalized "others": working-class Mizrahi Jews; legal, temporary foreign laborers; and undocumented migrant workers. While the narrative of the "White City" has become a story by and for Israeli Jews of European origin, says Rotbard, the "Black City" has risen in darkness and remains at the edges of the same city (Rotbard 2015).

Hatikva's separation from Tel Aviv "proper" was thus rooted in the city's early development, one that nurtured the growth of the north and permitted the stagnation of the south. As Bernstein notes, more than sixty years after the establishment of the State of Israel, "the dividing line between north and south is accepted today as a central principle in the physical, social, and cultural layout of Tel-Aviv. People, especially youngsters, are identified, and/or identify themselves as 'northern' (*tsfoni*) or 'southern' (*dromi*). In many respects, the two are seen as polar opposites" (2012, 135). And these opposite communities that Bernstein identifies in the physical and social landscapes of Tel Aviv, unfortunately, largely remain the wealthy and the poor, the nurtured and the neglected, the Ashkenazim and the Mizrahim.

Making the Abstract Concrete

During the early months of my fieldwork, I learned from residents of Shchunat Hatikva that they defined South Tel Aviv as much by what it is not as by what it is. It is not North Tel Aviv. They said the south of the city is neither clean nor quiet nor considered safe. In the north, they said, where Tel Aviv University and major museums are located, wealthier Israelis live in tall, modern apartment buildings with their windows and doors closed to protect their possessions. This view would soon crystallize as I became aware of the historical events that had placed Hatikva in a situation of conceptual and physical neglect.

Project Renewal was one of the key historical events that shed light on the relationship between Hatikva and greater Tel Aviv. In 1978, the government of Israel and the Jewish Agency for Israel jointly founded a national rehabilitation initiative called Project Renewal, which aimed at decreasing socioeconomic gaps in Israeli society through the rehabilitation of infrastructure in distressed communities. The *Jewish Telegraphic Agency* reported that at the inaugural dinner for the project, held in New York City on March 17, 1980, Mayors Ed Koch of New

York and Shlomo Lahat of Tel Aviv celebrated putting one hundred million dollars "in philanthropic and public funds to work over the [following] several years in strengthening the social fabrics of neighborhoods in the world's two largest Jewish cities, New York and Tel Aviv" (March 19, 1980).[3] The mayoral dinner speeches at the event focused on Shchunat Hatikva as "the slum neighborhood on the fringe of Israel's largest city that has been 'adopted' by New York's Jewish community as part of Project Renewal/Israel." The *Jewish Telegraphic Agency* outlined the plan for Hatikva's rehabilitation:

> Hatikvah is regarded as the worst of 160 slum areas in Israel where some 45,000 immigrant families, mostly from North Africa and East Europe, comprising 300,000 individuals, dwell in poverty and deprivation, Lahat said. Project Renewal/Israel, undertaken at the urging of Premier Menachem Begin, aims to speed the integration of these Jews, who constitute what has been called the "second Israel," into the mainstream of Israeli life, he stated.
>
> The estimated $1.2 billion in financing required to break the cycle of poverty in which they live is to be provided half by the government of Israel and half by world Jewry through the Jewish Agency . . . The program to be implemented in Hatikvah . . . includes rehabilitation of existing and construction of some new housing; expansion and renovation of such community facilities; intensification of social services for youths and the aged, tutoring and career guidance for adolescents, and training of parents in home management and family guidance. (May 19, 1980)

The plan was extensive and the planners were hopeful, but the designs they had formulated from above could not all be achieved on the ground.

One planner for Project Renewal who was featured in the *Journal of the American Institute of Architects* detailed the failure. In the December issue, Charley J. Levine (1979) described an urban design proposal for the redevelopment of Hatikva's dilapidated housing—one of the physical infrastructure goals in Project Renewal. "A bold but controversial urban design scheme by architect Israel M. Goodovitch may bring order and badly needed new housing to a troubled slum area of southern Tel Aviv," the article began, and although it continued to discuss physical details of the design scheme more than the neighborhood's social life, it shed new light on the residents' relationship to their surroundings. Israel M. Goodovitch had proposed replacing Hatikva's original housing with modern, prefabricated structures built on reclaimed land, one closed-down street at a time. Residents could remain in their old houses as the adjacent construction took place, eliminating the need for relocation, which Goodovitch surmised was a key point of resistance. Upon completion of the new structures, the old housing would be razed and replaced with green space. "The first principle that anyone who hopes to improve this situation must realize," Goodovitch said, "is that Hatikva residents will not move. No matter how much this complicates things, this is *their* neighborhood, and there is no way that any kind of relocation program might succeed" (Levine 1979, 44). Goodovitch believed this was the only feasible redevelopment plan for Hatikva's "slum" housing, and when asked what would happen if any residents refused the new housing he was offering, he replied: "Peer pressure, which is strong in this close-knit kind of place, will help remove any such obstacles . . . and free, modern housing right in front of one's nose is an enticing proposition. If worse comes to worst, however, the city engineer will declare the old structures unsafe and condemn them, or the housing authority can declare the right of public domain and enforce cooperation" (45). His response, informed by his outside impression of the community, was unyielding. Goodovitch believed in his view of the community's circumstances and psychology so adamantly that the article's author indicated, "Goodovitch is not only convinced that his idea will work, he is positive that it is the only plan that *can* work" (45). The article framed Goodovitch's controversial design plan with a brief but dramatic review of Hatikva's socioeconomic history to convey Hatikva's looming deterioration:

> The Hatikva neighborhood was first settled in 1935 by streams of homeless newcomers. Land was parceled out in narrow, miniscule plots of only 120 square meters (140 square yards) each and families were determined to take advantage of every square inch purchased. There were no restrictive building codes. There was no social pressure to conform to communal standards. There was only a frenetic drive to build one's house with the business of living inside it.
>
> Already a decade before the state of Israel was born with the stirring song "Hatikva" (the hope) adopted as the national anthem, the Hatikva quarter was already rushing toward its present state of premature dilapidation. Inadequate basic services and insufficient living space have created a blight that is unusual for Israel. (45)

The article continued with demographic information, notably commenting that 75 percent of the people were "of Afro-Asian background, the so-called 'other Israel,' rather than the minority of European Jews that has traditionally set the country's cultural pace." This was a community of physical and social marginalization, balancing social ills such as "drugs, juvenile delinquency, and prostitution" with "remarkable strengths, foremost among them a profound sense of community." Returning to Goodovitch's redevelopment plan, the article finally tied the community's spirit and the neighborhood's design together to highlight the actual circumstances facing redevelopers such as Goodovitch: "The residents know they have critical problems and want to solve them, but they will accept solutions only within certain parameters. New housing, for example, is a coveted goal, but highrise apartment buildings would never be accepted in the quarter. Lowrise buildings are traditional here, and the people intend to maintain the tradition. They also want more open spaces, more playgrounds, more parking areas, and better schools for their children. But, above all else, they do not want to be dictated to, and they will not countenance hypothetical solutions dropped on their doorsteps without prior consultation" (45). The redesign of Hatikva's housing was not only a physical challenge due to old, winding streets that were occupied by crumbling, two-story structures; it was a social challenge as well. City planners needed to confront the people who lived on these narrow streets and in these chipping structures—people who felt simultaneously deserving of this municipal attention and wary of the city, which was the source of its depressed state over decades of neglect.

Three years after the article's publication, in 1982, social anthropologist Emanuel Marx reviewed the socioeconomic state of Shchunat Hatikva, one of the first seventy sites selected for Project Renewal. Marx assessed the neighborhood's condition at this point in the project to evaluate how effective the government's rehabilitation effort might be in practice. "Hatikva," wrote Marx, "located at the centre of a belt of so-called slums crossing the Tel-Aviv conurbation from east to west," had been selected as a prototypical working-class neighborhood considered in public opinion to be a "slum" (1982, 40). He credited this popular opinion to the Israeli news media's representation of Hatikva, which he said filtered its representation through a sensational lens: "In the public mind [Hatikva] is associated with crime, youth gangs, and football. Reports on these subjects appear in the media in the wake of police raids on the quarter in search of narcotics dealers or fugitive criminals, or after a group of young criminals are apprehended (as in the case of the Ma'ats gang in 1977), or when the local football club 'Bnei Yehuda' is involved in a spectacular game or when its supporters vandalize property in the quarter. The coverage is usually negative and generalizes from single instances to the whole population" (41). Marx concluded that Hatikva was "a typical instance of a stigmatized community."

Sociologist Erving Goffman created a list of symptoms that could be attributed to stigmatized individuals;[4] Marx applies it here to the case of this neighborhood, declaring, that "the stigma attached to [Hatikva], the inconsiderate intervention of the wider society, and the inhabitants' acceptance of the stigma when confronting representatives of that wider society, are all there."[5] He labeled this condition a "perceived defect" rather than "objective reality" and identified its deleterious cause and result: "The heart of the issue," wrote Marx, "is the relative powerlessness of the residents. This is a longstanding condition which has led to a gradual deterioration of the quarter" (1982, 41).

Marx noted that the particular dynamics of social control wielded by national, municipal, and local representatives undercut any sense of authority that Hatikva's residents might possess. He found the lack of political power rather than economic weakness to be the source of Hatikva's socioeconomic distress, and he stated that this rehabilitation project was simply another demonstration of the entrenched power struggle between local organizations and national authorities that perpetuated Hatikva's status as a slum:

> Central government works against voluntary associations that could represent the inhabitants. While associations can be set up relatively easily, they are then co-opted by the authorities and thus lose their power. Or if they persist in remaining independent, the authorities fear them and put obstacles in their way. As centralization also prevents the formation of groups within the state and municipalities, these organizations do indeed become vulnerable to coercion by individuals and groups. Officials therefore fear that inhabitants may engage in organized violence against them, and tend to suppress attempts to organize. This reluctance to allow inhabitants to organize and negotiate, eventually leads some of the inhabitants into organized violence, in an attempt to establish contact with the authorities. Thus in December 1980 a group of young men from the Hatikva Quarter forcibly occupied the Mayor's office in order to coerce him to accede to their demands. The police arrested the group, and the municipal authorities are seeking to curb their activities.
> There seems to be no way out of the dilemma, no way to increase the power of the inhabitants. (44)

Marx's report was an honest, if pessimistic, assessment of the potential of the government's rehabilitation program to provide deep and lasting improvements in the neighborhood's social and physical infrastructure.

Cycles of Neglect

Almost twenty years later, in 2010, with new facades plastered on buildings, a renovated *shuk* (outdoor market), and a new community center (Beit Dani)—all due to the rehabilitation effort—Israeli news reports continued to confirm Marx's analysis of the ongoing power struggle between Hatikva's residents and the Israeli government. In the context of the increasing, contested migration of thousands of Eritrean and Sudanese asylum seekers into South Tel Aviv beginning in 2005 and continuing into 2010, the placement of a new, disadvantaged population among the country's already-depressed communities led to local demonstrations that decried the government's neglect of its disenfranchised populations. After a wave of protests across South Tel Aviv in which working-class communities demanded that newly arrived individuals be distributed across the northern, wealthier neighborhoods of the city or deported back to their home countries, Prime Minister Benyamin Netanyahu released a videotaped response to address the broiling discontent. His message was summed up in the two sentences of his address that became headline news the following day: "I ask one thing, and I will be adamant about it. The citizens of Israel cannot take the law into their own hands—they cannot take part in violence or degradation" (in an article by Barak Ravid in the *Haaretz Daily Newspaper*, December 22, 2010).

The reaction to Netanyahu's video in Hatikva made clear that the struggle that Marx had identified in 1982 still continued. Residents were pleased that the prime minister had acknowledged their frustrations as well as their ability to take matters into their own hands if the government did not respond to their demands, but they still did not believe that he would offer anything but empty words. I observed Hatikva's internal strength and its guarded attitude toward outside authority in a more intimate context as well. Commenting on topical headlines or local social strife, residents taught me about what binds Israel's southern populations together and separates them from the politics and social standards that they feel exist to the north. Throughout the duration of my fieldwork, I would witness this dynamic stressed to greater and lesser degrees, first during the Eritrean/Sudanese migration into South Tel Aviv, and then during the housing demonstrations in South Tel Aviv and greater Israel in the summer of 2011.

Marx had described Hatikva as part of the "the commercial and industrial hub of Israel" that has attracted a steady stream of new arrivals from other parts of the country, "many of whom establish a first foothold in the low-rent slum belt" with the hope of establishing themselves before moving on to higher status neighborhoods (1982, 40). Today, Hatikva is home to the city's transient populations. However, Hatikva—and South Tel Aviv more broadly—has been marked by a history of attracting not only Jewish immigrants but non-Jewish migrants as well, making possible the rebuilding of many lives in this new land, but all at a social cost.[6]

In personal histories that Hatikva's veteran Jewish residents shared with me, I heard recollections of early immigration to Israel that were beset by bias and disrespect for the cultural and ethnic identities of immigrants of Middle Eastern and North African origin (*Mizrahim*).[7] My acquaintances shared stories that offered countless examples of governmental discrimination against Hatikva's Mizrahi residents. For instance, I heard of individuals who were compelled to change their Mizrahi names to Ashkenazi-sounding substitutes in order to receive telephone service in this southern quarter of the city. I also heard families recall how their fathers and uncles, who had arrived from Yemen in the 1930s and 1940s, worked in construction for Ashkenazi employers with the promise of pay at the close of the day that was repeatedly never received—an exploitation of their labor that has formed the basis of their current distrust of Israel's upper classes. Elderly women at Beit Dani, the community center in Shchunat Hatikva where I volunteered, collectively recounted memories of the Ayalon River's historic floods in the 1950s when rainstorms deluged the neighborhood's inadequate drainage systems, causing damage that gave them personal reason to call this southern area Tel Aviv's "urban frontier."

In addition to individual memories of neglect, the Tel Aviv Municipal Archive contains a written history of persistently unanswered calls for attention by Hatikva's residents from as early as the 1930s. In the archive, annual files are filled with handwritten notes and typed petitions by men and women of South Tel Aviv requesting attention to the poor sanitation and lack of public services in their neighborhoods. Nearly all of these petitions were marked with a stamp of receipt by the Office of the Mayor, but nothing more. Today, although an awareness of the mechanisms that perpetuate Israel's social inequalities has advanced, residents of Shchunat Hatikva have frequently shared with me their lingering memories and continuing experiences of ethnic and class inequality.

Ashkenazi and Mizrahi

As a woman of Ashkenazi heritage conducting ethnographic research among the majority Mizrahi population, my personal experience gave new dimension to the oral histories I was collecting, many of which concerned ethnic and cultural differences between Ashkenazi and Mizrahi Jews. I occupied a position of difference as an American woman learning about Hatikva's residents and social history through participation in neighborhood life. Before my fieldwork began, I had not been self-consciously aware of my Ashkenazi identity more than to recognize that my family's roots reached back to Germany, Romania, Hungary, and Palestine. In fact, it was almost difficult to recognize my Jewish identity at all while being raised in densely Jewish New York City. As residents of Hatikva increasingly trusted and welcomed me into their lives, however, I began to realize that the light color of my skin, which signified my Ashkenazi cultural heritage for them, was one of my most distinctive identifiers, and a constant by which I could measure my insider-outsider status during my time there.

Over the sixteen months that I spent in the neighborhood, the perception of my insider/outsider status offered me continual insights into the community's history and social boundaries. While skin color is a visual characteristic, other aspects of my identity that spanned the range of visibility contributed to my level of acceptance in the community. I was Jewish (insider) but of Ashkenazi heritage (outsider); my father was born in Israel and his family still lives there (insider), but I was born in the United States and still live there (outsider); I had studied Hebrew (insider), but English was my native language (outsider); some members of my family are observant Jews (insider) but I did not consider myself so (outsider); I was a single woman interested in marriage and family (insider), but I was working toward a doctorate at the age of thirty instead of getting married (outsider); and, last but not least, my skin tone was light in comparison to the skin tones of my friends from Hatikva (outsider). Simultaneously and conversely, however, the colors of my skin and those of Hatikva's Jewish residents were lighter than the darker skin colors of the Sudanese and Eritrean migrants who were newly arriving to the neighborhood, often repositioning me as an insider in this context. These flexible cultural, ethnic, linguistic, religious, gendered, and racial components of my personhood placed me in a variable position in Hatikva, giving me access to a multifaceted and nuanced perspective on Ashkenazi-Mizrahi relations.

For part of my time in Hatikva, I was enlightened as an insider, praised for demonstrating a commitment to the neighborhood and its residents through my ongoing presence—through the length of my stay, my participation in residents' lives, and my genuine interest in neighborhood social events and local politics. For the other part of the time, I was educated as an outsider, my Ashkenazi heritage prompting jokes about Ashkenazi-Mizrahi cultural differences and friendly banter about that supposed contrast. Learning from both positions, I became aware of the social gap that still exists between Israel's Ashkenazi and Mizrahi populations in Tel Aviv. Residents shared their memories and observations that reaffirmed the stereotypes that regularly circulated throughout the community.

Mealtimes in Shchunat Hatikva offered some of the richest opportunities to learn about Ashkenazi-Mizrahi distinctions. When hosts offered me a cup of coffee or a bowl of soup, they also offered lessons about my position in the community, about Ashkenazi and Mizrahi characterizations, and about their personal and cultural beliefs on health and social values. I accepted all foods that were presented to me—especially foods I had never seen before—and expressed particular interest in learning about "traditional" foods. I affirmed that my research included all expressive forms of self, culture, and society, so that stories of food preparation and consumption were included in my area of interest, which gained me great approval as an eager eater. I share the following mealtime vignettes to elucidate a tension between Ashkenazim and Mizrahim that I felt permeated daily life in Shchunat Hatikva.[8]

I hardly entered a home in Hatikva where I was not immediately offered food and drink. When Sharona, a young woman of Iraqi-Yemeni descent, heated water for our four o'clock tea, she told me that I was warm—not like the color of my skin, the color of Ashkenazim—and she smiled to make sure that I knew she said this as a friend. Most often, we sat in her kitchen with her mother, Suad; several of her adult brothers; and a gaggle of nieces running around—all of us gathered around a small table covered with bowls of food: sautéed okra in tomato sauce, hummus, or a fresh soup made by Suad. Early in our days together, at this table, Sharona offered me *skhug*—a spicy condiment of Yemenite origin that accompanied most meals I was served in Hatikva. It is typically made of fresh, hot green (or red) peppers, cilantro, garlic, cumin, salt, and olive oil. Sharona and her mother watched me gently tap a dab into my soup, and when I said it was delicious, they breathed out a sigh of relief and surprise, praising me for my excellent sense of taste. My appreciation of the spicy condiment set me apart from other Ashkenazi people, they said, whose personalities were like the bland, white foods they associated with Ashkenazi culture.[9]

In less familiar homes, I also encountered stereotypes in the kitchen. During my first Sukkot in Hatikva, when friends and family visited each other during the hot hours of the day, I would wander Hatikva's streets to photograph the ritual structures. One afternoon, I found a woman hanging laundry in a courtyard below a terrace sukkah I was photographing. She introduced herself as Yaffa, the builder of the sukkah, and invited me upstairs for tea. As I told her the story of my recent arrival in Hatikva, she opened her refrigerator to reach for fresh *nana* (mint) leaves, and I could not help but remark how beautifully stacked the inside of her refrigerator was—a colorful array of containers and towers of fresh produce balanced atop each other with precision. She smiled at me and said that Mizrahi Jews spend their money on food, unlike Ashkenazi Jews, who spend their money on education and careers. She equated food with love, family, warmth, trust, respect, and heritage—an association that I encountered many times thereafter in the neighborhood. As I drank my tea, Yaffa told me about how she eats with her grandchildren and neighbors in her sukkah every night, and how special she believes the Hatikva community to be. "People from all over the world live right next door to each other, and in peace," she said, pointing out her window to the homes of her Ethiopian, Moroccan, and Bukharan neighbors. "Only in the government do people think that everyone has a problem with each other. Outside the neighborhood, no one knows what life here is really like," she said. We talked through our tea until Yaffa had to resume her day's duties. I thanked her and returned to my rounds.

Not only was I always offered food and drink when I arrived in people's homes, I was always given food to take home when I left. If I refused the food, I was probed for my reason, and most often I was convinced to revoke my reluctance by the conversation's end. Only once did I refuse with success—and remorse. I was visiting an elderly woman named Yaffa (the name is common in this neighborhood and in Israel more generally) whom I had met at the Bukharan senior women's social group that met every Monday in Hatikva's community center.

Yaffa was the only one of the twelve elderly women who spoke fluent Hebrew in addition to Bukharit and Russian, and she called me over to sit with her so that she could translate the social exchanges for me. After an hour of pickled fish and stuffed dumplings, one woman plugged in a CD player, placed a bejeweled Bukharan headdress atop her head, and started dancing to an Uzbeki tune that the rest of the women instantly recognized. Several others jumped up to join her, and soon I too was called up for wrist-twirling in the middle of the room. At the close of the evening, I thanked Yaffa for her help in translation, and agreed to visit her at her home as soon as possible to hear about her story of childhood immigration from Samarkind, Uzbekistan.

When that day arrived some weeks later, I headed to Yaffa's home directly from another neighborly visit where I had unexpectedly been served a meal. I was too full to eat more and as much as I did not want to offend Yaffa, I politely declined her offers to cook for me as we entered her home. Yaffa relented asking after several attempts, and we sat at her empty table as she told me about her life. She began with her current life in Hatikva, for which she expressed both love and lament. "People think that Hatikva's people are trash," she said, "but the people who work in our streets, we ask them, 'Do you want tea? Coffee? Water?' In the north of Tel Aviv, they don't even offer them water from the tap! We are from the heart." She was saddened that as a child, her daughter was ashamed to tell her friends that she was born in Hatikva. Yaffa added that she is still saddened by her daughter's continued discontent with Yaffa's insistence on remaining there. Her daughter wants Yaffa to move out of the neighborhood to a higher status community, just as she has, but Yaffa said she would never leave. She pointed outside to the large garden and sukkah in her backyard and said that this was what she loved. She would never find space for such a garden or sukkah anywhere else in Tel Aviv.

We walked outside and watered the plants on the side of the sukkah as she recited to me the names of her favorites. At the end of my visit, Yaffa closed her gate and watched me begin to bike away. Halfway down her street, and almost out of earshot, I heard her cry out after me: "You know it's not healthy to run around all day and not eat! God forbid, you might get an ulcer!" Yaffa's message was clear: preparing food for someone was an act of respect, serving it was a gesture of affection, and accepting it honored these gracious efforts. To refuse to eat together was to refuse to be together, and to be alone was unhealthy.

Informal comments about the relationship of food and survival by residents of the neighborhood reinforced this association between eating and community health. One resident described for me the economic distress of Hatikva's population but ended by affirming that despite the situation, "No one is hungry here." In the same context, another acquaintance said, "Where there's nothing, there's food," and from another resident, "Where there's no money, there's food." Pnina Cohen recalled the poverty of her youth when many family members slept in one room together. "Times were very hard," she said, "but no one was ever hungry."

I learned this lesson from Pnina's family, one of the families with whom I became closest in Shchunat Hatikva. Pnina is of Yemenite descent, and her home, on the border of the neighborhood, was one I visited regularly. The first time I stopped by, Pnina told me that her door was always open and I should come over any time, day or night. Open doors welcomed unannounced visitors, and pots of food on the stovetop always rewarded those unexpected guests.[10]

One afternoon, I visited Pnina's house unannounced. She was making *malawach*, a Yemenite dish of layered fried dough served with *resek* (grated tomato) and a hardboiled egg, and she insisted that we sit and eat while we talked. As we peeled away the layers of fried pancake and dipped them in resek and skhug, Pnina told me that years ago, the Ashkenazi mayor of Tel Aviv, Ron Huldai, refused to eat the malawach that was served to him when he visited Shchunat Hatikva. "He didn't want to lower himself to our level, to eat our food," she said with pain seemingly reserved from years ago. For Pnina, eating a traditional Yemenite dish meant accepting all that came with it—the history, the culture, and, most importantly, the people. To refuse it was to refuse her history, culture, and community.

In her study, "Hummus Is Best When It Is Fresh and Made by Arabs: The Gourmetization of Hummus in Israel and the Return of the epressed Arab," Dafna Hirsch presents a cultural biography of hummus that frames it as a material that different people use at particular times as means to distinct ends. She argues that "the Arab identity of hummus functions as a resource employed by actors who are embedded in various political, social, and economic projects" (2011, 618). Rather than analyze the consumption of hummus as a symbol of ethnic heritage or political action, Hirsch examines the continual exploitation of "the Arab identity of hummus" across social, political, and religious spaces. In a similar way, narratives about the consumption or refusal to consume food of Middle Eastern and North African Jewish origin in Hatikva are shifting but potent assessments of historic and current-day social relations between Ashkenazi and Mizrahi Jews. A food item in isolation is not a commodified object symbolic of cultural status or value. Rather, each food is in dynamic relation to its maker and to its potential consumer, inscribed with new history and value each time it mediates social interaction. Food becomes a prop in the expression of identity and performance of history.

Economic status, social acceptance, and power relations are all invoked in eating practices in Hatikva, with particular attention to Ashkenazi-Mizrahi cultural distinction. The Ashkenazi-Mizrahi divide in Israeli social history has had a negative impact on Mizrahi access to educational, economic, and political opportunity. These vignettes illustrate how that divide has seeped into the consciousness of individuals as well, and how it is expressed in the intimacy of their homes.

Israeli and Foreign

At the start of my fieldwork, I was interested in learning about the perception and practice of Jewish rituals in the context of Hatikva's Jewish ethnic and cultural diversity, but I did not know how the demographic changes taking place in South Tel Aviv would affect my research. Public outcry by Hatikva's residents in response to the Israeli government placing waves of Eritrean and Sudanese asylum seekers in their neighborhood throughout 2010 and 2011, however, provided insight into not only how Hatikva's veteran residents viewed the newcomers, but also how they viewed the government, more privileged Israelis, and themselves. These were all critical perspectives on the "self" and "other" that informed my understanding of their social and cultural practices. In this last section, I examine the tense, triangulated relationships between temporary, non-Jewish residents of South Tel Aviv; veteran Jewish residents of South Tel Aviv; and the Israeli population of greater Tel Aviv. The North–South and Mizrahi-Ashkenazi divisions described in the previous two sections remain the key sources of friction between Hatikva's residents and those who live outside its borders, but in the current context of social unrest in South Tel Aviv, perceptions of belonging and exclusion become even more layered.

In their article "Bubbling Over: The Contestation of Urban Space and Possibilities for Joint Struggle in Tel Aviv" (2009), Maya Shapiro and Matan Kaminer highlight how the dubbing of Tel Aviv as a "bubble" reveals the tensions between fantasy and reality and between stability and collapse, which characterize this city's atmosphere. The Israeli bubble metaphor, they write, "presents the city, on the one hand, as a self-contained world of frivolity, money and sex, deliberately oblivious to the crushing realities around it—primary among which is, of course, the Israeli-Palestinian conflict. On the other hand," they continue, "the bubble metaphor also highlights the ways in which Tel Aviv is a precarious delusion, liable to 'pop' at any moment and implode under the weight of the everyday violence from which it is so desperate to escape." Such tension may be experienced in cities all over the world; thus they turn to another "bubble" in the city that makes Tel Aviv distinct: "If there is a 'bubble,'" they write, "then its borders can be traced—and those large tracts of the municipal zone which are excluded from its borders, while formally part of the polity, are often seen as 'not really' Tel Avivi." These excluded tracts make up the city's southern half.[11] Shapiro and Kaminer sketch this alternative bubble environment in which the "invisible inhabitants" of these ostracized areas live:

Tel Aviv is a city whose South (called 'the black city' by architect Sharon Rotbard) has always been populated by Mizrahim, marginalized and proletarianized Jews of Middle Eastern origin . . . Their position in the shadows of Tel Aviv means that they live surrounded by the city's most dirty, denigrated and dangerous activities. In the geographic center of its South lies the country's largest bus terminal, and within walking distance of this polluting eyesore one can find such amenities as a morgue, a jail, a methadone clinic and a red-light district.

Tens of thousands of non-Jewish migrants from over 72 countries in the global South [have] come to Israel and settled in Tel Aviv to fill shortages in low-wage, urban-centered labour sectors. While they often share the experiences of precarity vis-à-vis their status and marginality in the labour market, these migrants are not a homogeneous group. 'Foreign workers,' mostly from China, Thailand, the Philippines and the Indian subcontinent, are hired on contract through a labour recruitment program initiated by the Ministry of the Interior but largely managed by unregulated manpower agencies. Another significant number of migrants are asylum seekers that arrive from Eritrea and Sudan and are issued United Nations identification numbers that grant them temporary residency privileges and do not always include work permits. Still more "illegal aliens" have arrived from South America (primarily from Colombia and Ecuador) and West Africa (Nigeria, Ivory Coast and Ghana), entering the country with a three month tourist visa and settling in Tel Aviv hoping to find informal employment in domestic service, restaurant work, or construction . . . This is Tel Aviv. (Shapiro and Kaminer 2009)

This is the shadowed Tel Aviv that lives in a precarious existence, a delicate bubble, ready to burst. Tel Aviv's transnational population and the multitudes of languages, cultures, and ethnicities that are represented within its municipal bounds make it a global capital. Its distinction, however, lies in the unique and complex of relationships that have developed among its diverse Jewish majority and non-Jewish minority, on whom Shapiro and Kaminer focus rare attention in the above passage. Shapiro and Kaminer highlight the political implications of the social and geographic divisions in Tel Aviv, hinting at the deeper consequences of this spatial and social separation: "The disparity between the rich and the rest of the city—in spatial terms, between the North on the one hand and the center and South on the other—exerts a strong pull over the terms in which political claims in the city are framed—from the anti-immigration demonstrations of Southerners to the demand for rent control in the center of the city." Tel Aviv is considered an oasis of cultural diversity, liberal-minded politics, and creative expression in a country more often identified with religious conservatism, militaristic strategy, and a self-conscious interest in maintaining a Jewish identity; however, in the South Tel Aviv bubble, a complex of power relations and dynamics of oppression are sealed and revealed.

The diverse area that surrounds Tel Aviv's New Central Bus Station, tucked beneath the shadow of the highway overpass, offers low-income housing to newly arrived immigrants and migrants and a possibility to begin life anew. Amidst continual population turnover in this area, veteran residents struggle to maintain social cohesion in their neighborhoods. Since 1990, foreign workers from South Asia, South America, and Africa have settled in South Tel Aviv with temporary work visas in order to earn money for families back home in their native countries. Filipino women are one such case. The structure of their temporary lives in Israel, outlined here to illustrate the greater sector of society of which they are a part, follows a given pattern: Filipino women leave children, siblings, and parents in the Philippines and pay significant fees to secure multi-year work contracts in Israel through unregulated manpower agencies. They are offered wages higher than what they could make in their home country, and they must undergo a competitive application and sponsorship process before being selected. Often they wait years in the Philippines after submitting their application before they are approved and hired. Once in Israel, these women are trained in Israeli social, cultural, and historical background and given a fundamental introduction to the Hebrew language. They are then placed with elderly individuals across Israel as in-home attendants, and they spend twenty-four hours a day for weeks and years at a time living with and caring for homebound senior citizens. They send most of their paychecks back home to their families, but a large majority of the workers are devoted to paying off their travel and placement fees to the manpower agencies; they are often in debt for months, and perhaps years, after their arrival. These women typically take off one weekend per month to travel from their employers' homes to South Tel Aviv where they often rent an apartment with other home-care attendants or with family and friends also hired as temporary laborers in Israel. There, they share a jointly rented apartment near the Central Bus Station or, when possible, all meet up together when vacation days overlap.

South Tel Aviv is crowded with migrant workers from all over the world living in conditions such as this, or in even worse conditions when situations are less regulated. Its streets are filled with billboards in Tagalog, corner stores selling international phone cards, and specialty food markets stocking Thai noodles and Indian spices. These foreign workers' employment is formally and informally designated according to the workers' permits and skills, which create generalized categories such as Filipino women working in home care, Thai men in agriculture, Chinese men in construction, and South American and African women in domestic work.[12]

The most recent population influx into Israel, beginning in late 2005 and continuing until today, is made up of Eritrean and Sudanese migrants and asylum seekers who have fled their home countries in search of refuge and a means of survival. In 2008, a report on the growing migration published by the Euro-Mediterranean Study Commission outlined the cause of the new demographic trend and alluded to the ambiguous status of the tens of thousands of new migrants crossing into Israel, a trend that would later cause great controversy:

> After serious clashes between African refugees and the Egyptian authorities in Cairo in the last months of 2005, Israel became a more viable destination for these migrants. This led to the development of a new movement in the illegal immigration routes, with migrants departing from Egypt, being smuggled through the Sinai desert, before then reaching the long and largely un-populated border between Israel and Egypt, much of which is physically open. Conflicts in their countries of origin, and a seeming lack of a coordinated Israeli response, led to a very significant influx that brought more than 13,000 African asylum seekers and illegal immigrants into Israel.
>
> The difficulty of distinguishing between regular migrant workers in an illegal situation and classical asylum seekers escaping from real crisis scenarios is part of challenge faced by Israel in dealing with this issue. Against the backdrop of the history of the Jewish people, there appears to be a certain readiness to offer refugees special protection in Israel. However, a substantial rise in illegal immigrants could trigger several social and economic problems. Moreover, questions concerning the "Jewish" character of Israel may clearly also have an impact given that the vast majority of these migrants, refugees and asylum seekers are Muslim or Christians. (Martins 2009, 7)[13]

Since this report in 2009, the number of migrants and asylum seekers in Israel has steadily grown, with over sixty thousand Eritrean and Sudanese individuals now having crossed the border into Israel.[14] Journeying on foot across Egypt at risk of being shot by Egyptian soldiers, they are then at risk of being kidnapped by Bedouin criminal gangs in the Sinai Peninsula situated close to the Egyptian-Israeli border, often enduring torture while being held hostage for ransom from families in their home countries for sums of up to fifty thousand dollars. If they survive to reach Israel's border, they are taken in as asylum seekers and placed on buses for transfer to one of several underprivileged areas in Israel, such as South Tel Aviv. There, at last, they momentarily end their journeys without money, shelter, governmental support, or recognized status.

These migrant individuals occupy a liminal position in Israeli society. They are denied work permits and subsist on insufficient means of support (largely from a network of NGOs that assist refugees and foreign migrant workers living in South Tel Aviv, such as African Refugee Development Center [ARDC], Aid Organization for Refugees, and Asylum Seekers in Israel [ASSAF]). They are, however, allowed to enter the country in search of asylum in accordance with the 1951 UN Refugee Convention, which Israel supports both in theory and practice.[15] Israel's inadequate current immigration policy has thus led to unhealthy, overcrowded living conditions for the new migrants. This has resulted in rent increases in neighborhoods such as Shchunat Hatikva, where up to twenty migrants have been reported renting a single unit; the use of parks and street corners for congregating and sleeping; and an alleged increase in crime that has instilled fear in long-time residents who blame the government for placing tens of thousands of desperate individuals in the nation's poorest areas.[16] The veteran residents of these areas also express concern for the Jewish identity of their neighborhood, which seems threatened as the area absorbs high numbers of non-Jews with new social, cultural, ethnic, and linguistic practices.

Shchunat Hatikva's weak socioeconomic infrastructure, which has developed out of a history of discrimination and sense of exclusion, is expressing itself anew through this rapid change in demography. An historic class struggle between the Ashkenazim and Mizrahim is being fueled now by the continual placement and neglect of new non-Jewish populations in low-income communities without adequate support for their safety and survival. The existing populations in these communities, such as those in South Tel Aviv, face a graver and more complicated struggle to improve their own living conditions and withstand the looming threat of the disruption of the foundation of their lives. Underprivileged Mizrahim, foreign workers, and recently arrived asylum seekers—each group with its own rights and expectations as distinct residents of south Tel Aviv—share physical space and social stresses in neighborhoods such as Shchunat Hatikva as they compete for governmental care.[17]

Uneven Distribution

In the winter of 2010, when neighborhood council meetings and demonstrations against the influx of the new population in Hatikva began, one of the first demands made by the community was the even distribution of the incoming migrants throughout Tel Aviv and the country at large. The goal was not only to settle the newest population group throughout the state, but also to increase awareness of the issues surrounding their migration beyond South Tel Aviv. They wanted the middle and upper classes to recognize the escalating socioeconomic discontent among the disadvantaged populations in the south and to share the burden of responsibility. As individuals voiced their concerns about the government's inadequate immigration policy and discriminatory management of the asylum seekers, veteran residents of the neighborhood repeatedly reminded the community to be vigilant about language when discussing the issue in public, for the liberal news media and upper classes would grab any opportunity to misunderstand their grievance and misrepresent Hatikva as racist. The fear of such an accusation had grown out of the political exploitation of the situation by controversial right-wing politicians adamantly opposed to allowing foreign migrants into the country.

Weeks later, at an antigovernment demonstration in Hatikva's shuk, Hatikva residents waved signs that read, "Send the infiltrators home" as well as "No to racism, yes to neighborhoods."[18] Although media reporters who attended this and other demonstrations in South Tel Aviv quoted the slogans in their articles, more often they emphasized appearances by extremist political figures, who quickly became associated with the protests of these communities. Such figures included Michael Ben-Ari, an anti-migrant member of parliament for Israel's far right-wing National Union Party, and Baruch Marzel, leader of the far right-wing political party Jewish National Front; they used these opportunities to show support for South Tel Aviv's disadvantaged communities and to express their views on the place of non-Jewish foreigners in Israel. Consequently, Hatikva's call for assistance repeatedly appeared in the media as an attempt to exclude the migrants rather than as a cry for assistance for themselves.

Following this antigovernment demonstration, Yair Lapid—liberal journalist, Chairman of the Yesh Atid Party as of April 2012, and Minister of Finance as of March 2013—published an op-ed piece in *Yedidot Ahronot* entitled, "This Is Not Racism: Demonstrations Against Illegal Migrants Have Nothing to Do with Their Skin Color" (December 22, 2010). Lapid claimed that "those who argue that the recent rallies against migrants are racist are self-righteous, and worse than that, they seek easy solutions. The poor are not the ones who are supposed to handle the State of Israel's welfare problems, the poor are not supposed to take care of our policing problems, they are not supposed to resolve the issue of housing for even poorer people than them, and they are not supposed to, and cannot, deal with the infiltrators. Things are difficult for them as it is" (Lapid 2010). Beyond the claim by Hatikva's residents that the Israeli government was neglecting its responsibilities to its own disadvantaged citizens as well as to the newest incoming populations, Lapid's remarks highlighted the accusations of racism that became prevalent in the news media as it publicized Hatikva's protest efforts.

My informal talks with Hatikva's veteran residents gave me further understanding of their perspectives on the neighborhood's unrest. During conversations about Sukkot observance, several people connected the holiday's narrative to the current experience of the Eritrean and Sudanese asylum seekers crossing into Israel in search of safety and opportunity.[19] This parallel was noted with expressions of empathy for the homeless foreigner, but also with reservations.

Dror Kahalani, a resident of Hatikva, articulated the uncomfortable contradiction between empathy and opposition: "God told us to remember that you too were in Egypt. Don't forget that you were foreigners . . . We need to remember that our fathers were also [outsiders] in a foreign country." However, like others who spoke about the tensions in the neighborhood, Dror added: "But it's written in the Talmud: 'Your own city's poor before the poor of another city.'"[20] The qualified reactions of these individuals to the plight of the migrants appeared to be complicated by reasons beyond their primary concern with survival. Although they expressed empathy for another homeless people, they resented the government's historic and chronic neglect of Israel's lower-income classes, especially as the displaced poor of other nations were being moved into their space.

In May 2011, a young leftist activist involved in South Tel Aviv's social struggle interviewed Dror about yet another upcoming demonstration against the government that the Hatikva community would be holding. She wanted to understand the goal of the protest, the position of Hatikva's residents in the struggle, and why young, liberal Israelis living outside South Tel Aviv should join the effort. In his response (the interview was uploaded to YouTube and emailed to Hatikva's residents), Dror said:

> The main problem is that all these people who make decisions in the government and the municipalities neglect us, neglect foreigners of all kinds . . . The easiest solution is to throw them here—the weak ones with weak ones. Work it out amongst yourselves. But the government needs to take responsibility . . . They can solve it only if they want to . . . they don't care, not about us and not about the various foreigners. This is the root of the problem. If there is crime here, it's the result of great negligence and the serious fault is on the part of decision makers in the city, the government, and Interior Ministry . . .
>
> I told you once and I will tell you again. It doesn't matter if he is Sudanese or Eritrean, it doesn't matter who he is. He has a body, and he has a soul. He went through things that I'm not sure some of us would have survived. That's a very important thing. He passed through seven chambers of hell. What can you expect? That you put them here and everything will be honey, milk, and sugar? That's not right. A person can't sleep in the street all his life . . . It doesn't matter if it is us or them. If you want them

to be here as human beings, they need the minimum of the minimum. It can't be that the government decides that they are here but nothing is done about it . . .

We want people to come to this demonstration in multitudes so the government will understand that we are a big body, and we may be second-class, but if we gather all the second-class people together, we are power. If we all unite and aim at the same target, believe me, someone will hear us.[21]

Dror spoke of Hatikva as part of a broader marginalized sector of society that includes other South Tel Aviv Jewish and non-Jewish populations—all of whom comprise Israel's "second class." His recognition of the strength to be gained in unity is significant for its implied critique of the policies of those in power: the notion that government keeps this sector of society in place by keeping it divided. However, instead of acting with other neglected populations as a single underclass group living in shared impoverished conditions, voicing demands for survival together, Hatikva has felt the need to defend its own needs against the needs of others in a moment of social crisis, such as this, and to compete for its disadvantaged place in society.

Pitting needy populations against each other by competing for resources was challenged at other critical moments during my fieldwork as well. In particular, the widespread housing demonstrations that took place in streets and parks throughout Israel beginning in July 2011 created many opportunities for the exchange and development of ideas on social and economic inequality in Israeli society today. In the tent encampments—both in Hatikva's public areas and Levinsky Park by the Central Bus Station—I repeatedly witnessed local Jewish residents of the area, young leftist activists, and Arab Israelis sharing concerns and finding common ground in their individual struggles.

One afternoon in Levinsky Park—the public park in which many Eritrean and Sudanese men slept—I sat on the grass with a cluster of individuals in heated debate about the reasons for the housing protests and the obstacles they expected to face. At that early point in the demonstrations, various camps had sprung up across South Tel Aviv and Jaffa, separate pockets of resistance without connection to their neighboring efforts. Tensions had begun to develop regarding the media attention and donations (food, clothing, and so on) that only some camps were receiving—primarily, the camp of young leftist activists and asylum seekers in Levinsky Park. Hatikva's residents were once again becoming frustrated by the preferential treatment that reflected historic Ashkenazi-Mizrahi and North-South class divisions. Three representatives from the Hatikva camp had therefore decided that they should visit the other South Tel Aviv camps to try to form alliances rather than allow rifts to develop between the marginalized bodies.

When they arrived in Levinsky Park, one young Ashkenazi activist who had come to volunteer with the Eritrean and Sudanese asylum seekers began an impassioned exchange with Yossi, a young man of Yemenite descent born and living in Hatikva who had come as one of the three Hatikva representatives to join forces with other South Tel Aviv-Jaffa protesters. Seated on the ground with the young activists and Eritrean and Sudanese men, Yossi was suddenly deep in discussion about such issues as the social and political dynamics among South Tel Aviv residents, the incoming homeless migrants around the Central Bus Station, and the government. The conversation was forthright and intense, each individual compelled to defend his own experience, and yet simultaneously intrigued about the position of the others. At one tense moment, the young activist said to Yossi, "But people in Hatikva are racist. How do you explain how you think about and treat the Eritreans and Sudanese in the area?" Yossi responded without hesitation, "We're not racist! We're a big salad there! Jews, Arabs, Ethiopians, homosexuals. I'm married to an Ethiopian and my sister's a lesbian—first things first, people are people! That's how we see them." He continued to dispel the activist's accusation by explaining his view of the government's manipulation by pitting the weaker populations against one another with false representations spread through the media. He told the young activist to visit the Hatikva camp and meet the residents there to understand the neighborhood's situation for himself. At the close of the conversation, the activist extended his hand and Yossi shook it. As they gripped each other in recognition of the common ground they now occupied, the activist looked intently at Yossi and said, "We're together till the end," and they both nodded.

Moments of informal education and alliance building such as this were complemented by the more formal creation of the "Periphera" coalition during the summer protests. The coalition was created by members of disadvantaged communities across South Tel Aviv-Jaffa, such as Shchunat Hatikva, Shapira, Jesse Cohen, Jaffa, Kfar Shalem, and Bat Yam, as well as others. This banding together of marginalized neighborhoods was meant to overcome the alienated feeling that the coalition members said the government had engendered: the feeling that each population was an isolated competitor with every other one, which enabled the government to retain control. The Periphera coalition would hold regular meetings throughout the summer months of demonstration, jointly organize and attend protests, create a listserv and website for internal communication and public awareness, draft its own concerns and demands of the government as a newly unified lower class, and most importantly, recognize their own struggles in each other's situation.

During several interviews about Sukkot, individuals raised the issue of *Dor HaMidbar* with me—"the Generation of the Desert" or "the Wilderness Generation"—an expression that refers to the generation of Israelites who were commanded to wander in the Sinai Desert for forty years without a permanent home after worshipping a golden calf and abandoning their faith in God. This generation was burdened with the guilt and pain of their wrongdoing, and they would bear it as a punishment and perish with it in the desert. Only then would a new generation be born and be allowed to enter the Promised Land, free of sin and the memory of suffering. The term Dor HaMidbar is used more broadly today to refer to people in transition or to periods in which learning, suffering, and growth are required to move beyond a troubled past into a future of fulfilled promise. Although I spoke with my interviewees about this notion in the abstract, I observed it in the experience of residents of Shchunat Hatikva, and South Tel Aviv more broadly, who perceived themselves as a modern-day Generation of the Desert—not yet liberated of its suffering, and not yet received in the Promised Land.

Notes

1. Although features of Shchunat Hatikva's neighborhood and community were frequently described to me as "authentic" in complimentary and even admiring ways by individuals living outside the neighborhood, controversial implications of the notion of "authenticity" are actively debated in the fields of folklore and anthropology. In these fields of cultural study, questions of "authenticity" are inextricably tied to questions of "traditionality." One may trace the conversation through touchstone arguments presented in Eric Hobsbawm and Terence Ranger's *The Invention of Tradition* (1983), Richard Handler and Jocelyn Linnekin's "Tradition, Genuine or Spurious" (1984), Charles Briggs's "The Politics of Discursive Authority in Research on the 'Invention of Tradition'" (1996), Richard Bauman and Charles L. Briggs's *Voices of Modernity: Language Ideologies and the Politics of Inequality* (2003), Barbara Kirshenblatt-Gimblett's "Intangible Heritage as Metacultural Production" (2004), Dorothy Noyes's "The Judgment of Solomon: Global Protections for Tradition and the Problem of Community Ownership" (2006), Jason Baird Jackson's "Traditionalization in Ceremonial Ground Oratory: Native American Speechmaking in Eastern Oklahoma" (2008), Regina Bendix's *In Search of Authenticity: The Formation of Folklore Studies* (1997), and Debora Kodish's "Envisioning Folklore Activism" (2011). These and other authors probe the politics of a search for "authenticity" and the problematic and static dichotomies implicated in this search—"traditional" versus "modern," "folklore" versus "fakelore," "original" versus "copy," and so on.

Today, as global institutions such the United Nations Educational, Scientific, and Cultural Organization (UNESCO) spearhead new efforts to identify and "protect" sites of tangible and intangible heritage around the world, questions of "authenticity" are raised on policy levels with new and greater economic and political consequences for the places and practices involved. Addressing the potential problems with a global recognition of "authentic" sources of world heritage, Dorothy Noyes highlights the risk in associating impoverishment with authenticity: "The projection of culture and community onto poverty has economic consequences that will in turn shape policy. Local culture has become sought-after raw material, extracted by multinational corporations for refinement into cultural commodity. As with the environment, the extent to which local culture is a renewable resource is unclear and much disputed. The ideological opposition between modernity and authenticity suggests that the best culture is proper to a disappearing premodern world. The criterion of authenticity turns culture into a scarce resource and a rival good, creating competition to define one's own lodes as purer and deeper than those of other communities" (2006, 31). Noyes emphasizes how an historic search for "authentic" cultural products and processes is perpetuated through implementation of such global heritage policies, and without deep regard for the lasting effects in local contexts.

In contrast, Debora Kodish identifies how the notion of "authenticity" can be of productive purpose when understood from the emic perspective. She comments that, "In the context of inequality (and terrible times), authenticity is not merely a rhetorical strategy or an abstraction. When you cannot recognize yourself in the way that you are treated and in the names that you are called—but when you still have a hope, a belief that you are not what they say you are—authenticity can be a name for a space where you can breathe" (2011, 36). As a folklorist committed to the social activist change that public folklore work can help bring about, Kodish recognizes that a sense of "authenticity" can create a positive space of empowerment that mediates between the spaces of struggle and justice.

I include this note because descriptions of the Hatikva neighborhood and culture as "authentic," while laudatory, evoked critiques of the notion mentioned above. While scholars have written widely about the essentialization and commodification of Mizrahi cultural expression, often musical expression, in Israeli society (Shohat 1997; Regev and Seroussi 2004; Horowitz 2010), more is to be learned about Israelis' impressions of the "authentic food" and "authentic culture" in Shchunat Hatikva to understand how these impressions may carry the negative or positive forces that Noyes and Kodish, among others, identify.

2. Over the past decades, scholars have critiqued Israel's historically dominant Zionist discourse for its modernizing and nation-building objectives (Shohat 1997; Khazzoom 2003; Massad 1996). In Israel's founding years, this mentality shaped a new Israeli identity that was disproportionately based on the image of the Western European Jew. That project, writes Ella Shohat, was founded on the notion that, "Asian and African Jews [came] from 'primitive,' 'backward,' 'underdeveloped,' 'pre-modern' societies and, therefore, [needed] modernization" (1997, 5)—a belief that has eroded over the past 60 years of Israel's development, but whose sting I discovered to be still keenly felt in the memories of the older Mizrahi immigrants who lived through that early period. My observations of the memory remnants of this historic prejudice are discussed more deeply later in this chapter.

3. "Mayors of NYC and Tel Aviv Launch $100 Million Project Renewal for Neighborhoods in Both Cities." *Jewish Telegraphic Agency*, 1980.

4. Erving Goffman, *Stigma: Notes on the Management of Spoiled Identity*. Harmondsworth: Penguin, 1968, pp. 136–137.

5. Ibid.

6. While I examine Hatikva's neighborhood life from the perspective of folklore and folklife studies, the class structures and social dynamics that sustain it would benefit from the consideration of other scholarly approaches as well, particularly that of urban sociology. Specifically, scholars of the Chicago School of Sociology, active in the 1920s and 1930s, proposed that physical surroundings shape human behavior as reliably as genetics and personal traits had been given credit for doing. Robert E. Park and Ernest W. Burgess, two founders of this school of thought, focused on the city as an environment that parallels the natural world and nurtures its same forces, such as competition and survival (Park and Burgess 1925). They proposed the notion of "succession" to understand the migration and resettlement of populations in urban neighborhoods, producing environments marked by increasing economic competition and social reorganization (an expression of which is known today as "gentrification").

Additionally, Park and Burgess produced the concentric zone model that conceptualizes a city's structure as five concentric rings, the middle (the city center) containing the greatest social and economic disintegration, and the outer rings (the city's periphery) characterized by more social and economic strength. While my own study of Hatikva illustrates the reversal of their model (Hatikva and other "peripheral" neighborhoods experiencing ongoing social and economic strife while the center of Tel Aviv prospers), I mention Park and Burgess to gesture to the important scholarship on urban ecology that has developed out of their work. Although it is not within the purview of this research, such perspectives can contribute great insights into the study of social dynamics in stigmatized neighborhoods such as Shchunat Hatikva.

7. The term *Mizrahi* (or Eastern) broadly refers to Jews whose ancestors descended from countries of a Muslim majority. The term is controversial for its tendency to conflate ethnic groups and because the individual groups within the Mizrahi label often did not refer to themselves by this name. However, it is used popularly today in Israel to differentiate from Jews of Ashkenazi descent.

8. Historically, within Israeli anthropology and sociology, the folklore of Mizrahi Jews has been presented as the only (simplistic) frame through which to view Mizrahi cultures and histories. Ella Shohat has critiqued "the converging discourses of the Enlightenment, progress, and modernization [that] are central to the Zionist master narrative" and which purport to have saved Mizrahi Jews from Arab "captors." In this master narrative, and in the "civilized, modern society" into which the "Oriental Jews" were initiated, she notes critically that Mizrahi Jews "have won new appreciation for their 'traditional cultural values,' for their folkloric music, their rich cuisine, and warm hospitality." Although mainstream recognition of such Mizrahi cultural values and expressive forms historically passed as a "humane" form of appreciation, Shohat importantly reframes this response by highlighting its greater context: "The projection of third world identities and cultural practices as untouched by modernity and postmodernity often is subliminally implicated with a view of the third world as 'underdeveloped,' or 'developing,' as if it lived in . . . another time zone apart from the global system of the late capitalist world. . . . In Israeli modernization discourse, Mizrahim always seem to lag behind, not only economically but also culturally." Shohat further observes that beyond these socioeconomic inequalities within Israeli society, such essentialized perspectives have also nurtured a "national export industry of Sephardi 'folklore,' which circulates (the often expropriated) goods—dresses, jewelry, liturgical objects, photos—among Western Jewish institutions eager for Jewish exotica" (1997, 6–9). I note this to make clear that my brief focus on foodways and eating customs in Shchunat Hatikva is in no way meant to contribute to any perpetuation of essentialized Mizrahi stereotypes in Israeli academic discourse or society. In contrast, I present these examples for the insights they provide into strained Mizrahi-Ashkenazi relations that I found to persist still today.

9. *Skhug* is the Hebrew name of this condiment transliterated into English. The transliteration of its Yemeni Arabic name would be *sahaawig*. While I do not here explore the significance of the Kahalanis' use of the Hebrew word for this food item, rather than the Yemeni Arabic word, that distinction should be noted for the nuance it adds to their sense of connection to Yemeni identity and culture, especially through the expressive means of food and language. I am grateful to Ari Ariel for recognizing this distinction.

10. It took me several weeks to understand that the pots of food that constantly sat on the stovetop nurtured a different pattern of eating and socializing than I was used to. Rather than eating three meals all together at the table, family members (as well as friends and unexpected guests) often arrived home at various points throughout the day and served themselves food

that they ate individually and according to their own schedules. While at first this seemed to me to be a disjointed pattern of eating, I soon recognized this system in many homes in Hatikva and learned that it accommodated different work schedules and encouraged unexpected visits by extended families and friends to the matriarch's home (most often, the mother in the family would cook for her grown and growing children, as well as elderly relatives). Friday night meals were typically eaten all together at the start of Shabbat, but during the week, pots of food predictably sat on the stovetop and invited anyone to eat in one's home.

11. *Tel Avivi* is an adjective coined and used by Israelis to describe anything of the city—residents, fashion styles, concepts, material goods, etc.

12. There is a great amount of research on the development of this international migrant labor class in Israel. The following sample of citations provides greater background on the populations and socio-economic factors involved in this development: Kemp, Adriana. "Labour Migration and Racialisation: Labour Market Mechanisms and Labour Migration Control Policies in Israel," *Social Identities* 10 (2004): 267–292; Kemp, Adriana, Rebeca Raijman, Julia Resnik, and Silvina Schammah Gesser, "Contesting the Limits of Political Participation: Latinos and Black African Migrant Workers in Israel," *Ethnic and Racial Studies* 23 (2000): 94–119; Kalir, Barak. *Latino Migrants in the Jewish State: Undocumented Lives in Israel* (Bloomington: Indiana University Press, 2010); Raijman, Rebeca, Silvina Schammah-Gesser, and Adriana Kemp. "International Migration, Domestic Work, and Care Work: Undocumented Latina Migrants in Israel." *Gender & Society* 17 (2003): 727–749; Kama, Amit. "Labor Migrants' Self-empowerment via Participation in a Diasporic Magazine: Filipinos at Manila-Tel Aviv," *Asian Journal of Communication* 18 (2008): 223–238; Liebelt, Claudia. *Caring for the "Holy Land": Transnational Filipina Domestic Workers in the Israeli Migration Regime* (New York: Berghahn Books, 2011); Liebelt, Claudia. "On Gendered Journeys, Spiritual Transformations and Ethical Formations in Diaspora: Filipina Care Workers in Israel," *Feminist Review* 97 (2011): 74–91; Liebelt, Claudia. "On Sentimental Orientalists, Christian Zionists, and Working Class Cosmopolitans: Filipina Domestic Workers' Journeys to Israel and Beyond," *Critical Asian Studies* 40 (2008): 567–585.

13. "Paper 81: Undocumented Migrants, Asylum Seekers, and Refugees in Israel." Euro-Mediterranean Study Commission, accessed March 2013. http://www.euromesco.net/index.php?option=com_content&task=view&id=1162&Itemid=48.

14. According to statistics published in the March 2013 Israeli Authority on Population and Immigration's "Report on Foreigners in Israel," available on the Israeli Government's website: http://www.piba.gov.il/PublicationAndTender/ForeignWorkersStat/Documents/foreign_stat_032013.pdf, accessed March 2013. In this report, as of February 28, 2013, the exact figures listed are: 64,638 "infiltrators" entered Israel; 55,195 "infiltrators" currently reside in Israel; 70,584 legal foreign workers in Israel; 14,549 illegal foreign workers in Israel.

15. The ethical conflict for Israeli Jews of belonging to a country that was created to protect persecuted Jewish refugees and immigrants, and yet now feeling threatened by the presence of another persecuted population crossing over its borders, is expressed in coverage of Israel's recently amended "infiltrator" law: Isabel Kershner, "Crackdown on Migrants Tugs at Souls of Israelis," *The New York Times* (June 18, 2012).

16. National and international reports of the poor living conditions of South Tel Aviv's newest migrant population are prolific but vary in their figures. A typical report appeared in *Le Monde Diplomatique* in July 2012, stating that "while the state issues the asylum seekers visas, it calls them 'illegal infiltrators' and does not allow them to work. So they scrape by on odd jobs and crowd into inexpensive apartments, sleeping as many as twenty to one room. Some refugees live in south Tel Aviv's parks" (Mya Guarnieri, "South Tel Aviv Land Grab").

17. For broader international coverage of the trafficking of Eritrean and Sudanese migrants in the Sinai Peninsula and their entrance into Israel, see the Amnesty International briefing, "Egypt/Sudan: Refugees and Asylum Seekers Face Brutal Treatment, Kidnapping for Ransom, and Human Trafficking" (April 2013); and, Lynch, Sarah, "Sinai Becomes Prison for African Migrants," *The New York Times* (November 1, 2012). For Israeli coverage, see The Hotline for Migrant Workers and Physicians for Human Rights' report, "Tortured in Sinai, Jailed in Israel: Detention of Torture and Slavery Survivors under the Anti-Infiltration Law" (June-September 2012); the Israeli Ministry of Foreign Affairs' communiqué, "Israel to Take Significant Steps to Block Infiltrators from Africa" (July 19, 2010), available online: http://www.mfa.gov.il/MFA/Government/Communiques/2010/Israel_block_infiltrators_Africa_19-Jul-2010.htm; and, Shtrasler, Nehemia, "Why not move Israel's African migrants to north Tel Aviv?," *Haaretz* (January 7, 2013).

18. Regarding the terminology used to refer to the Eritrean and Sudanese individuals in Israel: *mistananim*, or "infiltrators," is the official and most common term used by the Israeli government and residents of Shchunat Hatikva. According to the Israeli Authority on Population and Migration, "infiltrators" are defined as "foreigners who entered Israel through the Egyptian border illegally and were located at the border (with their entry) or within the State of Israel (at a later time)" (http://www.piba.gov.il/PublicationAndTender/ForeignWorkersStat/Documents/foreign_stat_032013.pdf, accessed April 4, 2013). *Plitim*, or "refugees," is also used by various governmental and nongovernmental bodies in discussion of the situation, but the legitimacy of each term is adamantly contested due to opposing opinions of the individuals' reasons for coming to Israel and the difficulty of tracking the status of the new migrants.

I have chosen to use the term "asylum seekers" to refer to the Eritrean and Sudanese populations arriving in Israel, according to the United Nations High Commissioner for Refugees' definition of the term: "An asylum-seeker is someone who says he or she is a refugee, but whose claim has not yet been definitively evaluated" (http://www.unhcr.org/pages/49c3646c137.html, accessed March 10, 2013). This description is most accurate to the situation of the Eritrean and Sudanese migrants in Israel during my period of research, and it remains as value-neutral as possible to allow for the various voices in dialogue to express their own views.

19. See note 18, page 26.
20. Babylonian Talmud, Bava Metzia 71a.
21. "The Real Problem of South Tel Aviv," YouTube video, 5:10, May 13, 2012, http://www.youtube.com/watch?v=_37U5bYTMhU.

3 Within Shchunat Hatikva: Values and Spaces

THE HISTORICAL SKETCH of Shchunat Hatikva in the previous chapter presented an image of the neighborhood that has been popularly accepted in Israel since the neighborhood's founding in 1935: an urban enclave marred by neglect, despair, and danger. However, the primary social and cultural values that animate Hatikva's community through the daily practice and social life of its residents create a second view of the neighborhood. The neighborhood's relationship with the rest of the city may define it from the outside, but the social life that flourishes within its borders—on its streets, in its markets, and in its cultural and religious centers—defines the neighborhood from within.

The relationships that individuals develop with the physical environments they occupy provide insight into their personal and communal histories, current experiences, and belief systems. Three physical spaces in Shchunat Hatikva stand apart from the rest of the neighborhood for their ability to transcend their physical boundaries through the residents' interpretation and use. They are the outdoor market, the neighborhood soccer stadium, and a network of devotional spaces, with the synagogue at the center. These sites are exceptional in that they foster the expression of two core values that sustain, and are sustained by, the community: sociality and hope. Through social connections and the affirmation of hope, borders of difference blur and a unified society emerges.

Shuk Hatikva

Today, in northern and central Tel Aviv, Israeli students sip cappuccinos in street corner cafés, and tourists admire the city's Bauhaus architecture, chic boutiques, fine art markets, and seaside ports. These commercial and cultural attractions do not exist in Hatikva, however, where small, local businesses provide necessary services and practical goods to the community. Bicycle and shoe repairmen sit on chairs in front of their corner shops; containers of *amba*, a pickled mango condiment of Iraqi origin, and hot *sahlab*, a milky pudding dessert eaten throughout the Mediterranean, fill the stalls in Hatikva's shuk.

Fig. 3.1. The center aisle of Shuk Hatikva, the outdoor market in Shchunat Hatikva. Tel Aviv, Israel. 2011.

Richard Bauman begins his study of the verbal arts of a Mexican marketplace by noting, "Open-air markets are display events par excellence in Roger Abrahams' [1981] sense of the term, 'public occasions . . . in which actions and objects are invested with meaning and values are put "on display"'" (2004, 58). *Shuk Hatikva*, the open-air market in the center of Shchunat Hatikva, is replete with a rich diversity of buyers, sellers, material goods, visual displays, and verbal and social exchanges. Spread across several streets that intersect with Etsel Street, the main thoroughfare of Hatikva, the shuk is the beating heart of the neighborhood. Traversing the neighborhood by foot, bicycle, motorbike, car, bus, or minibus, waves of people flood the pedestrian pathways toward the shuk as oversized trucks blocking streets deliver goods to the market stalls from morning until evening. Shoppers on Etsel Street are easily tempted from the congested sidewalks into the inner crevices of the shuk by its alluring fragrances, sights, and sounds. Vendors line the main strip, where they hawk seasonal fruits and vegetables, meats, cheeses, olives, spices, breads, and on Sundays only, household items and Bukharian ceremonial clothing. Significantly, the shuk's location on Hatikva Street makes the name of the neighborhood, Hatikva, synonymous with this site of vibrant social and economic exchange. Only from Friday afternoon to Saturday evening does the bustling life of the shuk halt as Hatikva's residents retreat from this scene of commerce for the quiet observance of Shabbat. The shuk embraces old-timers and engulfs newcomers, sheltering all its visitors from the beating summer sun and pounding winter rain with canopy covers and a steadfast presence in the neighborhood's changing environment.

Shmuel is a juice vendor in his midforties who stands behind his stall on the corner of Hanoch Street, a small side street off the shuk's main artery. He flashes a toothy grin to all those who pass by; in the fall he juices the mountains of pomegranates in front of him, and all year round he fills plastic pints with orange and carrot juice. His father, with rounded shoulders, makes concentrated pomegranate syrup by hand in the room behind the stall, as their family has done for generations. Shmuel insisted on giving me free samples of fresh pomegranate juice and a rose water slushy the first time I walked by, and I happily accepted, offering my introduction in exchange when he refused payment.

As I sipped the scarlet juice, a steady stream of Shmuel's regulars passed by for their daily doses of fresh-pressed sweetness. Most men donned a *yarmulkeh* (skullcap worn by observant Jewish men) that Shmuel made available atop a pile of oranges for his observant customers' use as they recited the blessing over the

Fig. 3.2. Shmuel, a vendor who juices fresh fruit, stands on a side street of Shuk Hatikva. Shchunat Hatikva, Israel. 2011.

juice before taking their first sip. Standing in the street, they would hold their cup in one hand and the yarmulkeh on their head with the other; they whispered the short prayer under their breath and took a small sip, then returned the yarmulkeh to the pile of oranges again and stepped aside to down the rest of the juice. While people blessed their cups of juice and threw their heads back in satisfaction, I watched Shmuel press fruit and I listened to stories of his family's life in Hatikva. From this day on, Shmuel always called me over for a cup of fresh juice whenever I passed his stall, whether on bike or by foot. In place of payment, which he always refused, he asked for updates on my research or, more often, told me what he had learned in his most recent Torah study lesson. He often suggested that I meet someone in the neighborhood who he thought might offer me insights on Sukkot, which he knew I was studying. I would write down the name, finish my juice, thank Shmuel, and bid him goodbye until the next time he would wave me over, which, most likely, would be the following day.

Encounters such as this with strangers and friends in Hatikva's shuk are inevitable, and they give one a sense of belonging. With subtly layered, quotidian banter, they mask riptides of social meaning that tug at people's hearts and minds. Shmuel was not the only vendor who routinely called me over as I rode by on my bicycle. Another vendor who sold household goods near the entrance to the shuk befriended me the first time I entered and, after some minutes of conversation, wrote down the name of a local scholar of Israeli folk dance who he thought I might like to meet. Thereafter, he would call me over and ask how my research was progressing, how my friendship with the local scholar had fared, and what other work I was involved in, to see if he could help.

Vendors would often express an interest in helping not only those they knew but strangers as well. One evening, I was purchasing cookies in the shuk when at the cash register, I discovered I was short of change. I had no time to return home for more money or to search for other items, so in a moment of hope, I crossed the market's aisle to ask the man selling bread rolls if I could borrow the difference to cover the cost of the cookies. I promised to return his money the following day. This man had sold me pita several weeks earlier, and although I remembered him, he barely knew me as one of the innumerable customers he served each day. Regardless, he smiled, rang open the register, and dropped the coin into my palm. I smiled with relief and thanked him for his willingness and trust. I returned the following day to repay him, and our new friendship solidified. Such unexpected interactions occur regularly in this environment, where honesty and trust support individuals and engender social connections and a collective sense of belonging.

Over time, I gradually learned the styles and meanings of market interactions, and I discovered that an ability to "flow" rested at the core of its communication. Throughout the year, my new neighborhood friends commended me for this ability "to flow" (*lizrom*)—a quality defined by flexibility and trust, they said, and consequently the absence of fear or judgment. On several occasions, they vouched for my presence at unfamiliar gatherings by telling their friends, "*He beseder, he zoremet*," or "She's fine, she flows." The ability to be spontaneous, open, and trusting was a mode of behavior whose display, through daily interactions, confirmed the bonds of connection.

Hatikva's shuk reliably cultivates the social cohesion that takes place there. The permanence of its framed structure and the promise of renewing familiar social encounters inside make it a site of guaranteed community engagement.[1] The variety of that engagement is great, however, making this public space one that serves both individuals and groups, the disadvantaged and the secure, buyers and sellers. Hatikva's shuk is a place of regeneration and affirmation, where people come for food and friendship; a place of hardship and despair, where homeless individuals and skeletal cats, together, sort through piles of discarded produce at the day's end; and a place of protest and unity, where residents gather at its entrance, an entrance to the neighborhood, to protest government neglect of their needs. It is a place characterized by predictability and change as vendors attend to veteran customers and new migrants alike, standing in line together. Hatikva's shuk is a microcosm of the larger social world of which the neighborhood is a part, where community forms, solidifies, and breaks apart according to social necessities and economic pressures.

Bnei Yehuda

Bnei Yehuda is the name of the local football (soccer) team of Shchunat Hatikva—the only member of the Israeli Premier League that represents a region or town rather than a city in Israel. The team was formed in 1936 by Yemenite residents of the neighborhood and rose to Israel's top division in 1959. Over its more than seventy years of existence, this football club has achieved unexpected national prominence; it has made Shchunat Hatikva famous for its skilled players who, decade after decade, have improbably defeated larger, wealthier teams across the country and around the world.

From 1936 until 2004, Bnei Yehuda faced opponents on its home field, constructed in the center of the Hatikva neighborhood. Since 2004, however, games have been hosted in Bloomfield Stadium, purposely located outside the Hatikva neighborhood on a relatively empty plot of land just across the border of Tel Aviv in Jaffa. Bnei Yehuda shares Bloomfield Stadium as its home field with two other Israeli Premier League football teams, Maccabi Tel Aviv and Hapoel Tel Aviv. Bnei Yehuda's home field redesignation in the last decade from the Hatikva neighborhood stadium to an anonymous shared stadium outside the neighborhood was not without resistance by Bnei Yehuda's fans: the move was and still is actively denounced as a social and political offense to the Hatikva community.

When I asked Hatikva residents about the stadium move, they frequently responded by recalling the atmosphere of the neighborhood when Bnei Yehuda played in the Hatikva stadium. The whole neighborhood would come out for the games, they said, bleachers packed with loyal fans cheering for family and friends on their backyard field, now hosting some of the best athletes in the country. The waves of nonresidents flowing into Hatikva, as well as such public media attention on the neighborhood on game days and nights, were rarities that filled the neighborhood with excitement and pride. When a match ended, crowds filled with emotion would pour onto Hatikva's narrow streets and often overwhelm the police. Victories were celebrations of pure elation, and losses could result in street brawls between opposing fans. The police could not handle these postgame encounters, especially in Hatikva's small quarters, so the city finally transferred Bnei Yehuda to a larger stadium in which the masses might be better managed by security forces. Bnei Yehuda was evicted from its home, leaving empty one of Hatikva's defining public spaces, one that helped narrate its history, create a sense of self-worth, and bring its community together.

In 2003, preceding Tel Aviv's mayoral elections, candidate Ron Huldai visited Shchunat Hatikva and declared to its community what he knew would gain their favor: if elected, he would keep Bnei Yehuda in the Hatikva neighborhood stadium. His words made an impression; residents still consider his unfulfilled promise a dishonest example of his character and public service. In the years that have passed since his election, Bnei Yehuda fans have hung large orange banners in the new Bloomfield Stadium that read, "Bnei Yehuda Above All Else," "Bnei Yehuda Queen of the Neighborhood," and "6 Years Without a Home." Similar banners are attached to fences around Shchunat Hatikva whenever Huldai visits the neighborhood, even when the reason for his visit has no connection to the team's return, which it almost never does. Huldai gave his word and has not honored it, they say, adding his betrayal of trust to their list of government offenses.

Beit Dani, the community center in Hatikva where I volunteered, is located just adjacent to the Bnei Yehuda stadium, where large banners wave on the orange concrete walls, protesting the team's loss of its home. Adi Cohen, a man in his late thirties who early became a close friend of mine, was an avid Bnei Yehuda fan. When I asked him about the banners, he said that if I really wanted to learn about the neighborhood, I had to go to a Bnei Yehuda game. He had season tickets and would bring me as his guest, he said, pleased to introduce a potential fan to the crowd. For the rest of the year, I attended Bnei Yehuda games at Bloomfield Stadium with Adi, his friends, and his brothers whenever the team played home matches, gradually learning from the stories fans told about the team's history and place in the neighborhood.

Fig. 3.3. Bnei Yehuda plays a game in Bloomfield Stadium as fans sit on the left and right sides of the field. The two orange banners on the bottom left read, "6 Years Without a Home" and "Queen of the Neighborhood." The orange banner on the top right reads, "Bnei Yehuda Above All." Tel Aviv, Israel. 2011.

Most fans who enter Bloomfield Stadium to attend Bnei Yehuda's soccer games are men wearing orange scarves, shirts, and hats—the official color of the Bnei Yehuda team—carrying season passes in one hand and bags of sunflower seeds in the other. They arrive en masse and on time, except to Saturday evening matches, when religiously observant fans miss games or arrive after the first quarter, waiting until dusk has fallen on Shabbat. These avid fans—teenagers, young adults, and aging seniors—are friends, family, and neighbors, and they are there as much for each other as for the game.

The scene at the matches was reliably the same each time I attended, and our participation followed an informal but familiar pattern. From our seats in the center of the stands, Adi, his friends, and I would watch the opposing team's band across Bloomfield Stadium play spirited songs as fans shouted rousing synchronized cheers. On our side of the stadium, Bnei Yehuda's side, the bleachers were packed with men passing bags of sunflower seeds down the rows, drinking black coffee in small Styrofoam cups, and smoking cigarettes with eyes intensely fixed on the field. When a crucial play was made, in place of an upbeat song from a shiny band, the mostly male crowd would jump up and let out cries of anger, excitement, or frustration. They would then break into songs and chants that usually featured a militaristic chorus such as, "Bnei Yehuda, war!" or "Bnei Yehuda fights!"—cheers that were just as coordinated and impassioned as the opposing team's musical numbers but that conveyed a playful and sharp sense of rivalry that the Bnei Yehuda fans clearly enjoyed. In between outbursts of angst and glee, Bnei Yehuda's fans dissected each play and commiserated or celebrated with each other.

During the season, I attended several games in which Bnei Yehuda played Maccabi Tel Aviv. This was a team to which a Hatikva-born native and former Bnei Yehuda player, Eliran Atar, had been transferred in May 2010 for $1.2 million and a four-year contract. The transfer had not been the young athlete's choice, and yet every time Atar received the ball on the field, Bnei Yehuda's fans reacted with spite and insult, jeering their former star player, brother, neighbor, and friend, whom they all had known from childhood. I once asked Adi why the fans disproportionately heckled Atar, the one member of Maccabi Tel Aviv who was from Hatikva. He said that although they knew Atar was not responsible for his transfer, he was part of a system that works against them. He represented disloyalty, and although only a pawn in the process, Atar was treated as a traitor to publicly affirm the strength of their community.

Adi emphasized his point by describing the neighborhood's character more generally. Bnei Yehuda and popular singer Ofra Haza had once been the two successful symbols of the neighborhood.[2] Haza was the only singer ever to perform in Hatikva's neighborhood stadium, he said. When she passed away in 2000 and Bnei Yehuda was moved to Bloomfield four years later, the neighborhood lost its two sources of pride, ones that had brought the outside world into Hatikva.

After I had attended almost a year of Bnei Yehuda games with Adi, he told me that he wanted to show me a special film—a documentary about the team. The video, called *Shomrim al Hatikva*, or "Guarding Hope," narrated Bnei Yehuda's 1998–1999 season, when they nearly fell into Israel's second division. The three-part documentary was very emotional, Adi warned me, admitting that he cried in parts two and three every time he watched it. Adi was transfixed as soon as we began to stream the video. It alternated between clips of Bnei Yehuda's last three games of the 1998–1999 season and interviews with the team's players in their modest homes in Hatikva. Conversations with Hatikva's veteran residents and Bnei Yehuda's fans were interspersed throughout the story, depicting the strong relationship between the team and its home community.

Throughout the video, Bnei Yehuda's fans and players repeatedly spoke of Hatikva's *ahnashim pshutim*, or "simple people," the neighborhood's residents who believe in and rely upon the team's glory. One of the star players, Sahar Mizrahi, sat at his parents' kitchen table in Hatikva, looked into the camera, and said, "Professors don't come out of this neighborhood; lawyers don't come out. Maybe you become a football player or possibly, in the case of Ofra Haza, bless her memory, a singer, but there aren't many paths in the neighborhood. Because of this, it's very important that Bnei Yehuda does well, to give the children something to believe in, something to aspire to."[3] The relationship between Hatikva's children and the team is significant, and a Bnei Yehuda youth soccer league that practices in the neighborhood stadium today enables children to don orange uniforms and train from a young age. When Bnei Yehuda scored a crucial goal in the final game of the documentary, a fan on the sidelines yelled out, "For the neighborhood! For the children of the neighborhood!" Hope is a future-oriented belief, and in Hatikva, children are important carriers of this belief forward. Bnei Yehuda's journey from the heart of Hatikva into national and international arenas represents the opportunities that lie beyond the neighborhood's borders, and for their fans, that dream rides on each of their victories.

During a final vignette, Hezi Shirazi, another star player, sits on his couch and quietly explains, "People need to understand that Bnei Yehuda's community takes the results home with them on Shabbat, all throughout the week. When the team succeeds, there's calm; people are calm. When they don't succeed, people are irritable in the neighborhood, and nothing will help; their whole lives are Bnei Yehuda." Bnei Yehuda's wins and losses linger in the neighborhood because they affect residents' beliefs in themselves, in their community, and in their ability to hope for the future. Believing in Bnei Yehuda is an expression of hope, just as believing in God might be, a parallel that is made explicit by the team and its fans through several ritualistic practices on the field.

At the beginning of the documentary, for example, just prior to the start of the match, two Bnei Yehuda coaches take eggs whose shells have the number "3" printed on them to the stadium's goalposts. They crack them on the metal poles to bring good luck. They then sprinkle salt on the sidelines to ward off the evil eye, and in one match, the documentary presents a coach running around the field to the players almost in position so that he can swing a live chicken over their heads, evoking the *kapparot* purification ritual performed before Yom Kippur.[4] When Bnei Yehuda surprises fans by scoring a winning goal in a final minute of a match, the camera spans across the field to capture fans and players alike with arms outstretched toward the sky and crying, "There *is* a God! There *is* a God in the heavens!" At such moments of triumph and despair, Adi paused the film and said to me, "*That's* the neighborhood!" Bnei Yehuda represents the community's need for hope. When validated, through Bnei Yehuda, this hope brings the outside world into the neighborhood in recognition of Hatikva's talent and strength, and it brings Hatikva into the outside world to interact with those beyond its borders.

In contrast to the reliable presence of the shuk as a site of togetherness, Bnei Yehuda and the space that it occupies in Hatikva are marked by unreliability. The social cohesion that does occur within the physical space of its stadium and the social space of its fandom are inextricably tied to the unpredictability of the team's performance. Social relationships are not built upon an exchange of material goods and social connection, such as occurs in the market, but through shared belief and hope.

Houses of Worship and Sites of Belonging

During my first weeks in Shchunat Hatikva, I spent my days walking up and down Hatikva's streets to observe its physical conditions and the social lives that unfold within them. I walked by one- and two-story houses, senior and community centers, schools, bakeries, pharmacies, restaurants, the outdoor market, clothing stores, spice shops, and synagogues. Amid the random arrangement of community and commercial establishments, synagogues consistently marked the landscape. When I asked various residents and the local librarian where the synagogues were located in the neighborhood, I always received the same response, with a smile: "There are seventy-two synagogues in Hatikva and seventy-two streets, one per street." Although today in Hatikva you will find some streets with synagogues whose doors are locked and other streets with at least two synagogues in use, the message of the saying holds true: the physical face of the neighborhood reveals its residents' values, with devotion at its core.

Synagogues in Hatikva are typically small, approximately the same height as the houses that abut them, with doors opening into one main room. The exteriors are simple but usually defined by one special feature—an unexpected color of paint such as pistachio green, a wrought-iron Jewish star on a front gate, or the name of the congregation carved into a faded façade. When the heavy metal chains and padlocks are removed from undecorated front doors, the view of the single-room sanctuaries is surprisingly rich, with walls that are covered with memorial plaques and varied light fixtures. Elaborate material expressions of love and loss communicate the loyalty that members of each congregation, who live on that synagogue's surrounding streets, feel towards their social and spiritual community.

Residents today reminisce about their ancestors who settled in Shchunat Hatikva in the 1930s and 1940s and built these small synagogues for their families' use. Explaining the great number of houses of worship, they say that men built synagogues for their individual families, as neighbors often did not get along. Strong views and a dedication to faith are respected qualities in this community, and they are the legacies of Hatikva's early residents that their children now recall

Fig. 3.4 (top), Fig. 3.5 (bottom), and Fig. 3.6 (page 90). Three of the dozens of synagogues in Shchunat Hatikva, typically one room wide. Tel Aviv, Israel. 2010.

Fig. 3.6. *Continued.*

with pride. Today, Hatikva's synagogues are generally open to all and attended by people other than the original families for whom they were built. Although many congregations struggle to find a *minyan* (a quorum of ten Jewish men required for certain religious rituals) for daily prayer and the walls of their synagogues are cracking from lack of maintenance, the presence of the synagogues in great numbers confirms a community committed to faith and family.

While each synagogue in Hatikva functions independently, together they make up a network of devotional spaces. Restaurants and private homes also belong to this network, but as secondary sites. These three devotional spaces—the synagogue, the restaurant, and the home—are all places in which connection unites with hope through the expression of faith.

Devotion in the Restaurant

The first prayer service that I attended in Shchunat Hatikva was held in a small white Yemenite synagogue on Talmon Street called *Hesed L'Avraham*, or "Grace for Abraham." The intimate sanctuary seats a maximum of twenty-five men, who line the room's walls and fill its center sitting on wooden benches. A handful of women sit in a narrow side room designated as the women's space, which once was the synagogue's kitchen. A large refrigerator with a padlock on its door still hums in the corner of this room.

I discovered this synagogue when Simon Tobi invited me there the first time I walked into his restaurant on Haganah Street, the main artery that traverses the neighborhood's northern border. The blue sign above his restaurant's entrance read, "Simon's Restaurant: Food from the Heart," with a solid white heart painted below. In Hatikva, invitations to social, cultural, and religious gatherings are casual and customary, always spontaneous, and often consequential. Simon's informal invitation to join him at his synagogue, Hesed L'Avraham, was one such example, paving the various paths that I followed thereafter in the neighborhood.

Simon Tobi, whose name in Hebrew means "a good sign," was born in Yemen in 1936 and immigrated with his family to Palestine in 1944. He has lived in Shchunat Hatikva long enough to recall, with nostalgia, when Arabs and Jews lived next door to each other, mingling on street corners and sharing pita that his father made in the *taboon* (outdoor bread oven) that he had brought from Yemen. He remembers that the grandfather of his current neighbor Dror Kahalani brought two young wives from Yemen during his lifetime in Hatikva, and that he lived until he was 117 years old, walking around with bare feet his entire life for fear that he would fall ill if he wore shoes. He also remembers the waves of different immigrant populations settling in Hatikva since his own arrival, inhabiting each of Hatikva's streets according to their ethnic group—Yemenite Jews next to Iraqi Jews next to Persian Jews, and so on. Throughout the late 1970s and into the 1980s, Simon served as Chairman of the Hatikva Neighborhood Council Board, and he is as familiar with Hatikva's clan-like social history and its neighborhood politics as with the Torah, which he has studied since his youth and consistently cites in casual conversation. As his synagogue's leader and one of the neighborhood's unofficial rabbis, he has long led the services at Hesed L'Avraham in Yemenite and Hebrew. He is one of few individuals still in the neighborhood with so high a level of Torah and Yemenite cultural knowledge that his name is respected both by those who have known him for decades and by those who have only just heard of him. The spaces in which Simon spends his life—his restaurant and his synagogue—are benchmarks by which to measure change in Hatikva.

Simon's restaurant is fronted by a room-wide corrugated metal door, which can be pulled down and pushed up as on a garage to expose the entire width of the room to the sidewalk during its open hours. The first time I passed by the restaurant's open front with a room full of empty tables and chairs calling to passersby, Simon was silently seated in the far back left of the room. I walked in and looked up to see twelve long, bare florescent light bulbs fastened to the high ceiling in the shape of two shining Stars of David. The walls were covered with photographs of a younger Simon accepting service and education awards from state officials, venerated rabbis such as Yosef Ovadia wearing his trademark sunglasses and ceremonial robe, and a group of young boys in Yemen seated in a circle on the earth around their *mori* (teacher) learning Torah. Months later, a current photograph

Fig. 3.7. Simon Tobi's restaurant sign reads, "Simon's Restaurant. Food from the whole ♥ at Simon's. Original Yemenite foods. Spicy delicacies. Strictly kosher." Shchunat Hatikva, Israel. 2010.

of Simon proudly holding a football-sized etrog that I had taken during Sukkot and presented to him would join the photography display. Hand-drawn Kabbalistic illustrations and a *hamsa* (hand-shaped amulet believed to ward off the evil eye) hung above a small sink in the corner, and a plaque displaying a prayer for prosperity in business hung beside a case of refrigerated drinks. The functional and decorative interior design of Simon's restaurant narrates his personal history, the history of his community, and the history of his culture, as they come together in this space, his restaurant.

Nothing is the way it used to be, and Simon regularly reminds me of this. Today in Hatikva, people lock their windows and doors, food has no flavor and causes illness (such as diabetes, which plagues much of Hatikva's population), and synagogues no longer teem with life as they once did. Jewish community life in the neighborhood has diminished due to the waning devotion of younger generations and the increasing number of non-Jewish immigrants settling in the area. At seventy-four years of age, with constant leg pains and a lifetime of work behind him, Simon now spends his days sitting in a tall, tattered black leather chair in the back corner of his restaurant, waiting for customers. He once employed six servers and ran out of food several times during the day, he says, but

Fig. 3.8. Simon Tobi sits in the back of his restaurant and holds the *etrog* that he has just purchased for prayer during Sukkot. Shchunat Hatikva, Israel. 2010.

today only one kind man with bony, rounded shoulders named Danny helps out in the kitchen, and cooked food sits in large silver pots until the day's end. While Simon sits in the back and sips the hot tea that Danny brings him, Danny leans in the entranceway and smokes cigarettes, both men silently watching the neighborhood rush by. Loyal friends and longtime patrons stop in these days to visit Simon, as much out of respect for him as for his delicious and locally respected Yemenite beef soup. They stop in for a bowl, share with Simon the latest news of the neighborhood, and listen to his responses in the form of parables from the Torah, full of moral direction.

Most often, individuals come in to speak with Simon about matters related to his synagogue—to prepare for an upcoming holiday service or donate money to the congregation, which he collects as the *gabbai* (Hebrew: the gabbai is typically the treasurer and overseer in a synagogue; however, in this case, Simon performs a role closer to rabbi, and is locally referred to as such). If individuals have a sick member of their family, someone who has passed away, or someone who has recently escaped harm's way, they visit the restaurant to offer a donation to the synagogue in exchange for inclusion in Simon's prayer during the coming Shabbat service. The prayer will be for safety and gratitude for good health. Simon, in his black chair, takes out a pencil and small piece of paper and writes down the name of the ill, deceased, or spared individual and accepts the donation. He slips the small piece of paper back into his shirt pocket until Saturday morning's service, and the visitors bid him goodbye. Every day, seated across from the large covered bin of pita at the back of his restaurant, Simon hears his neighbors' pains, prayers, and faith in salvation.

Devotion in the Synagogue

The first day that I walked into his restaurant, over a bowl of his homemade *hummus ful* (hummus topped with fava beans, tahini, and a hard-boiled egg), Simon invited me to his synagogue. I had briefly introduced myself and explained my reason for coming to Shchunat Hatikva and was enjoying his homemade hummus at his own recommendation when Simon began to speak. "Are you Jewish?" he asked. "Yes," I said. "Then you should come to my synagogue tomorrow for Rosh Hashanah," he replied. I accepted his invitation, and he dictated directions into the heart of the neighborhood according to landmarks rather than street names. As I thanked him and exited into the blinding sunlight, Simon cried out after me from the back of the room, "Come early so you don't miss me blowing the *shofar* [ram's horn]! It's a blessing for the new year!"

I woke up at seven o'clock the next morning and walked down Hatikva's quiet cobblestone streets to a short white building on Talmon Street with graffiti scrawled across the bottom of its front wall. I pushed open a white gate onto a white-tiled outdoor patio that held a table, a few plastic chairs, some plants, and a sink. As I walked through the gate, a man exited the synagogue's main sanctuary, handed me a *siddur* (prayer book) and a cup of water, and returned to his bench inside. As Simon read from the Torah at the *bimah* (or high place, referring to the raised platform from which the Torah is read) in the center of the men's sanctuary, I took my seat next to four other women in the women's side room on the other side of the wall that divides the congregants by gender. I could not see clearly through the barred window that divided these rooms due to the lace cloth over the bars, but I recognized Simon's voice. The room was full of men seated around Simon and murmuring in quiet individual prayer. Periodically through the hours, the Ark—a simple set of doors at the back of the sanctuary padlocked with a heavy chain—would be opened to reveal the synagogue's set of Torah scrolls. Men would reach into the closet and lift out large cylinders of silver and gold taller than their torsos and shinier than any plaque on the wall. These Torah covers were beautiful, ornate, and heavy, and bells jingled from the crowns that capped each scroll. Next to the buzzing refrigerator in the women's section, below unforgiving florescent lighting, inside the crumbling and graffiti-scrawled plaster walls, these scrolls appeared as materially inspiring as spiritually sanctified.

Fig. 3.9. The Yemenite *Hesed L'Avraham* synagogue in Shchunat Hatikva where Simon Tobi leads services, morning and evening. Shchunat Hatikva, Israel. 2010.

More women showed up as the hours passed by, some with children, and soon the maximum capacity of eight in the women's room was reached. New arrivals spilled onto the patio and needed to find plastic chairs and clear an outdoor wooden bench before they could join in prayer. Hearing the men lead the service through the window on the women's side was more difficult for those seated outside the room, and in the hottest of months, as I would later learn from experience, sitting for long periods of time in the stifling outdoor air (the inside room was air conditioned) made it an even greater challenge. Outdoor attendees thus inevitably commiserated about the inaudible sound and stifling conditions, and they compensated for their disadvantage by quietly sharing neighborhood news with each other. Thus they belonged in an alternate way—through social, not only spiritual, connection. Those outside would sit across from each other and speak about events in their families and the community and would gently question any newcomers to the synagogue (for months, me) about their background and current life. Social space and devotional space within the synagogue's gated boundaries overlapped in this way, strengthening these women's roles socially and spiritually.[5]

As the months passed, I learned that the synagogue's outdoor patio was also an important social space for the male congregants of Hesed L'Avraham. During each Saturday morning Shabbat service, men would take short breaks during prayer to sit outside on the patio and catch up with each other over small cups of *café shachor* (black coffee: Turkish-style, typically served with sugar) or *café lavan* (white coffee: a Yemenite herbal tea made of ground corn, ginger, cardamom, and typically served with sugar). One morning, with no other women in attendance, I sat on the patio sipping café lavan with three men who were taking a break from the service. They spoke about current issues and, in particular, the Eritrean and Sudanese migrants who were settling in the neighborhood. No one had answers, but all three had questions about the stability of their neighborhood's future and its Jewish identity. What would it mean for Christian and Muslims residents to play loud music on the Sabbath when observant Jews did not use electricity-powered equipment? And what if the newcomers held outdoor barbecues on holy days of fasting such as Yom Kippur? They each asked each other such questions and shared stories of having encountered these experiences in the landscapes of their lives.

Dror Kahalani, one of the three men seated at the table and by then a close acquaintance of mine, eventually turned to his uncle Yossi to shift the discussion to a lighter subject. He said it was good to see Yossi there that morning—a rare occurrence. Yossi is one of Dror's few relatives who lives in North Tel Aviv, constantly reminding his family in South Tel Aviv as often as possible of the wealth that exists elsewhere, anywhere, beyond Hatikva's borders. At Dror's comment, Yossi smiled and thanked him; yes, he said, he was happy to visit Hatikva but he insisted that we should visit *his* synagogue in North Tel Aviv. "It's rich," he said, "and the size of it—you wouldn't believe how many people attend!" We would be amazed, he exclaimed—there is never a problem finding a minyan there!

Dror shook his head and said he would never exchange this synagogue for another, not even for the richest in all of Tel Aviv. He pointed to me and said, "Gabi's rich, and I'm also rich. Being rich is not all about money. A man with bread and margarine can be the happiest man. Give him a can of tuna, and he feels like a king!" Yossi shook his head silently with a knowing smile. Dror then pointed to six exposed tips of metal beams that protruded from the wall above the synagogue's door. "See those metal beams up there?" he asked us, and we all looked up. "They talk about me," he said, and he leaned back in his chair. His uncle shook his head again, still smiling.

"You don't know what you're missing in North Tel Aviv," he said to Dror, and he stood up with the third man to rejoin the service. Dror and I remained seated outside to finish our coffee.

"Why those beams?" I asked Dror once the others had left. "What do they say?"

"I helped put those beams in!" Dror burst out. "That wall has watched me come here for forty years," he said, and we looked at it together again in silence.

We stood up, threw our cups in the trashcan, and returned to our respective rooms for the remainder of the service. Dror has participated in this community not only through the devotional and social worlds that exist inside the synagogue's walls, but also through the creation of the synagogue itself. Immigrants to Hatikva constructed these houses of worship, and their descendants honor and sustain them, strengthening their community through work and use.

Although the synagogue is a concentrated site of spiritual devotion in Hatikva, residents express their faith in secondary spaces of devotion as well, their restaurants and their homes. My first meeting with Dror Kahalani had begun in the synagogue but continued in one of these secondary spaces. After the conclusion of the first Rosh Hashanah morning service at Hesed L'Avraham, women and men milled around in front of the building to catch up with each other and wish each other well on the New Year holiday. I stood to the side of the gate and said goodbye to the women with whom I had shared a bench inside, and as people began to walk home, I saw the man who had brought me the siddur and cup of water when I arrived hours before. I walked over to thank him, and he introduced himself—this was Dror. He said he knew who I was, as Simon had told him to look out for me and make sure I was comfortable when I arrived at the synagogue. When I thanked him, he asked what I was doing just then. I admitted that I had no plans, and Dror invited me to walk with him to his parents' house a few streets down to say *kiddush* (blessing over wine to sanctify a holy day) and share lunch. I gladly accepted the offer, and he locked the synagogue's doors and closed the gate. We walked down several streets and along the market to Azay Street, where Dror was born, passing a parade of neighbors returning home from their synagogues. Most residents were dressed in white for the holiday, wishing each other *Shana Tova* (Good Year) and sending regards to each other's families as they passed by.

Devotion in the Home

Before Dror and I reached his parents' gate, we stopped at a large metal door across the street and knocked. In this house lived Dror's brother Doron; his wife, Fani; and their daughter Talia. Dror's sister, Sharona, lived on the third floor of the building where his parents lived on the second floor. On the first floor lived another brother, Zohar, with his family, and three houses down the road lived their youngest brother, Ronen. Only two siblings had moved off Azay Street: Dror, who lived with his family just across Haganah Street, the main road bordering Hatikva's north side, and a more distant brother who lived in a nearby suburb. Dror's grandmother lived one block down by the market's entrance, and various cousins and twelve half-siblings were spread throughout South Tel Aviv. The Kahalani family is large, but the core is concentrated, and when you stand on the roof of his parents' building and call out to the siblings who live on Azay Street, they answer readily, despite closed doors and gated windows.

Sharona answered our knock on the door and invited us in to Doron and Fani's kitchen. Dror introduced me as a guest in the neighborhood and we all exchanged a few words of introduction before falling silent as the men recited the kiddush. After the blessing, Dror and I wished them a Happy New Year and bid goodbye. We crossed the street, walked up one flight of stairs, and pushed open the unlocked door to Dror's parents' apartment. Dror's mother, Suad, was standing over the stove in the kitchen, frying round pieces of dough. When she saw us enter, she approached us to say hello and immediately offered us sweet hot tea and cake. Dror and I sat with our tea in the small kitchen as Suad finished preparing *zalabiyah* (fried round pieces of dough popular in Middle Eastern countries, sometimes covered with sugar, and sometimes served with a hard-boiled egg and grated tomato) for the holiday meal.

This visit to the Kahalani family was my first, and it founded my lasting relationships with each member of their family that continually enlightened me about family and community life in Hatikva. From this day forward, whenever Dror or his siblings would invite me to their social gatherings, they would explain our friendship to those whom I had not yet met by recalling our first meeting. Dror would say, "Gabi came by herself to my synagogue on Rosh Hashanah, and I met her outside. I invited her to my parents' house after the service, and now she's part of our family!" He told the story each time with the same surprise, as if the serendipity of our encounter was meant to be.

Following the Kahalani family's direction I rarely called to announce my visits to them, and whenever I left, one of the family members would call out, "When are you coming back? Come back soon! Don't disappear!" I felt expected when I walked through their unlocked door, and I came to learn that consistent, casual stop-by visits characterized their daily social life and home environment.

Suad Kahalani, Dror's mother, is the master of her house. Six months after I met her, when I asked if I could record a conversation about her life story, we sat down on her twin bed to talk. I requested that she please say her name and where she was born into my audio recorder. She responded without hesitation: "My name is Tikva, and I was born in the Land of Israel." Until then, I had known her as Suad, and her children had all told me that she was born in Iraq. However, she spoke the name Tikva (which means "hope" in Hebrew) into the recorder with confidence, and she admitted that she thinks it is much more beautiful than her Iraqi name, Suad (which means "happiness" in Arabic). Tikva is the Hebrew name she chose for herself, but no one calls her by it, Suad had declared with the same confidence that she was born in Israel although she immigrated to Israel at age one with her mother. Her narrative choices helped ground her in her world and conveyed her sense of belonging.

Upon arrival in Israel, Suad and her mother first lived in *ma'abarot* (refugee and immigrant encampments) before moving to South Tel Aviv. She remembers the Shchunat Hatikva of her youth in the early 1950s as a very different place from the neighborhood in which she lives today. Suad has spent her entire life in this neighborhood—first as a child, then a young bride, then a mother of six, and now also a grandmother of seven—never having left the country, nor hardly South Tel Aviv. Her memory is faithful, and she began her life story for me with a grin by recalling the trouble she gave her parents as a young girl. When she was twelve years old, her mother wanted to marry her off to an older Iraqi man who was wealthy but blind. It would secure her future, her parents told her, but Suad resisted. "I didn't want to marry him!" she cried out to me, still exasperated by the thought of it fifty years later. She decided to run away from home to find another suitor, and she did, staying with friends and acquaintances in the neighborhood in the meantime. Several years later, she returned home with Saadia, a Yemenite man several years older than she and very handsome, she recalled. She knew her parents would disapprove of her marrying a man of Yemenite descent, but at the age of sixteen, against her parents' will, she married Saadia anyway, her mother refusing to attend their wedding.

Half a century after that occasion, as I sat with Suad on the second floor of the building that she bought from Halamish (a public housing company) while raising five young children on her own, she described to me the life she has endured. Through self-conscious smiles and giggles, she recounted an abusive marriage, the death of a child, and continued caretaking of her now bedridden husband: "I've suffered my whole life. I've had a hard life, a hard life," she whispered so as not to wake her husband, who slept in the next room and whose waking would prompt a string of demands. Suad smiled as she paused between tales of suffering, and I finally had to ask her, "But you smile and laugh all the time! How do you seem so happy?" Suad replied, "Why should I cry? How will it help me to cry?" And she smiled widely again, silently. She then continued with the story of the death of her second daughter, a child who was so beautiful, she said, but who drowned in the Mediterranean Sea at the age of eight. "God gave me a strong blow, and no one could help."

Suad's life story is marked by moments of physical and emotional pain, but she remains loyal to her God and to her family. *B'ezrat HaShem*, or "With the help of God," she often repeats after recounting mundane commitments or wishes for the future. A wooden plaque with a prayer to God hangs above her bed; *mezuzot* grace all her doorframes, and she lights two candles in her kitchen as the sun sets every Friday night without fail.[6]

When news of a massive impending earthquake spread throughout Israel in January 2010, emergency preparedness workshops were repeatedly offered around Hatikva. Suad had no interest in attending the workshops and told me not worry. "This country is full of people who pray. God will protect us," she said calmly, smiling. Suad's faith gives her strength and a sense of control in an environment scarred by hardship. As I became closer to her, I increasingly understood why she holds the name Tikva, "hope," so close. She spends every day cooking and caring for the four generations that surround her—her children and grandchildren, her husband, mother, and mother-in-law. And, she spends every evening cleaning her own house, and then her mother's house in the adjacent neighborhood to which she travels by public bus as her unknowing husband sleeps. Suad is the central link in her family chain, pulled in all directions and working continually to keep the bonds between the links strong.

Suad's cooking is a daily expression of her dedication to sustaining the relationships around her. Throughout the day, family and friends visit and sit in her kitchen or on her terrace with hot food and drinks that fill her refrigerator and sit on her stovetop. Her food and drinks nourish the unannounced visitors to her home and make unplanned, shared meals a regular occurrence. While enjoying food, drinks, and social time together in Suad's home reinforces the connections between family and friends, this use of her domestic space also plays an important role in the family's religious practice.

The concept of "domestic religion" illuminates the greater significance of Suad's practical and devotional activities in her home. In her ethnographic study of elderly Kurdish and Yemenite women in Jerusalem, Susan Sered comments that the concept of domestic religion is "one of the few aspects of Jewish women's religiosity for which we have evidence concerning a number of ethnic groups" (1992, 90–91). Domestic religion provides a frame for the informal practice and transmission of Jewish values and identities, with particular focus on women, in contrast to the explicit performance of Jewish religious duties in the more structured settings of the synagogue or in public, as practiced by men. Regarding the preparation of food in women's homes—and cooking was a significant responsibility of the women whom I came to know in Shchunat Hatikva as well—Sered observes that "a major aspect of the role of spiritual guardianship of one's family is to preserve the Jewish identity of children and grandchildren. They use traditional dishes (which their children love) to that end. But food is also necessary for physical survival. The women know that when they cook for their families they are, in the most basic sense of the word, nurturing, allowing their families to live. Giving prepared food to the poor is the greatest religious act that a woman can perform . . . This is the quintessential women's *mitzvah*" (92). Beyond performing this greatest mitzvah in the everyday context of their lives by cooking for their families, women also cook for the holidays, which, Sered notes, lends them even greater religious autonomy and authority: "The fact that women prepare for holidays means that it is the women who are the ritual experts, the guardians of law and tradition, the ones with the power to *make* or *create*, not simply to participate. For these women food preparation is sacred because it embodies, concretizes, dramatizes, and ritualizes the central elements of Judaism, as understood by the women themselves" (102). Sered's notion of domestic religion places the food-based practices of the women whom I describe in this study in greater perspective—one that grants them the due meaning of their actions.[7]

Every Saturday after the morning service in their synagogues, Suad's sons arrive at her kitchen to eat fresh, hot *jachnun* (Yemenite dish of slow-baked, rolled dough served with a hard-boiled egg and grated tomato), wrapping packages of it to take home and share with their children. On holidays, Suad faithfully fries basketfuls of *zalabiyah* for her sons' synagogue congregations when they stay up late through the night in prayer and study sessions. And every Friday night after family dinners with their respective spouses and children, Suad's children convene in her kitchen around nine o'clock to prepare countless small plates of nuts, sunflower seeds, and chips for their Shabbat evening gatherings on the roof of the building. During these regular gatherings, the Kahalani family and their friends sit with snacks, sweet kosher wine, and beer that fuel hours of boisterous conversation. I soon learned that these Friday nights together were a tradition, and if I saw Dror in the neighborhood on a Friday morning, he would typically bid me goodbye by saying, "See you tonight at my mother's!" I became a regular on Friday nights at Suad's home, and the more I attended, the more I appreciated how this social time together provided relief from the weary routines of daily life, strengthened family ties, and renewed hope.

The Kahalani siblings are employed in various working-class jobs in Tel Aviv. They wake up before the sun rises, work unusual shifts, and return home weary from full days of physical labor. Sharona traverses South Tel Aviv neighborhoods by foot, delivering mail in the early morning hours. Her husband, Yair, works in construction late into the day. Doron works in maintenance at a high school; his wife, Fani, cleans a different high school. Dror works in maintenance at a theater school in the neighborhood, and Ronen is a garbage collector in North Tel Aviv. This list does not account for all the siblings, only the ones that regularly attended Suad's Friday night gatherings. On Friday nights, after cleaning their homes, showering, dressing in special formal attire, attending synagogue, cooking, and enjoying sit-down meals with their families, they retire to Suad's second-floor kitchen and terrace, or to Sharona's third-floor roof, for postdinner snacks, drinks, and laughter late into the night. It is the scene of an intimate party, lacking only an audible soundtrack, as they do not play music out loud on Friday nights out of respect for Shabbat observance in the neighborhood.

For most of the year in comfortable weather, the gatherings that I attended were held on the roof, all of us seated around a white plastic table that faced an outdoor television set. It showed either a popular Friday night sketch comedy program (*Eretz Nehederet*) or the reality show of the moment (Israeli "Big Brother" or "Who Wants to be a Millionaire"), the sound muted with captions displayed. In colder winter months, we would gather in the small living room of Sharona's apartment, just large enough to fit a loveseat in front of a coffee table and large television. Most evenings, almost ten guests had to sit on chairs that blocked the television for lack of space in the room. These nights were always crowded and loud, friends arriving throughout the evening hours and Suad coming up to sit with us for short visits in between cleaning and attending to her husband downstairs. Whenever Suad appeared in Sharona's doorway, we would all cheer her arrival, Dror immediately pouring her a glass of sweet wine and offering her a chair. She would sit silently for a few moments, smiling, cupping her glass of wine and a few almonds in her hands, and soon either her eyes would close and she would fall asleep sitting up, or she would sneak out to finish her duties downstairs. The time together was never more than a few hours, but those hours were special and separate from the rest of the week.

On most Friday nights, one of three topics of conversation would keep the voices tangled in debate: money, gender, and belief. However, by the end of these lively contests, most opinions would unite. When speaking about money, for example, the group typically concluded that they were victims of a corrupt socio-economic system, and regardless, money causes more trouble than happiness. If the topic was gender, they would often debate passages from the Torah, texts that prescribed rules for how men and women should each practice daily and ritual activities. Men want freedom, and women want cooperation, they often claimed, citing this as the underlying cause of behavioral differences both in and out of the religious context.

When debating belief, they would describe the beliefs of different ethnic groups and compare them to search for similarities or differences that might reveal deeper meaning. One night, while discussing food customs, Sharona said that Yemenite Jews believe that if you borrow an egg from a neighbor, you must offer a shekel (Israeli currency) in its place and then always return the egg, for every egg has a soul. A friend of Moroccan origin then said that Moroccans believe that you should not pass knives between hands for fear that this will provoke a fight. You must pass all sharp objects on a table. When you buy someone a pair of shoes, Fani said next, the recipient must offer a shekel in exchange when the shoes are presented. Everyone was familiar with this belief and agreed, but no one knew the reason. Iris, another friend who was present that night, interrupted to say that she did not believe in any of these notions. She said that her mother, of Yemenite descent, told her when she was a child that "all the business with hamsas and amulets for good luck are foolish, and if you really want to ward off the evil eye, just wear a tiny little safety pin on the inside of your shirt." The group considered this and moved on.

Within Shchunat Hatikva: Values and Spaces | 103

Fig. 3.10. The Kahalanis' post-dinner gatherings every Friday night for Shabbat. In fall, spring, and summer months, they gather on the roof of their building. Shchunat Hatikva, Israel. 2010.

Fig. 3.11. In the winter months, the Kahalani family gathers in Sharona's third-floor apartment for Friday night socializing. Shchunat Hatikva, Israel. 2010.

Fig. 3.12. The table full of post-dinner snacks served each Friday night after dinner: an assortment of nuts and chips and a hummus plate keep visitors sated. Shchunat Hatikva, Israel. 2010.

These evening discussions presented an array of beliefs, values, and life experiences. In each debate, at least one individual was challenged to prove the strength of her or his character through the persuasiveness of her or his argument—stamina and determination resulted in success. Quick wit, insightful interpretation of the Torah, and interrogation of a system of belief were the methods by which each person displayed her or his social, cultural, and religious beliefs.

These Shabbat evening gatherings in Suad's and Sharona's homes were structured by the ritual of Shabbat observance, but they served a purpose beyond the religion as well: they created a space in the homes and the lives of those who attended for the expression and evaluation of their ideas and principles. On Friday nights, kitchens, living rooms, and rooftops became sites of devotion to family, friends, and the self, as well as a means of enacting local culture through practice and discourse.[8]

Hatikva's shuk, the Bnei Yehuda stadium, and a network of devotional sites, including the synagogue, restaurant, and home, narrate the neighborhood's social history and experience from the inside out. Collectively, they bring individuals together in the construction of belief and community. Within the neighborhood, each space represents a part of Hatikva's consciousness that reflects the social values and circumstances of the people who live within its borders. These spaces also possess meaning beyond the neighborhood, however, as each one has the power to break down Hatikva's social and physical borders: the shuk invites outsiders from other parts of Tel Aviv and beyond into the neighborhood to experience "authentic" Mizrahi specialties; Bnei Yehuda takes the neighborhood's name and community into national and international arenas; and Hatikva's varied sites of devotion enable residents to transcend their physical boundaries through spiritual practice and belief. The ability to cross Hatikva's borders through the power of these spaces forges social connections and helps sustain the community within. Whether public or private, secular or spiritual, permanent or changing, these sites ground residents in their home environment and empower them to reach beyond.

Notes

1. The dependable sociality that the shuk nurtures and upon which Hatikva's residents rely may be contrasted to the anonymity and surface sociality that characterize consumer relations in more structured commercial environments, such as supermarket chains or malls. Daniel Miller (2001) is one scholar who studies such consumerism in places such as in North London to understand the deeper social and cultural functions of the give and take of material goods.

2. Ofra Haza was a Yemenite Jewish singer born and raised in Shchunat Hatikva who became known as Israel's first "pop star" in the 1980s. Her music is credited as having bridged Eastern, Western, traditional, and popular musical styles, making her rise to success among European, American, Arab, and Jewish Israeli audiences. Throughout her career, she spoke about her love of Yemenite Jewish music as well her childhood in the neglected Hatikva neighborhood, sharing how she drew upon the strength and positivity by which she characterized Hatikva's community. She died in 2000 from AIDS-related pneumonia at the age of forty-two. In 2007, the Tel Aviv municipality renamed a section of the public park in the Hatikva neighborhood in her honor.

3. Interviews from part two of the three-part documentary, "Shomrim al HaTikva":http://www.youtube.com/watch?v=4UJuK52TXfQ&feature=relmfu, accessed May 14, 2016.

4. A parallel can be drawn between this sanctification of the Bnei Yehuda football field in Shchunat Hatikva and more formalized cultural and religious sanctifications of public space. Jason Baird Jackson's observation of the Yuchi people's purification of ceremonial grounds prior to the annual Arbor Dance offers one such example: "Taking a handful of the plants from his assistant, the chief begins doctoring the arbors by tapping and sweeping the flower blossoms over the bench . . . At each arbor he begins with the right front bench, followed by the right front post. This process continues with the chief alternating between the posts and bench sections . . . Everything that relates to the square ground and its rituals is expected to be in a pure or purified state" (2003, 182, 198). Jackson describes the physical and spiritual

preparations for the Arbor Dance as an expression of Yuchi ritualism more broadly, and while I am not claiming that the sanctification of the Bnei Yehuda stadium is an expression of Jewish ritualism, I believe that it is an expression of greater social and culture belief systems at work in the Hatikva neighborhood.

5. Although I do not undertake a thorough analysis of all the roles that the synagogue plays in Hatikva's community life, I do acknowledge the synagogue as a space that provides for the individual expression of faith as well as for communal devotional and social activities. For a detailed study of how the synagogue space may host a range of activities and perform a variety of functions, see Samuel Heilman's *Synagogue Life: A Study in Symbolic Interaction* (1998). In his examination of how individuals realize the synagogue's multiple purposes as a house of prayer, house of study, and house of assembly, sometimes simultaneously, Heilman begins by informing his readers that "a prayer service is more than simply a time for praying; study sessions are more than merely occasions for learning; and assembly is far more than just getting together ... the reader must be prepared to sacrifice concise categories at times in order to have a truer picture of the setting. A close probe of the action may even temporarily leave him in doubt as to why people are in shul—to pray, study, or socialize—since they will be doing all three, and more" (65). In my recognition that Hatikva's synagogues nurture hope and sociality by providing spaces for personal and shared expressions of ordinary and extraordinary beliefs, I value Heilman's nuanced analysis of the shifting contexts of performance that may take place within a single setting.

6. *Mezuzot* pieces of parchment inscribed with verses from the Torah and contained in cases that are attached to doorframes in Jewish homes to fulfill a commandment in the Torah.

7. I have identified the home as a "secondary" space of devotion after the synagogue, but I do not mean to imply that any "domestic religion" performed by women at home is secondary to that of men in synagogue. I simply use the term "secondary" to help conceptualize the degree of structure that characterizes devotional spaces in the neighborhood. The synagogue has a primary structure, being a formal and public space for devotion. The restaurant and the home have secondary structures, being less formal and more private settings for devotion.

8. I have chosen to focus on the Kahalani family in depth because I was able to observe and participate in their social and religious gatherings on a nearly daily basis during my research period in Shchunat Hatikva. While their behaviors and beliefs may not represent those of all other families in the neighborhood, I found their family structure and history to be in line with the historical majority of Hatikva's population. Of Yemenite and Iraqi origin, the Kahalanis represent two of the majority ethnicities in the neighborhood, and they had immigrated to Israel just as the State had formed, experiencing the development of the Hatikva neighborhood over several generations already. In contrast to some families in the neighborhood who had immigrated at the same time but whose first, second, or third generation had moved out of Hatikva if and when possible, the immediate Kahalani family had remained living in close proximity of each other at the center of the neighborhood, four generations now interacting daily. Evoking an extended family clan-like social structure that was described to me as prevalent in Hatikva in the 1950s, 1960s, and 1970s, the Kahalani family has adapted to changes in the neighborhood over the decades but has maintained social relationships, values, and practices that are rooted in those earlier decades. For their ability to integrate their historic and current social and cultural conditions, the Kahalani family represented to me both the past and present experiences of a majority of Hatikva's population.

4 *Sukkot* in Shchunat Hatikva

As the sun sets on the holiest of Jewish days, the Day of Atonement or *Yom Kippur*, the sound of the *shofar* (ram's horn) is heard echoing across the streets of Shchunat Hatikva. The gates of prayer and day-long fasts come to a close as Jewish residents step out of the myriad synagogues into the streets, reach into bowls full of sliced, raw, green *khavoosh* (quince) and apple with which to break their fasts, and look up into the dark night sky. Entire congregations, numbering between fifteen and eighty members each, stand together in the streets and hold prayer books up high with their outstretched arms. With eyes fixed on the moon, they recite the *Birkat HaLevanah*, a prayer for the sanctification of the new moon. With this prayer, Yom Kippur has ended and individuals disperse to share coffee and cake with family and friends at their homes. The prayer for pardon is followed by a ritual celebration of joy. Walking through the neighborhood at this hour, one sees clusters of people sitting together in brightly lit kitchens, on terraces, and on streets outside their front doors. They savor a few sweet bites as the sound of hammering begins to ring throughout the neighborhoods, ushering in the next ceremonial affair, Sukkot.

Sukkot is heralded in on the heels of Yom Kippur's twenty-five hours of solemn repentance. Atonement for one's sins from the previous year is instantly replaced by preparation for a festival of joy according to a decree in the *Shulchan Aruch* (a Jewish legal code book compiled by Joseph Karo in 1563) stipulating that one mitzvah should be followed by another. Although Sukkot officially begins at sundown four days after Yom Kippur concludes, the material preparation for the festival—hammering the first nails into the sukkah's frame on the evening that Yom Kippur finishes—is the ritual action that honors this decree. As the celestial cry of the hollow shofar gives way to the solid pounding of metal on wood, Hatikva seamlessly transitions from a state of individual repentance to one of collective celebration.

Sukkot in Practice

When I arrived in Shchunat Hatikva in July of 2010, I began volunteering at the local community center, Beit Dani, working with the neighborhood's elderly

Fig. 4.1. In preparation for Sukkot, residents transport home palm-tree branches on the tops of their cars to construct the roofing of their sukkah. Residents of Hatikva remembered using bicycles, rather than cars, in the past to drag branches. Shchunat Hatikva, Israel. 2010.

Fig. 4.2. People gather brush for the sukkah's roofing from street corners in the neighborhood where the city has piled high tree branches for community use. Shchunat Hatikva, Israel. 2010.

Fig. 4.3. Framed images of venerated rabbis and religious scholars are among the decorations hawked on the street in the week prior to Sukkot. These images adorn the sukkah's interior. Shchunat Hatikva, Israel. 2010.

female residents. From that locus of communal activity, I started to learn about local histories and social networks. Word-of-mouth invitations to family meals and social celebrations soon followed as acquaintances from Beit Dani learned about my research project. With Beit Dani as my base, I slowly moved into the community and gained increasing access to cultural events and social circles, which allowed me to establish relationships with Hatikva's residents. Two months after my arrival, during Sukkot of 2010, I documented the ritual constructions of Beit Dani's senior members, whom I had befriended, as well as the sukkot of other residents whom I had met by then in Hatikva's restaurants, synagogues, shuk, and community gatherings. I photographed more than fifty sukkot that autumn and the following one, measuring and making material documentations of nearly forty. These sukkot were built by Yemenite, Iraqi, Iranian, Syrian, Moroccan, Bukharan, Afghani, Egyptian, and Libyan individuals whose families spanned three generations—from the eldest, who had immigrated to Israel, to the youngest who were born as first- and second-generation Israelis.

My visibility as a volunteer in the neighborhood community center and my consistent presence in core neighborhood spaces such as the shuk, the synagogues, and the restaurants, gained me trust and recognition over the months, enabling me to pursue three forms of fieldwork: documentation of material culture, participation in neighborhood life, and open-ended interviews with residents. In particular, conducting interviews about Sukkot ritual practice, which were most often ongoing conversations rather than single, formal sessions, became possible because of my ongoing presence in Hatikva's community life. Although Sukkot served as the initial and central focus of my inquiries, my conversations with residents included discussions of their life histories, religious practice, foodways, social customs, cultural beliefs, local politics, and national and international news. Each of these issues illuminated for me the social standards, personal ethics, and cultural values that informed these individuals' Sukkot ritual practices, so that their narratives did not stand alone as isolated texts, but were layered with surrounding contexts of meaning.

The transformation of the sukkah from written to material form is accomplished through two stages of expression: interpretation and creation. However, these expressions are not only tools of transformation; they are tools of tradition that make possible the adaptation of an inherited practice, uniting people and places across different time periods. Over time, individuals weave the most meaningful parts of former practices together to create patterns. These patterns may be designed through a process of "selective retrieval," or the intentional perpetuation of particular elements of the past to advance the creation of an envisioned future.[1] This process of weaving selected elements of inherited practice into a pattern—tradition—brings us to the moment in which residents of Shchunat Hatikva build new sukkot each year. With each reconstruction of the sukkah in the lived experience of Sukkot observers, the sukkah becomes an increasingly layered physical and metaphysical object.

Articulated in distinctive ways by each individual, the reasons for Sukkot observance involve more than the recollection of biblical history or the affirmation of shared Jewish values; they involve the particular contexts of the worlds in which these individuals currently live.[2] The following case studies offer glimpses into the creative and existential possibilities that manifest themselves in the observance of Sukkot in South Tel Aviv today. Through ritual practice, sukkah builders and users align themselves with those values of the holiday that they hold close, and they claim this occasion for the intentional expression of fundamental beliefs. Although Sukkot ritual practice has been passed down for thousands of years, it is invested with new meaning each time it is performed in the specific environment in which it occurs—in this case, an urban Israeli neighborhood, home to ethnically diverse, working-class immigrant populations. In this environment, this ritual of construction creates a space that is otherwise hard to find amid the national and international forces that simultaneously sustain and fragment the neighborhood. Religious conflicts, socioeconomic struggles, and issues of national security characterize Israel's national context. The international context in which this ritual is implicated is characterized by imposing forces such as globalization and commodification that trickle down to affect enduring practices. The occasion of Sukkot in South Tel Aviv therefore carves out a reliable space in an unreliable environment for the intensified expression of one's beliefs and for safe, social relations. For the duration of the holiday week, routines are interrupted to reminisce about what life once was and to dream of what it should be.

These following three case studies present a diversity of Sukkot ritual practice by current residents of Shchunat Hatikva. Uriel Zada, Yoram Meshumar, and Dror Kahalani are all first-generation Israeli men born to Jewish parents of Iranian, Yemenite, and Yemenite-Iraqi descent, respectively. Their parents settled in Tel Aviv after immigrating to Israel and were all still living in Shchunat Hatikva when I met them in the summer of 2010. These three men, their parents, their siblings, and their children opened their homes to me during my sixteen months of research, and they invited me to participate in their daily lives. They have parallel but differing life stories that have culminated in each family's settling in this dense neighborhood of South Tel Aviv, where they annually build sukkot.

Place and Protection

Uriel Zada

On the first day of Sukkot, September 22, 2010, I pedaled my bicycle up and down the streets of Hatikva to photograph sukkot and, hopefully, meet their builders and users. This was my plan, with no destination in mind, no schedule to follow, and no acquaintance expecting my arrival. I began heading toward Hatikva's public park, Gan Hatikva, which lies at the edge of the neighborhood. In the two months I had spent there by then, I had walked through the heart of the neighborhood every day, taking different routes on my commute between the community center, the shuk, various synagogues, and community events. But Gan Hatikva was a green space used by residents for exercise and relaxation, and I had not yet had a reason to visit. I biked around the edge of the park on this sunny morning, however, and noticed the properties lining the periphery of the park. Rows of nondescript one- and two-story houses and short apartment buildings with chipped cream-colored plaster and concrete facades abutted the edge of the park. I biked slowly enough to glance down the alleys in between the buildings where sukkot might stand and soon passed a backyard enclosed by tattered tarps woven into a metal fence. The visible part of the space was filled with materials—disassembled desks and tall bookcases holding unneeded household items, children's bicycles, a toy motorbike, a large standing lamp, several two-foot-tall silver gas tanks, plastic bins brimming with concealed objects, and brooms. In the center of the yard, however, stood a lace-walled sukkah, built into the mass of material and yet clearly standing apart. The sukkah's delicate white lace walls waved in the breeze, contrasting with the neighborhood's uniform landscape of dilapidated concrete. Unable to see beyond the exterior of the sukkah whose entrance faced the opposite wall of the house, I locked up my bike and set out to find the builder to ask for a closer look.

I entered the apartment building on the opposite side of the yard and knocked on the only door on the first floor. After a second knock, an adolescent boy dressed in black pants and a white shirt with *tzitzis* (knotted ritual fringes attached to the edges of prayer shawls, worn by observant Jewish men) peeking out from below his shirt opened the door and said, "Yes?" I introduced myself, explaining that I was researching Sukkot observance and that I had seen what I assumed was their sukkah from the road. If it was theirs, I wondered if I could meet those who had built it. He told me to wait in the dark hallway for a moment and called for his father. An older man came to the door and introduced himself as Uriel, then welcomed me into their kitchen where he resumed the preparation of his lunch. I explained my interest in the sukkah to him; pleased to hear about my project, he immediately led me outside to the back patio where the sukkah stood. Uriel said it was empty inside because they were still making final preparations for that first evening's gathering. He still had to set up a large stereo system in the sukkah's corner to play religious music during the week, which they had all enjoyed in previous years, and to supply the table, chairs, and floor covering. We walked around the outside of the sukkah, and Uriel pointed to a white wooden door that lay horizontally against one wall of the rusted metal sukkah frame, as well as a bookcase that leaned up against another. These items of furniture ensured the *kosher* status of the ritual structure, he said, in accordance with Jewish law that dictates that the sukkah's walls, while temporary, must remain secure against the blowing wind. The furniture created partially solid walls that compensated for the lace walls that waved in the breeze.

Uriel did not take notice of the other items that lay scattered around the patio beyond the sukkah's frame, but stood among the plastic bins and bikes piled up high around him and described the space within the sukkah as holier than the space of the synagogue. He would have loved to speak more about the meaning of the holiday, he said, but was busy with his final preparations and warmly invited me back another day to continue. I gratefully accepted and photographed Uriel with two of his sons standing proudly in front of their sukkah before I thanked him and biked away.

I came back to Uriel's home five weeks later, welcomed at the door as if I were an old friend. His wife and all six children were also home this evening. Uriel carried two religious texts under his arm as we walked into the dining room where we would sit and speak while his wife helped the children study in the kitchen. As we sat down, Uriel nodded to his wife, who was leaning over the kitchen table

Fig. 4.4. Uriel Zada stands with his two sons in front of their backyard sukkah. Shchunat Hatikva, Israel. 2010.

Fig. 4.5. Uriel Zada's sukkah peaks over the fence that surrounds his backyard on the day prior to the start of Sukkot. Shchunat Hatikva, Israel. 2010.

with one of their daughters assessing a homework assignment, and said, "Education in the home is so important. If she were not teaching the children right now, you and I could not sit together and study about Sukkot." In the brief time of our friendship, Uriel had already described his family as *datiya* (religious), in contrast to *masortit* (traditional), which others in the neighborhood had used more frequently used to explain their families' religious affiliation. The gendered division of labor in Uriel's home followed a stricter allegiance to religious prescription than expressed in the homes of other Hatikva residents whom I had visited, and recognizing this fact helped me understand the relationship between his reading of Jewish texts and the structuring of his daily life.

I turned on my recorder and Uriel began his story. Forty-six years ago, he was born to David and Edna Zada, who had individually emigrated as young teenagers from Persia.[3] He was one of six children born and raised in Shchunat Hatikva, and he had lived in the neighborhood his whole life. Recalling his childhood in the 1970s, Uriel described a different Hatikva than the neighborhood of today. Hatikva was a "crime neighborhood," he said, where "even the police were afraid to come." Criminals had control of the area and as a result, Uriel stated, "people of Hatikva were considered a waste of time." The two characteristics that Uriel used to describe the neighborhood's history were Hatikva's reputation for criminality and constant incoming waves of immigrants who settled there because of the low cost of living.

Not long after new public housing projects had provided some relief to incoming immigrants, Hatikva was once again under pressure. Russian immigration began in 1991 and new residents flooded the neighborhood. Three to four years passed before most of the Russians were integrated into the community. Some left and some advanced, said Uriel, and now, "the Eritreans and Sudanese have moved in and it's more crowded than ever. There isn't an open room in Hatikva—it's overblown." Uriel ended his description of the neighborhood's development over the forty-six years of his life with a reflection upon its effect on his own development. Although this was what his family grew up with, he asserted that they learned to cope in this environment through their faith. He said:

> We thank God. We thank God, our family does, that we are religious. We were more religious than our friends growing up, and we grew apart from them. A lot of people I knew growing up have turned to drugs—they became addicts and they died from drugs and were murdered in road accidents and theft. And thank God our parents kept us here, in this stench of a place in the right way, and that we knew how to guard ourselves. That's the greatness. We did not have to move Ramat Aviv Gimmel to guard ourselves. Here in this place, we were safeguarded.

Uriel had embraced his family's faith and ritual practice in a volatile and changing environment. Although he still remembered that to be religious in the Hatikva of his youth was "to be laughed at—you were in the Third League, a miserable man," he was grateful for the religious faith that had sheltered his family in uncertain surroundings.

Uriel described religion as a protective shelter not only in memories of his childhood, but also during our discussion of Sukkot. He began by recounting what he considered to be one of the most beautiful Sukkot stories he had heard:

> There was a war some fifty, sixty years ago, and the enemy outside of Israel came and bombed it by plane. There was a Rav by the name Ben Zion Abba Shaul, I think, who was a friend of Rabbi Ovadia, and who died, peace be upon him. During Sukkot, they were sleeping in the sukkah when they were informed that bombardments were taking place. Israel was weak, and as they were dropping bombs, the Rav said, "I am going to run to the bomb shelter!" There was a righteous Rav there too, and he said, "It is stated that the sukkah has protective qualities. Being in a sukkah is like being in a shelter, nothing will happen to you. Do not be afraid. Sit down. Do not be afraid." The other one cried, "No, no! I'm going to the shelter." As he left, a missile fell down on him. Luckily, he only lost a leg, and survived. And so, it is said how important the issue of faith is in the sukkah. This is a very, very important subject.

"Faith provided the ultimate shelter," said Uriel. "The sukkah," he continued, "comes from the Torah, and therefore has extra sanctity. The one who said we should build this sukkah is God. God said, 'Make me a sanctuary and I will dwell in it.' This is the Temple. The synagogues are from the sages." God commanded the creation of the sukkah, as decreed in the Torah—an unmediated communication that imbues the practice with its holiness. Inside the sukkah, Uriel said, one is forbidden to engage in certain activities—such as speaking profane words, drinking beer, watching television, or using a computer. "You may only speak sacred words in this space," he said, "which means learning the Torah, learning about Sukkot, learning Jewish laws. You may learn anything you want in there, but do not talk trivia in a sukkah."

The second manner in which the space of the sukkah is holier than that of other Jewish devotional spaces, concerns *mitzvot*. "There is a commandment in the Torah," Uriel said, "that the greatest mitzvah is to be happy . . . and it's the greatest commandment on Sukkot because on this holiday we must be happy." In this overlap between the general commandment to be happy and the specific commandment to rejoice on Sukkot, one fulfills the greatest mitzvah through this particular observance. Furthermore, he said, "Every second spent in the sukkah, a person is fulfilling a mitzvah." He explained this by comparing the mitzvah of dwelling inside a sukkah to other mitzvot one might perform, such as donating charity: "When a person offers a shekel, for example, his hand performs a mitzvah. If he goes to synagogue, his legs fulfill a commandment. If he holds a prayer book, his hands fulfill a commandment, and his eyes perform a mitzvah. But being inside the sukkah is a very, very special thing because his whole body is performing a single mitzvah at once." The sukkah offers the opportunity to give one's whole physical self over to the performance of a good deed. The ritual body and the ritual space are meaningfully entwined in an act of spiritual devotion.

Uriel emphasized the spiritual power of the sukkah but also acknowledged the significance of its physicality. As a child, Uriel said he always helped build his family's sukkah: "I used to go several miles to cut tree branches with my saw, climbing up like Tarzan, then binding the branches together, tying them to my bicycle, and bringing them home. The *schach* was then dirty from dragging it in the dust of the road, so I would take a hose and wash it. I would work hard, very hard, to make the sukkah, but the Torah says the more a person sweats to fulfill the mitzvah, the greater the mitzvah, the greater the reward." I asked him why then, given the satisfaction of such physical labor, does he now construct his sukkah with prefabricated metal poles and bamboo mats? "Today, everything has changed," he said, and continued:

> Truth be told, it should be done the old way, but you need the strength. Today I have six children. The time I told you about was when I was a child, twelve, fourteen, sixteen years old. Today, I have to support my family and work. I barely have time to make the sukkah. And my children do not act as their father did in this area. They are a little bit spoiled, as part of this "Bamba" generation.[4] I want it to be easy, so I have my mat. I keep it in the shed, and then I pull it out on Sukkot. Once, I used to go to the trees and cut it down all myself, and it was a mess and very, very difficult. Today we no longer have the strength to do these things. We have a mat, and it holds up well.

Despite his commitment to strict religious observance, Uriel adjusts his actions to his circumstances. If the spirit of the sukkah is constant, its physical structure may be variable, accommodating to changing conditions in order to enable continued observance.

Although Uriel may purchase a metal frame for his sukkah, the manner in which he constructs it still adheres to Talmudic prescription. "I have to build it in order," he said: "First all the walls and then the schach. If I build the schach first and then the walls, the sukkah is unacceptable. I would need to remove the schach and build it again. It's very important for the sukkah to be kosher, and, of course, I must make it the appropriate size for the family. It must not be too small because we like to bring in a few beds to sleep on, which is fun." He continued with other specifications of the construction that he observes to maintain the kosher status of the sukkah. These rules include not laying the schach directly on top of the metal frame, but placing wooden beams upon the metal so as not to defile the purity of the organic material; and leaning a door and bookcase against the sukkah's lace walls to assure their stability in the breezy wind.

Although aesthetic adornment of the sukkah is not commanded in the Torah, Uriel attends to the decoration of his sukkah, citing Exodus 15:2 as his guide: *zeh eli v'anvehoo*, or "This is my God and I will glorify Him." Honoring this statement and God, Uriel vows to bring beauty to all his acts of devotion. "We hang up the lace sheets for beauty," he says; "they do not make the sukkah kosher or impure, but they show our respect for God. We love to perform mitzvot with that respect, bringing as much beauty and perfection into them as we can." In both 2010 and 2011, I observed the same decoration of Uriel's sukkah. Crayon pictures of biblical scenes hand drawn by his children lined the upper interior walls of the sukkah, palm branches weighed down by bunches of golden dates arched over the sukkah's doorway, and tinsel and homemade paper chains dangled around photographs of respected rabbis and righteous Jewish leaders. Uriel said that he hangs these photographs and biblical images on the walls so that the family may gaze upon them when they sit in the sukkah, inspiring even more sanctity in this holy space and "giving the children piety." Aside from the wall decorations, a fluorescent lamp hangs from the center of the sukkah's roof, a stereo system connected in one corner plays religious music throughout the week, a large table and white plastic chairs stand in the center of the sukkah, and red Persian-style rugs cover the ground in the concrete backyard.

Against one wall, almost unnoticed, stands a child-sized plastic chair upon which a stack of religious books is piled. "We have another good practice," Uriel says when I ask about this small chair; "We take a chair and place on it holy books for Elijah the Prophet. It's called Elijah's Chair, but it's not just for Elijah. It's for others as well, so that guests should come." The chair is the material symbol of the custom known as ushpizin of welcoming guests into one's sukkah, both personal and biblical guests. Uriel explains this custom by recounting the order in which the biblical guests are said to visit:

> On the first night of Sukkot, the first guest is Abraham our father, peace be upon him. Abraham, our nation's elder, a graceful man, who loved only to give and not take. That's Abraham our father. With him, we eat dinner, breakfast, and lunch. That's Abraham. Then comes the second evening, and who enters? Isaac, his son. Who enters after him? Jacob, Isaac's son. Then Moses, and after him Aaron, the brother of Moses, and after him,

Joseph the Saint, who is one of the twelve tribes. Then King David, King of Israel, alive and well, is our seventh guest, and with him ends the festival of Sukkot. Before we enter the sukkah we say, "Enter holy and supreme guests." We are asking permission to enter the sukkah, the sukkah that is Abraham's, Isaac's, and so on.

Uriel stands in the doorway of his sukkah each night and recites the prayer to welcome in one of the biblical guests. After concluding, he steps inside and welcomes in the family members, friends, and newcomers to the dinner table. Through the custom of inviting the ushpizin into his sukkah, Uriel acknowledges a "homecoming" shared by his ancestors and those around him. With photographs of respected rabbis hanging on the walls, Elijah's Chair in the corner, invitations to biblical figures, and the sharing of meals with friends and family, Uriel and his family build, decorate, and use the ritual space of the sukkah to transcend their particular time and place. Their sukkah shelters righteous leaders, faithful followers, and unknown guests together in a celebration of gratitude, joy, and protection.

Despite the careful attention paid to the material construction of the structure, Uriel's ultimate goal in the sukkah's construction is "to be happy and to have as many people as possible sit and learn Torah there, and to offer hospitality—these are the important things. This is the tradition and that is how my parents taught it to me—to entertain, to be happy, and always look for what is best, not what is bad. This is joy." Although Uriel emphasizes the seriousness with which he builds the structure, he makes clear that the meaning of the space is not ultimately determined by its material form. "What makes the atmosphere in the sukkah are the people," he said, "not the sukkah. You can have the most beautiful sukkah in the world and have nothing come of it." On each night of Sukkot, Uriel's family sings, plays music, dances, and thanks God for safety in a celebration of happiness. "People create joy," Uriel concluded, "and if you understand that, you will be happy."

After our discussion, as I packed up to go, Uriel offered me a sample of the marmalade that his mother made from the *etrogim* (fruit of the citron tree that is ritually used in Sukkot observance) that they had collected from their backyard. It was translucent yellow and delicious. He told me that I should visit his parents and speak with them about Sukkot as well. They lived in the center of Hatikva in an apartment that they bought over forty years ago, he said, and they would love a visit.

David and Edna Zada

I had, in fact, already visited Uriel's parents just one week after I had met Uriel for the first time. He had told me then that his parents lived near Beit Dani, where I was volunteering, and that I should stop by to meet them. I had taken him up

Fig. 4.6. Uriel Zada and his family gather in their sukkah for dinner. Shchunat Hatikva, Israel. 2011.

Fig. 4.7. The lace walls of Uriel Zada's sukkah are illuminated at night. Shchunat Hatikva, Israel. 2011.

on the suggestion and biked to their apartment one day during Sukkot to photograph their sukkah. They saw me, kindly waved me over as I photographed their structure, and told me to return another day when I had time to sit down and talk. Uriel's suggestion to speak with them during my second visit with him was a welcome reminder.

After four weeks and several attempts to reach them by phone, I biked to their two-story, salmon-colored building and found them at home. Uriel's father, David was sweeping away debris that had blown into his backyard from the brick-paved street. When he saw me approach, he smiled and welcomed me back. He told me to go straight up to the second floor and he would join me shortly. I walked up and knocked on the door, and Edna, David's wife, answered, swinging her arms open as she invited me in. She asked how I had been since Sukkot and immediately offered me lunch, which was cooking on the stove. David soon joined us and we all sat down at the table as if this lunch had been planned long ago. Such was the typical unannounced visit in Hatikva.

Before we began eating, I asked if they would mind my recording our conversation for my research on Sukkot ritual practice. Of course not, they said, so I began the recorder and asked them their names and where they were born. From only those two questions, they shared their life stories. David carried the narrative thread and Edna added details while she served us roast chicken, white rice with golden raisins, stewed okra in tomato sauce, spiced chickpeas, and pickled peppers—Persian food, she said and smiled. It was delicious.

David explained that he and Edna were born in the late 1930s in Boushir, Persia, close to Hamanda, near the burial sites of the righteous Esther and Mordechai. After the establishment of the State of Israel, David's family decided to immigrate to Israel. They left Boushir and for a year and a half, waited in an immigration camp in Tehran near where the dead were buried—a cemetery that David still remembers well. The people and the conditions in the camp were poor, but they remained there until their family's turn to immigrate was called. David recalled a shelter that his family built during the cold winter in the camp: "There was no cement, just mud, so we would mix the mud with hay, what the cows eat, to hold it together. We lived in that house for more than six months." When their number was finally called, they boarded a plane for Israel. "When we descended from the plane," he remembered, "we bent down and kissed the earth. We gave respect to the land of Jerusalem." After this expression of gratitude, they rose from the ground and were welcomed by Israeli officials and nurses holding pumps containing DDT, an insecticide that would kill any diseases and lice they might have had. The officials pumped the DDT on all new arrivals from head to toe, said David so they would enter Israel clean. From there they were taken to Shaar Aliyah, an immigrant camp near Haifa that accommodated Jews who had emigrated from Persia, Iraq, and Kurdistan. They remained for three months until, again, their lottery number was called, and they were sent to live in Beit Shaan, near Afula.

For the next two years, from ages fifteen to seventeen, David helped his parents support themselves in their new land. He had studied in a Persian school through the sixth grade but could not study any more in Israel because his family was too poor. He took a barber's bag and walked from house to house in Beit Shaan, offering haircuts. One day, one of his customers told him that he had a sister in Persia whom he could send for if David would like to marry. Yes, said David he would like to meet her, and so Edna was sent for by letter. She arrived in Israel six months later at the age of sixteen, and they were soon married. "We got married in big poverty," said David "My parents had a one-room house with a small kitchen, so we took the kitchen to live in." They had their first child there, then applied to Amidar, a government subsidy organization, to rent a small apartment close to his parents' house, paying seventeen *lirot* per month.[5] "I opened a barber shop and also worked as a mover. It was very hard. Sometimes we didn't have the money to buy bread," he recalled. Almost ten years later, in 1964, they moved to Tel Aviv into the apartment in which they live today, in Shchunat Hatikva. They received a small mortgage from a bank and bought this building, already raising five young children with one more on the way. "I made part of the house a barber shop and worked very hard. Now we're old. I'm seventy-five years old and Edna's seventy-three. That's all. It's a long but interesting story," David concluded with a smile.

The apartment where they had lived for over forty years was small. The front door opened into a small kitchen to the right, which led into a main sitting room that barely held a dining table, a couch, a crib for when their grandchildren visited, and a big-screen television against the far wall. The white walls were covered almost completely with framed photographs of children, grandchildren, *tzaddikim* (righteous men), and respected rabbis, all which kept one's eyes from moving into a far corner of the room that led to several small bedrooms and the bathroom. Behind the table in the main room, glass doors slid open onto a small balcony on which they build their sukkah and that overlooked their street.

Although they used to build their sukkah in their yard downstairs when their children were young, in their older age, they now build it on the balcony to avoid walking up and down the stairs endlessly during the holiday week. They construct a metal-framed sukkah that fits the size of the balcony exactly, hanging sheets and lace cloths to create the top half of the walls, while the balcony's solid concrete walls enclose the bottom half of the structure. Bamboo mats cover the roof to which a single, long fluorescent light bulb is wired in the center. Colorful tinsel chains, fresh etrogim picked from their tree downstairs, pomegranates, and laminated photographs of esteemed rabbis hang on the walls and from the roof. A long, thin table on which sits holy Jewish texts and a tall bottle of

Fig. 4.8. David and Edna Zada build their sukkah on their second-floor terrace, relocated from their backyard for convenience. Shchunat Hatikva, Israel. 2010.

Fig. 4.9. A narrow table and mattress occupy the interior of David and Edna's sukkah. Shchunat Hatikva, Israel. 2010.

soda water occupies the center of the terrace, and two twin mattresses are double stacked against the left wall.

David and Edna told me that they had built a sukkah every year of their lives since they were children. I asked them how the sukkot in the Persia of their youth were constructed, and they both remembered that they were made entirely of wood. Fathers, uncles, and brothers would gather together and cut the wood from trees, arranging four corner beams at a height of about two meters. On the roof of the sukkah, they would lay willow and palm branches, and around the sukkah they would attach cloth sheets and decorate the walls with paper decorations, tapestries, children's drawings, and rugs. They would construct a special doorway entirely out of willow branches, which were green and beautiful, remembered David and every time they entered the sukkah, they would recite a blessing. The sukkah took one day to build, but if they had all the materials gathered and laid out, it might take only three hours with everyone working together. In his family's courtyard, said David his four uncles and four brothers all worked together to construct the sukkah. "Almost all the Jews in Persia made sukkot," he continued. "Those who didn't have the space to build a sukkah would go to a relative and build it at their house to fulfill the mitzvah so they could also eat inside and say the blessings." Edna added that there were no tables or chairs inside their sukkot as there are today: "We had carpets on the floor, and yes, we had pillows. We would sit on the floor and eat, as the Arabs do. We were like Muslims who lie on rugs. We did the same thing." There were no special ceremonial foods associated with Sukkot, she continued, just anything delicious that they made. When I asked how they felt about these differences in sukkah materials and designs between the wooden sukkot in Persia and their metal-framed sukkah today, Edna said that she preferred the sukkah made from scratch. David nodded in agreement but qualified it by noting, "It's okay. If you buy it, it's also a mitzvah."

The design of David and Edna's sukkah on their balcony was quite similar to the design of the main room in which we sat. A long table occupied the center of both spaces, photographs of respected rabbis hung on the surrounding walls, and the main room's couch and the sukkah's mattresses both sat on the left side of their respective spaces. Sitting at the dining room table and looking through the glass doors at the sukkah on their terrace, the ritual space appeared to be a physical and social replication of their home space. When I asked David what, for him, the most meaningful part of Sukkot observance was, the fundamental difference between the two spaces became clear. The most important part, he said without hesitation, was sleeping in the sukkah, as if it is your home.

> The sukkah is similar to a house, but the house is temporary—it comes and goes—while the sukkah is forever. It is like a person whose body leaves this earth but whose soul is always in the world to come. A house may last

Fig. 4.10. David and Edna Zada. Shchunat Hatikva, Israel. 2010.

> seventy or eighty years, but then it goes away. In the Talmud, it is written that the sukkah is a metaphor for what is eternal. Generations and generations of righteous people die and their bodies are dead but their souls are alive in heaven. The house is temporary, but the sukkah does not go away—it is of the world to come.

David recognized permanent shelter in the impermanent ritual dwelling. The distinction that he made between the permanence of his sukkah and the impermanence of his house grew out of his lifetime of displacement as well as by his consistent ritual practice.

The material world is an ephemeral world. David acknowledged this in his interpretation of the sukkah as a spiritual and everlasting home. When I asked

David and Edna what brought them the most happiness in their observance of Sukkot, they both responded, "to welcome guests." They pointed to the sheets that they hung as the walls of their sukkah and on which were printed the names of the seven ushpizin, the biblical guests they welcome each night of the festival week. "God loves hospitality," said David "Abraham, our father, searched for guests to host, for God said first you will respect hospitality, then you will respect me. God loves someone who welcomes guests into his home."

Folklorist Jason Baird Jackson describes tradition as "a symbol (a meaning, a feeling, a construction) that people form in the present about the nature of themselves and their beliefs in light of a particular understanding of a significant past" (2003, 279). Jackson's explanation illuminates how the events of the Zadas' lives come together in the celebration of Sukkot tradition, which offers them a framework for understanding themselves and their beliefs. Through their faith in a Jewish God, Jewish law, and Jewish custom, both Uriel and his parents, David and Edna, rely upon generations of authority to construct spiritual shelters in a world of unpredictability and neglect. Like so many others in Shchunat Hatikva, they often begin their sentences with the phrase, *Katuv b'Torah*, or "It is written in the Torah," paving a path forward by reaching back. The sukkah, a material expression of that which is written in the Torah, is one stone upon that path.

Gratitude and Grace

Yoram Chai Meshumar

The first time I met Yoram Chai Meshumar, he was sitting with his father, Mordechai, outside the house that Mordechai built on Tishbi Street. It was a hot Sunday, September 26, 2010, the fourth day of Sukkot, and the two men sat with their backs to the wall, each holding a paper cup of hot black coffee and looking over at their family's sukkah erected on the dirt lot across the street from the house. I had been photographing sukkot in Shchunat Hatikva that afternoon when I happened upon the pair and their ritual structure. They looked over at me as I walked down the narrow street, my bulky camera swinging from my shoulder, so I walked up to introduce myself. As I began my introduction, Yoram interrupted to say, "Wait a second, do you drink coffee?" Yes, I replied, and he disappeared into his father's house emerging moments later with a chair and another cup of black coffee for me. "Sit! Join us!" he said, and then invited me to continue. I thanked him and took a seat next to his smiling father.

Mordechai soaked up the afternoon sun in his little black hat and listened as Yoram told me of his father's immigration from Yemen, how he built this house that we were leaning against with his own hands, and what it was like for Yoram to grow up here in Hatikva. When he began to describe his family's religious history, I reached for my audio recorder and asked him if I might record the conversation. I told him of my research project and how I would love to hear his thoughts on his family's religious practice. He waved the recorder away with a smile and said, "No, no, not yet, this is just the beginning! Next time," said Yoram "next time you'll come for dinner and you can ask me anything you want and record it all." I agreed and thanked him for the invitation, which would be the first of many.

Yoram's introduction to his family and his Jewish observance that afternoon was brief but telling. Among the first reflections that he shared with me was his goal to build a larger sukkah the following year—four by six meters instead of four by four meters. He wanted to accommodate up to five beds inside, not just his own, as he had done this year. He could easily compare his real and ideal sukkah dimensions because the frame he was currently using was a standard metal structure that his family had purchased years ago and used ever since. This was not the sukkah of his youth, however, said Yoram, as he pointed behind us to the right side of the house where laundry lines now stretched down a narrow alleyway. There, his family had built a sukkah in his childhood, its frame made out of scrap wood, the roof from branches that he cut down from trees in the neighborhood and dragged home through the streets, the decorations made days in advance by hand. That construction took hours, he said, and it was exhausting, but his father, uncles, brothers, and cousins all helped to build it. "Today," Yoram said with a look of despair, "people are lazy, and they don't want to go to the trouble to expend energy on it." Two people can construct a prefabricated sukkah frame such as the one they now use in less than an hour and a half, he said. In his childhood years, however, everyone worked together, and while hammering the frame together, they talked, told jokes, laughed, sang songs, and sat together with coffee and cake during breaks; they had fun, he concluded. When the construction was finally complete and you entered that sukkah, he recalled, you felt connected to nature, standing inside a wooden structure draped with Eucalyptus leaves whose fragrance enveloped you. As our conversation slowed and our cups emptied, I asked Yoram if I could photograph their sukkah and take a portrait of him with his father. Yoram agreed without hesitation and put his arm around his father, half his height, both smiling broadly.

Yoram does not live in Hatikva today but in a neighborhood about twenty minutes away by motorbike, which he rides for his work as a medic for *Magen David Adom* (Red Star of David, Israel's national emergency medical service). My serendipitous afternoon with Yoram and Mordechai occurred because Yoram was visiting his father for Sukkot after the morning prayer service and before dinner in the sukkah with the rest of their family. They had welcomed me to join them for their afternoon time together during this break. The routine of the holiday led to our chance encounter and fostered my lasting relationships with Yoram; his sisters,

Fig. 4.11. Yoram Meshumar sits with his father Mordechai in front of Mordechai's house (left) and across from their family's sukkah (right). Shchunat Hatikva, Israel. 2010.

Fig. 4.12. Yoram Meshumar holds open the door to his family's sukkah. Shchunat Hatikva, Israel. 2010.

Yonah and Gila; all of their children; and the family patriarch, Mordechai. In this way, the structure of this week-long holiday and the structure of the sukkah perform a parallel function: they create a space in which to disrupt the natural order to spend time with family and friends and to talk about history and values.

As I bid Yoram and Mordechai good-bye, I thanked them for the hours of conversation and hospitality, and I said I would call to arrange a time to officially record more of Yoram's stories. He called out after me that he was looking forward to it. Weeks passed as Yoram and I exchanged phone messages trying to find a time to meet. At last we picked a date four months after our first meeting, and at two o'clock on an unusually warm day in January, I arrived at Mordechai's house on Tishbi Street to meet Yoram and his father a second time. As I leaned against the front wall of the house, I looked at the dirt lot across the street where their sukkah had stood four months earlier, and where three dirt-covered rugs now lay, the only remnants of the ritual domestic space that had existed there for a week in September. Fifteen minutes passed and I wondered if I had mistaken our meeting time, so I called Yoram to check. I caught him on his motorbike returning from work. He said he was on his way and apologized for the delay.

I sat down on the dusty curb that bordered the parking lot and looked up at the sun with closed eyes as Mordechai had done on my first visit. Forty-five more minutes passed. I thought Yoram must have hit traffic, for his workplace was not far from his father's home. As I considered whether to call again, an older woman walked by and stopped in front of me to ask me why I was sitting on the ground. Without waiting for my answer, she walked down the street toward a pile of cardboard, returned, and handed me a piece to sit on before inviting me to her house down the street for a cup of coffee. I thanked her but declined, explaining that I was waiting for Yoram and his father. She paused, stared at me, and said Mordechai had just passed away. "That can't be," I said; "I just spoke with Yoram and he's on his way here to meet me now." She said it was true; they were her neighbors and she had just heard the news. I was silent, in disbelief. "Call Yoram and check," she said, so reluctantly I pressed redial. Yoram answered the phone immediately, apologizing profusely for not showing up. He said his father had just died, and he sounded hollow and quiet. I apologized, he said thank you and that we would meet another time, and hung up. His neighbor, still standing with me in front of Mordechai's house, invited me for coffee at her house a second time, and I accepted.

As we turned the corner of Tishbi onto Etsel Street, she began to tell me about her own family history in the neighborhood. "Are you looking for a room to rent?" she asked as we walked up the stairs to her kitchen. She was looking for someone to live with her since her husband had died a year ago and she now occupied their five-room apartment alone. She led me directly to the room that she hoped to rent, empty but for a twin bed. We continued the tour up one more flight to visit her son, Yehuda, who had converted the top level of the building into his own apartment. He was sitting on his couch with a friend watching television when we entered, and his mother said she'd be right back with the coffee. I stood by the wall quietly as Yehuda and his friend complained to each other about how pretentious the reality show star was who just then was speaking on the program. When they next paused, they looked over at me watching them and the television and asked who I was. I told Yehuda his mother had found me waiting for their neighbor Yoram just down the road, Yoram whose father had just died. Yehuda said that only in Shchunat Hatikva would someone pass you on the street and invite you up to her house for coffee, take in a stranger just like that, and he and his friend smiled with satisfaction at the thought of this. Their neighborhood was different, they said.

As we all sat waiting for Yehuda's mother to return, I asked him and his friend about their lives in the neighborhood. Yehuda said his maternal grandfather had brought the whole family from Yemen to Israel, eight children in all, one of whom was his mother. They had settled in Shchunat Hatikva, where his father and his thirteen siblings had also all settled from Yemen. His parents had met and lived there ever since. As a child with twenty uncles in the vicinity at any time, said Yehuda, Hatikva was one big, tight family for him. Everyone knew everyone and all the doors were open. Today, the community he knew in his childhood is no longer, and if he had children, Yehuda said, he would not raise them here.

For several hours, Yehuda described to me changes he observed in Shchunat Hatikva over the course of his life, and how he had traveled to India in his early twenties in search of the values with which he had been raised in the community of his youth. He searched for hardworking, sincere individuals who were not defined by their material worth but by their generosity and happiness. Today, Yehuda said, no one is satisfied with what they have, and everyone wants more. As the sun began to set, Yehuda closed his story by saying that although he had found what he was looking for on his travels across India—those people whose happiness came from personal contentment—he had still returned to Hatikva to live. It may not be the neighborhood of his youth, but you couldn't find this place anywhere else, he said. The community values were still in the individuals even if the community itself had dissolved.

We turned off the television and walked downstairs to find Yehuda's mother in the kitchen, standing over her stove and stirring two large pots, one full of lentils and one full of rice.[6] She was preparing food to bring the Meshumar family when they would return from the cemetery later that evening. Given the Jewish law that burials must take place as soon as possible after one passes away, Mordechai's funeral had already been scheduled for six o'clock that evening, just one hour away. Yehuda asked me if I would attend the funeral and I replied that as sad as I was, I hardly knew the Meshumar family, and was not certain I should attend. He smirked and responded, "This is not America. You don't need a personal invitation to come to a funeral." His tone was biting but harmless, and I took what he said seriously. I had not yet experienced a death in Hatikva and was not familiar with its accepted customs in relation to mourning, which I realized in light of Yehuda's comment, so I thanked him for his honest response and said, in that case, I would go. His mother said they would look for a ride to the cemetery for me.

I walked downstairs to wait outside and saw the Meshumar family erecting a large white tent across from Mordechai's house. Yoram and his two sisters were in the center with neighbors and friends who were helping them construct the same metal frame that they had used for their sukkah, attaching its white cloth walls on the same spot where it had stood four months before during Sukkot. The sukkah would stand there again now, this time for seven days of mourning as family and friends "sat *shiva*" (a week of mourning) inside the structure, a ritual space reinvested with meaning through this new context of use.

As fate would have it, I did not attend the funeral after all. All the cars were all full and the buses too late. Yehuda and his mother apologized as they got into their packed car and I thanked them for their help as I watched the caravan of mourners drive away. I turned to walk home, disappointed that I could not be there for a family whom I hardly knew and a funeral that I had not expected four hours earlier. I walked down Etsel Street through the center of the neighborhood and noticed for the first time blocks of white and black notices plastered onto the street walls announcing deaths in the community. They included Mordechai's death and the funeral's location and time among them. In the past three hours, friends and family had pasted these announcements to sides of buildings, metal gates, and kiosks all along Etsel Street, askew and overlapping other signs that announced upcoming community concerts, religious lectures, holiday celebrations, and political meetings. I passed colorful posters pasted onto the walls of buildings in the streets all the time but had never before taken a close look at these smaller black and white messages layered in between. Now I could see they were everywhere, and not just with Mordechai's name in bold print in the center of the sheet, but with the names of innumerable individuals whom I would never know. These public posters announced to the community who had departed and where family, friends, and neighbors could join the funeral and visit the family in mourning during the week that would follow. Now seeing these daily announcements, death became an everyday presence as I walked to work or lunch or home, passing freshly printed pages of mortal gravity, the sheen of their still-drying wall glue glistening in the heat. Sometimes I avoided looking directly at the bolded names, worried I would discover a loss before the day had even begun. Beyond being reminders of death, however, these posters were reminders of the community that was still present as people came together to grieve.

Four days later, I came back to Tishbi Street to visit the Meshumar family as they sat shiva within the shelter of what had been the sukkah. When last it had been a space of happiness and gratitude for all their family had, now it was a space of sorrow and the recognition of what they had lost. The metal frame was this time cobbled together with extra wooden beams to expand its standard size. Long tables and at least seventy-five plastic chairs were set up inside, a cloth partition and extended tent cover separating the men's and women's places for prayer. When I entered the tented area, I found Yoram and his sister Yonah sitting on a low mattress on the ground in ceremonial fashion against the front cloth wall. Yoram had a white *tallis* (prayer shawl) draped over his head and rounded shoulders, and Yonah was wearing all black with a black headscarf covering her hair. Rain was pounding down on the tarps as a grandson and several male neighbors tried to secure the structure's roof beams, which were threatening to fall in the downpour. Yoram welcomed me in when he saw me in the doorway of the tent and said that the sky was crying. It had started crying when they got back from the cemetery four days ago and had not stopped yet. I said how sorry I was for their loss and what a sweet man their father had been that one afternoon that I had enjoyed with him. I then took out from my bag the photograph of Yoram with his father that I had taken during my unexpected first visit, which I had printed and framed as a gift for the family—I had planned to give it to them when I returned on my second visit, which had never taken place. Yoram took it in his hands and smiled his wide smile again as he had in the photograph, and said he was touched. It was the best gift I could have ever given them, he said, for other things such as food come and go, but the photograph and memory will remain. He showed it to every visitor who entered the tent while I sat with them and said that this moment captured his father when he was still well, which meant so much.

During the week of sitting shiva, as happens during the week of Sukkot, family, friends, and strangers freely entered the open space of the tent to visit the host family. The structure of the sukkah, or in this context, the space of mourning, allows for unexpected passersby and expected loved ones alike to pay their respects and share in the experience. During my visit, a thin, weary homeless man who wandered Hatikva's streets daily in a semilucid state and was commonly referred to by community members as *HaNarcomani*, or the Narcomaniac, passed by the tent. He stumbled inside and was immediately shooed out with irritation by the visiting relatives and friends, as was the typical reaction to his appearance at restaurant doors or storefront entrances. As he stumbled out, Yonah stood up to run after him and hand him a cookie from the small plates of food resting on the tables for the mourning visitors. He took the cookie and mumbled a prayer over it, after which Yonah and he said *amen* together, and then turned to walk away. When she reentered the tent, Yonah

Fig. 4.13. Yoram stands with his father Mordechai Meshumar, who emigrated from Yemen. Shchunat Hatikva, Israel. 2010.

said that he had cried when he found out that Mordechai had died. Mordechai had liked him, she said, a man whom everyone else turned away. Yoram said that it did not matter who the man was; Mordechai loved everyone and everyone loved him. I then bid the family good-bye and began my walk home. On my way, I ran into two acquaintances, as was common in walks through the neighborhood. They asked me where I had been and I told them, unexpectedly prompting their own memories of Mordechai—"a man of gold," the first woman said, and "a man who rode his bike everywhere, always smiling," recalled the second woman. They did not know him well, but they had seen the notices and knew who he was.

In Shchunat Hatikva, social relations structure and nurture rituals such as sitting in the sukkah or sitting shiva. Through the transformation of private space into public space (opening up one's home to the community during the week of mourning) and public space into private space (building a sukkah in a public parking lot, or plastering street walls with death announcements), the dynamic relationship between individuals and their community is made palpable.

I would return two more times that week to Tishbi Street: once on the last night of the week of shiva when the whole community was invited for a closing dinner and prayer, and then again at nine o'clock the next morning when I would accompany the family to the cemetery for a last ritual at Mordechai's grave. The family had invited me to both events and I had accepted, all of us seemingly touched by our presence in each other's lives, although not fully aware of how this had come to be. The community dinner was a community effort with enormous pots of soup, fish, and chicken dishes, and innumerable plates of salads prepared and served by neighbors and friends to over one hundred attendees throughout the night, preventing the Meshumar family from participating in the hosting activity in accordance with Jewish laws of mourning.[7] I sat on the women's side of the partition next to a neighbor who did not seem to have come with anyone else. She spoke to me about the dangers of marrying late in life, as she said she had done, and then packed up our remaining chicken and fish bones for her animals at home and left. The scene was one of giving and taking between the Meshumar family and those in the Hatikva community.

When I returned the next morning, the photograph that I had taken of Yoram and his father was standing amid lit candles on a small altar on a side table in the Meshumar's kitchen. The sukkah's frame had been dismantled and the dirt lot had been returned to its barren state again. Our visit to the cemetery was brief but emotional. The women in the family, all dressed in black, leaned down on their knees and wailed with their arms stretched out on Mordechai's grave, pulled away at last with patches of dirt pressed into their black skirts. The women lit candles, the men recited prayers, and we all washed our hands at the cemetery's gate as we left, as Jewish tradition requires. When we returned to Tishbi Street, Yonah invited me in for coffee, but I could not stay. They thanked me for coming, hugged me good-bye, and told me to come back soon.

One month later, I returned to attend Mordechai's *haskarah*, the one-month anniversary of his death. That day, I met the Meshumars at Tishbi Street at nine o'clock in the morning again, and we traveled to the cemetery together to see the headstone. When we got there, Yonah sat down by the stone and stroked it, crying *abba-le* (Dear Father). She and her niece bent down and sobbed as they kissed his grave. In the middle of saying *kaddish*, the prayer for the dead, an unknown woman in tears walked up to our circle and asked if our *minyan*, the quorum of men required to recite public prayers, would say kaddish for her mother too, who had passed away three months ago. She was visiting alone and could not, according to Jewish law, recite the prayer herself. Of course they would, they replied. She thanked them and stayed with us until the kaddish for Mordechai was complete. Yonah put her arm around the woman as they stood there in tears together, and they shared whispers about their respective father and mother, both loved and lost. This request from a stranger had occurred the first time we had come to the cemetery one month earlier as well. An unfamiliar man had asked our circle of men if they would join him to say kaddish for his mother and they willingly obliged; in turn, he stood with us with his head down in prayer over Mordechai. This custom of such coming together for kaddish is not unusual, but deeply felt nonetheless, as strangers sustain each other during these most vulnerable moments and places.

Over the coming months, I would stop by to say hello to the Meshumars whenever I biked by Tishbi Street, where Yonah and her son, Tomer, now lived in her father's house alone. I visited during Purim, Passover, Shavuot, Sukkot, and on Shabbat for coffee on the sidewalk or for a warm meal inside. Almost always, Yoram would bid me good-bye with the parting words, "Our door is always open. Come back soon!"

I would not meet Yoram for our "official" recorded interview until more than one year after our first meeting on Tishbi Street, and with a second Sukkot having by then passed and a year of mourning nearly complete. I could not have foreseen the road that our relationship would travel before I would finally sit down with Yoram and my audio recorder, but that journey paved the way for my understanding of his philosophy of family, community, ritual, and belief.

Setting the Scene on Tishbi Street

During my second Yom Kippur in Shchunat Hatikva, Yoram invited me to his father's house to take part in their sukkah construction that would begin immediately following the synagogue's evening service. I rode my bike over to Tishbi Street after evening services at the Hesed L'Avraham synagogue and found the whole Meshumar family sitting outside their front door with coffee cups in hand and half-eaten cakes covering the kitchen table inside. They kindly offered me both, as usual. The three siblings, Yoram, Yonah, and Gila, were all there with their five children and several more cousins and friends. Although only Yonah and her son now lived in Shchunat Hatikva, the whole family still gathered in Mordechai's home as they always had, even though he was no longer physically present.

As family members finished their coffee, they began retrieving sukkah materials from the house and laying them down on the dirt plot across the street. The metal beams for the frame were suspended horizontally from the roof's overhang, the cloth walls were rolled up in a corner of the house, and the newly purchased AstroTurf lining for the interior floor of the sukkah was still in its plastic wrap. The family milled around the lot arranging the metal beams in their proper order, and as the first pole was hammered into its hole, everyone paused and Yoram recited a blessing. When he finished the prayer, Yonah and Gila began to delegate tasks, demonstrating and suggesting how to perform various elements of the construction. Yoram followed their orders, as did the rest of the family, but teased his sisters while he worked. "Here's the architect!" he said with a small chuckle, nodding toward Yonah; "And here's the engineer!" he announced with a huge smile, gesturing toward Gila. Everyone laughed, for none in the group had any formal training in these skills, yet each one was undertaking the construction with complete and perhaps overconfidence, especially given that several poles had already been mismatched. Toward the end of the frame's construction, an hour later, Yonah's son, Tomer, handed me a short string with which to secure two wooden beams that would support the brush for the sukkah's roof. As he handed it to me, he looked in my eyes and said, "Do it, it's a mitzvah." With the women directing the construction crew and the men reciting religious prescriptions and prayers, the Meshumars' sukkah construction created two spaces of belonging: a shared social space in which family and friends could relate with cooperation and humor; and a spiritual space where participants could together enact through their work the beliefs to which they subscribed.

"Never Close the Door to the World"

Later that month, when I returned for my "official" interview with Yoram, he sat down, looked me in the eyes, and said, "What I'm going to tell you now you should write on your wall and never forget: Never close the door to the world." This was his motto, he said, and one that expressed his respect for the values he holds close, humility and generosity. "You never know what waits around the corner," Yoram added, and he had been right—I had not known the world I would enter when I rounded the corner of Tishbi Street over a year before. If there was one lesson Yoram wanted me to learn as our friendship grew, it was to remain open in the face of the unknown, and he illustrated this lesson through the telling of his life story.

"When I was a child," he began, "there were no doors. Neighbors just came in and said, 'How are you?' They took something out of the refrigerator and sat down. All day long we were with each other. If you didn't see a neighbor for one hour, you would go to his home and ask, 'What happened? Where are you?' We once had a neighbor who lived on the second floor of that house," he said, pointing out the window to a two-story building across the street. "We used to see her every morning when she would leave her home, between six and eight in the morning. One morning we didn't see her, so we rushed straight over to her home. She had fallen and lost consciousness. If we had waited and thought maybe she'd come out later, it might have been too late." In Yoram's youth, in the 1970s and 1980s, during the height of Shchunat Hatikva's problems with drugs and crime, the Meshumars' house on Tishbi Street stood opposite one of the most infamous drug houses in Tel Aviv. Despite the unpredictable street environment in which he lived, Yoram still describes the neighborhood of his youth as one where "there were no doors"—a description that other veteran residents of Hatikva offered me as well. Doors were open and windows were unlocked. The community that existed, surrounded by the perils of Hatikva's streets, sustained itself through social connection and mutual responsibility.

My conversation with Yoram moved seamlessly from his childhood memories of Hatikva to his interpretation of Sukkot, the notion of home bridging the two. "So what's it worth, building a house? What's it worth?" he asked me. "This sukkah teaches us that all the materialism in the world is worth nothing if it has no purpose." A massive earthquake had wreaked havoc in Turkey earlier that week and Yoram lamented it now, remarking how unreliable the material world was. "When you're at home in a concrete house, and suddenly it all shakes and rain is pouring down and it might collapse, you must be secure and have faith. That's in your hands, not materialism. When there is no belief in materialism, faith increases, and so does abundance." Yoram then asked me if I knew the greatest virtue of the ushpizin, the biblical guests who are invited each night of Sukkot. I said I did not. He quietly replied with one word: "Grace." He continued:

> And what is grace? It's the opposite of materialism. This is the greatest advantage of Sukkot. Once you go out of your castle, your so-called fortress, and move into something a little shaky that the wind can blow away, then you come to an understanding that everything is from above. Then you are glad that you earned a thousand shekels and you are not jealous that your girlfriend earned five thousand. You are not jealous that your neighbor bought larger pots or a bigger television than you. Then you are at peace with yourself. When you are at peace with yourself, you have calm, and you are rich.

The contrast between contentment and wealth was at the core of my conversations with Yoram about the meaning of Sukkot observance, as it was with so many others in Hatikva. The rejection of materialism and recognition of the richness of transcendence is a widely held interpretation of the ritual of Sukkot. In Hatikva, however, I found that individuals spoke of this awareness during conversations that focused on neighborhood life or personal history, as well as ones that related specifically to Sukkot. Yoram continued to emphasize this idea by quoting a verse from Ecclesiastes: "He who loves money is not satiated by money," he said, and then explained:

> The materialistic person is he who, from his childhood to his death, gathers, gathers, gathers, and doesn't enjoy. He collects money, another house, more shares, more of this and more of that. At the end of his time in this world, he lives like a dog, and does not enjoy anything, just money. And what happens? His child or brother then says, 'Look at this fool who died

and did nothing with his money.' So he starts spending it, and there's no value to that money. No value to life. And now look at poor people who have nothing at home, and nothing to eat, but they are happy.

"The essence of life is to be happy," Yoram concluded, "and you are happy when you are satisfied. If a man is satisfied with what he is given, then he no longer covets other things. It is enough for him if he has a house, a roof, food, and a place to sleep. Thank God. What God has given, thank you." In his observance of Sukkot, Yoram celebrates grace, offers gratitude, and reaffirms his understanding of the false link between materiality and contentment. The moral that Sukkot observance teaches Yoram is one that he carries with him before the holiday begins and after it ends: how to remain happy in a material world. This is his personal experience.

Yoram also finds meaning in the process of the sukkah's construction, however, which is a collective experience. "When we were kids," Yoram said, "it took two and a half or three hours to build, at least. How does it happen? We talk, I make you laugh, you make me laugh, this one talks, that one jokes, and a one-hour task takes three. It was wooden, not Lego—what I call these sukkot today. You cannot build a wooden sukkah alone; you need more time and more people, and it goes by with laughter, and it's fun. Today, you come like a robot. *Tack, tack, tack, tack*, four legs. So what? Twenty minutes on the clock and there's a sukkah." In Yoram's memory, people came together to build the sukkah. His disillusionment about the modern prefabricated sukkah kits lies in the speed with which the construction takes place and in the simplified process. As the construction time has shortened and the process has demanded less effort, social time has also shortened and reliance on others' help has diminished.[8] Yoram regrets the move in sukkah construction toward individualism and speed.

In this loss of time spent together, Yoram also identifies a loss of education. "The biggest issue is cooperation," he says, illustrating his point with a story:

> "Get me the cup," says an old man. This old man does not have to have you bring the cup to him. He does it to send two messages. The first message is to teach, through personal example, and the second message is that it was worth sharing this task—that the two sides benefit. I benefit by you supposedly helping me, and you feel satisfied that you helped. It is a two way street. A child gets warmth from his grandfather, and love, and he returns it. When he grows up, what happens? He transfers that to his children.

Yoram views the process of sukkah construction as an opportunity for older generations to transfer knowledge and values to the next—an opportunity that becomes increasingly rare as lives move more quickly and away from cooperative activity. In particular, he declares the principle of work, which he had earlier credited with giving value and meaning to material goods, to be the fundamental principle sacrificed in the move toward speed:

> Today, everything is done in an instant and you do as little as possible. Decorations are ready, chains are made. For two shekels I can get a chain from here to the end of the sukkah, so what do I need to make it myself? As kids though, we would cut paper into strips—yellow, blue, red—and to do the chains alone was a ritual that would take us two days. Two! We made flowers, cut out shapes, drew pictures, all by hand, then took glue and attached one end inside the other. It was work. Do not forget that this is a very good thing. It was therapy. If you give a child a task and let him make chains, he sits. He is busy. If you then want to bathe him or lull the child to sleep, he does not give you problems. He will shower, he will go to sleep. He does not cause problems because his curiosity has been provided for. A child who does not have his curiosity attended to remains hyperactive. There is no work today. No work. This is something very lacking.

In Yoram's worldview, the ritual occasion of sukkah construction is more than a commemoration of an historic period of displacement, more than a celebration of the Israelites' survival in the desert. It is a time and space created for the intentional education of a new generation. It is an activity in which the values of cooperation and generosity, gratitude and grace are taught and learned through hard work. For Yoram, this holiday, the value of which was once earned through expressions of work and social relation, is now marked by a lost art and appreciation of labor and a turn inward toward the self.

Yoram's childhood experience of a tightly knit social network that sustained him in an unstable urban environment, and his memories of building a sukkah each year with his entire family convey the ways in which he and those around him acted in common to create community.[9] As such intentional collective networking diminishes, unanticipated and virtual collective actions increasingly actualize his community. The unanticipated actions include the unpredictable death of his father and the seven days of communal mourning that followed, and the virtual actions include such daily routines as Yoram's DVD viewing of and singing along to live concerts by Tzion Golan (a popular Israeli singer of Yemenite origin who sings Mizrahi-style music in Yemeni dialects of Arabic and Hebrew). These extraordinary and ordinary events stand out as unintended and virtual instances of collective performance through which Yoram's community is created today. Yoram's observance of Sukkot remains an expression of his determination to continue creating community in his life through intentional collective performance as well. Through his belief in the values of hospitality and generosity, and through their intensified expression through his sukkah construction and use each year, Yoram both reinforces the networks of which he is a part and redraws their boundaries by constructing new doors that he may leave open to the world.

Relativism and Labor
Dror Kahalani

Dror Kahalani and I leaned back in the white plastic chairs placed in front of his sukkah, cups of café shachor and pistachios in hand. We had just finished weaving together the schach for the roof of his sukkah, the last part of the ritual construction before the holiday was to begin the following night. "You know what they say about this holiday," he said. "He who does not see simhat beit ha-sho'evah does not see happiness in his days." Simhat beit ha-sho'evah otherwise known as the Water Drawing Ceremony, is a ceremony within the holiday. The ritual originated as an offering of water libations after the daily morning sacrifices at the Temple in Jerusalem before it was destroyed. These offerings began on the second night of Sukkot and continued each remaining day of the holiday week. Oral tales and Jewish texts recount all-night singing and dancing, bonfires that raged across Jerusalem, and unbridled celebration around these ritual water libations. The axiom that Dror recalls for me about the joy fostered by this ceremonial practice conveys a core intention of Sukkot observance for him—that "you must be happy."

This evening's construction of Dror's sukkah was the second in which I participated, for I had also assisted him one year earlier in 2010, shortly after my arrival to Shchunat Hatikva. Dror had invited me to help him build his sukkah after learning about my research and remarking that I must construct a sukkah if I was studying the ritual. I gladly accepted his offer and soon realized that in addition to his interest in helping me further my work, Dror was the lone builder of his family's sukkah and my assistance could be of use. Although the majority of Dror's immediate family—his grandmother, parents, brothers and sisters-in-law, sister and brother-in-law, nieces, and cousins—all live nearly all on the same street, and only a five-minute drive from Dror's home, the construction of his sukkah is more or less a solitary endeavor in his backyard. Compared to the rest of the family's residences, Dror's home offers the most outdoor space in which to build the largest sukkah and host the greatest number of guests, which is his wish.[10]

Beyond the issue of space, however, Dror is the informally designated social and religious leader of his family. He is also an active figure throughout the neighborhood community, serving as the primary caretaker of the small Yemenite synagogue that he attends, where Simon Tobi leads services; as a volunteer member of the Hatikva neighborhood council; and as maintenance manager at Hatikva's theater school next door to the shuk. He is a respected member of the community often involved in the planning and hosting of social, political, and religious events for Hatikva's residents, and he is commonly called upon by neighbors and friends for his practical abilities to fix broken VCRs, plumbing problems, mangled bicycles, power outages, and other mechanical emergencies. The Kahalani family name is one of several well-known names in the neighborhood, and that recognition has cultivated a leadership role for Dror. He hosts most of the holiday celebrations for his family because he has a large backyard, but also because he embraces and respects the authority he has been given.

When I began my first recorded conversation with Dror some months after we met, he opened the conversation by saying, "My name is Dror Kahalani, and I was born in Shchunat Hatikva. I've lived here more than forty years now. I was born in '67 during the war, the Six Day War." Although he does not remember the experience, Dror said that he fell on the floor of the green bomb shelter on Etsel Street when he was only three days old, when everyone in the neighborhood ran for cover just days after his birth. He has been told this story many times, he said, and now recites it as the opening to his life story.

The memories with which he constructed his life narrative for me thereafter were similarly characterized by experiences of pain and his reflections upon them. After his first fall, the earliest memory that Dror recalls occurred just a few streets over from that green bomb shelter when he was six years old, playing with friends by his grandmother's house at the side entrance to the shuk. There, a large truck was parked as its drivers delivered towers of live caged chickens to the market. "We were playing, and I ran around the cages on the truck and suddenly everything fell on me. Blood was flowing from my head and I ran straight home, crying. Instead of my father saying, 'Oh, poor you,' it was *PACHHH*! [He gestured a slapping motion.] 'Why were you playing by the chicken cages?' My father did that, and then it didn't hurt anymore and everything was fine," Dror said, his tone matter-of-fact. "Why didn't it hurt anymore?" I asked him. "Because I had been hit," he said, "and that hurt too, so the first pain didn't hurt anymore. That's how it once was. If that happened today, there would immediately be ambulances and health insurance and chaos, and in the end, nothing. Back then, there was blood, I cried, I was hit, and boom, that's all. The first pain didn't hurt because the second pain did. I never forgot this all my life. This is a story that never left my mind, I've always kept it there. What did I learn? That if we want, it doesn't have to hurt." This lesson about relativism that Dror learned from that early experience is one that he has drawn upon in subsequent challenging moments in his life: on the crime-ridden streets of his youth in Hatikva, in the Israeli army as a young man, in arduous jobs, and in trying relationships. If something hurts, he remembers that there could be something else that might hurt even more, and that possibility lessens the pain.

Fig. 4.14. Dror Kahalani begins to construct his family's sukkah by hanging sheets for walls. Shchunat Hatikva, Israel. 2010.

Fig. 4.15. Dror Kahalani adjusts the wooden beams across which he will lay brush for the *schach*. Shchunat Hatikva, Israel. 2010.

I retell this memory not for its psychological insight, but because Dror repeatedly emphasized the importance of relativism to me throughout the narrative of his personal experiences. "In a dream world," Dror once said, "of course I might want a bigger car, a nicer house, or more money, but that's not what makes you happy. We may have little, but we feel rich because we have happiness without the worries that rich people have from all the precious things they own." Making modest salaries throughout his adulthood, Dror has been a satisfied taxi driver, bus driver, and now maintenance manager. Just as he has learned that the level of pain in his life may be relative, so too may be the level of joy. As he had told his well-to-do uncle in a discussion of the relationship between wealth and happiness, "A man with bread and margarine can be the happiest man. Give him a can of tuna and he feels like a king!" Dror's ability to locate his own experience within the greater context of human possibility enables him to maximize his contentment and minimize his suffering. He is aware of experiences beyond his own and he draws meaning from that perspective.

Beyond the world of emotions, however, Dror's relativism also knits together his thoughts and actions in the realms of work, politics, and religion. When speaking about his childhood in Hatikva during the 1970s, Dror told me that as children, he and his siblings would receive new shoes twice a year: a pair of sandals on Passover because it marked the start of summer, and a pair of closed shoes on Rosh Hashanah, as winter approached. They had to take care of these two pairs all year, he said, stitching and polishing them when needed because they were their only shoes. Today, he said, his daughters have seven or eight pairs each and they do not care for them as he once did for his two. "Everything had value back then," said Dror. "If I had a bike, I would protect it like nothing else. No one bought it for me—it would be the bike I made. Today, people buy and buy and buy and it's not enough." In the face of a growing consumer culture that measures worth by the standards of a distant market economy, Dror still finds value in earning and preserving his possessions rather than in easy acquisition and replacement. His scale of value is calibrated by the work of his own hands.

The notion of relativism gives meaning to his experience of religion as well and is a fundamental feature of Dror's belief system and ritual practice. On a material level, Dror disapproves of the increasing commercialization of the sukkah. While increasing accessibility to the ritual through commodification, the prefabricated kits and manufactured decorations have devalued the practice for him because he does not need to work as hard to create the structure. As a child, he made the sukkah from scratch out of scrap wood, sheets, and brush that he would cut down from trees. He still builds it largely by hand and prefers to make the decorations at home with his daughters rather than buy them ready made, despite his admission that it is easier to do the latter. He says, "If you take scissors, cut the paper, get the glue . . . it's hard work but it's more meaningful.

These are things you don't measure with money. We always took newspaper and made paper chains, and used to save all of them, but today we don't do that. There was education back then, but things change. There's no value today. It doesn't matter if I have the money or not—there was more meaning and value in it because I prepared it." Personal creation of the materials transmits an education that Dror sees disappearing—an education that is earned through physical labor.

Dror does not place his religious beliefs and practices in an isolated realm only to be accessed at particular times and in particular places. His religious practice is in his daily practice. When I once asked Dror what "God" meant to him, he replied, "God is nature. Everyone calls it by a different name. I call it God, but those who don't believe in God call it nature. They're the same thing." For Dror, God is the system that keeps order and a logic that provides direction. He continued with a rhetorical question, "If we don't believe in God, what do we believe in? God says, 'First of all, believe in yourself, and only after that, believe in God.' You can't believe in God if you don't believe in yourself first. God doesn't just give me a sukkah if I pray for it. I have to cut down the branches, build it myself . . . first of all, I have to believe in myself!" Dror does not expect to receive anything without working for it. Moreover, he believes that the value of the sukkah he builds will be determined by the amount of effort he devotes to the task. For him, the value of this ritual is relative, and it rests in his hands.

The first part of Dror's Sukkot ritual, the construction, is an individual endeavor in which he finds meaning through his relationship with God. He recounted an anecdote to me several times throughout the course of our friendship to explain his understanding of this relationship: "God requested that we build the sukkah. We don't ask why. When God was distributing the Torah, he first offered it to the Christians. They asked what was written in it, and then said they didn't want it. God then went to the Muslims. They asked what was written in it, and they said didn't want it. He then went to the Jews, and they didn't ask questions. They only responded, *na'aseh v'nishmah*—'We will do and we will hear'—so, first you do, then you ask why."[11] Dror constructs his sukkah each year without questioning, honoring an agreement to earn understanding after action.

The second part of Dror's Sukkot observance is his weeklong use of the sukkah. He measures the spiritual value of the meals, prayers, and social gatherings inside the sukkah by the social life that takes place inside—the more people he can host, the more meaning he derives. Dror described the scene of his childhood sukkah to illustrate his point:

> Many years ago, at my grandmother's house, we built a small sukkah and we didn't have space inside because it was so full of family. Everyone had five or six kids, so there was no room, but we managed. There was a

bed, maybe twelve people sat on it, and chairs and chairs and chairs, and another bed, and benches ... The big ones sat inside, the little ones outside. First the elderly sat down to eat, then the younger ones, then the kids. One group of people ate first, then they left and another group came inside to sit and eat, then another group—this happened three or four times. Maybe thirty or forty or fifty people ate. I love lots of people, a big family, always. All the time we work, run here, run there, but on this holiday we sit, eat, drink, rest, talk. In my opinion, it's okay if you build the sukkah another way from the way I build it because the atmosphere is the most important, the feeling that everyone's happy, eating, enjoying themselves. That's more important than if the sukkah's kosher or not.

While the process of building the sukkah each year is a ritual obligation to which Dror feels committed because of his personal relationship with God, the use of the sukkah manifests collective devotion through social performance.

Dror continued to describe his childhood in Hatikva to explain how it has shaped his social values. "We were lacking things. People slept on the floor, kids and adults. There was one bed or two beds, but we weren't cold because we were close together, eight or nine of us on the floor. It was warm because everyone was together. That's why it was good. It was a warm environment," he said. Dror's family and friends compensated with strong relationships and mutual support for the material resources that they were lacking. He continued: "Back then, there was not enough food, but everyone had enough. We all ate out of one big pot, mostly water with beans, but everyone was full. Today, there's a lot of food and everything is ready made and there's never enough." This paradox of current-day life, the excess of goods and dearth of satisfaction, discourages him. Dror concluded the memories of his youth with an observation about the environment in which he born, raised, and still lives: "Hatikva is a special place," he said. "Here, there is everything, and there is nothing."[12]

Over the years that Dror kept his lessons of relativism and the value of labor in mind, he has built from them a perspective on education. An excess of material goods has caused people to be spoiled today, he said, and as the scale of little to plenty disappears and everything is available at any time, value decreases. With this flat line of worth, nothing is better and nothing is worse.[13] This is the problem, he said. The overabundance of goods and the ease of commercial accessibility eliminate the need to learn how to make objects or maintain them, and in this, an education about creation is lost. The process of sukkah construction imbues the ritual dwelling with the value that Dror appreciated. He worked to build the ritual space that God commands, earning the honor, the architecture, and the worth of that space through belief in this physical action, in the social and spiritual experience that occur in the sukkah, and in himself.

Sukkot with the Kahalanis

On the first night of Sukkot of 2011, I arrived at Dror's apartment at eight thirty, after dinner had been served. I had also promised visits to two other families' sukkot that evening since it is on this first night that most families host their elaborate meals. The Kahalanis did not mind my late arrival because they knew about my research and they had said that they would prefer that I come to their sukkah last and stay late, rather than come first and leave early.

I walked through the kitchen to their backyard door and saw the green sukkah that Dror had spent all week constructing. It was illuminated by a single light bulb hanging down from the roofing, with paper chains, paper-cut snowflakes, and crayon illustrations drawn by his two daughters, all dangling from the surrounding tarp walls. A small group of men reclined around the small square table inside the sukkah and a large group of women gathered around a larger table outside, in front of the sukkah's entrance. Nearly twenty people were in attendance in total, and although the meal had concluded, plates of fruit, nuts, and cakes and glasses of beer and wine were scattered across the tables and replenished for hours to come, ensuring a long night full of storytelling and laughter.

Everyone welcomed me when I walked in and a chair was instantly pulled toward the large table and a warm plate of dinner leftovers placed in my hands. I sat with the women—Dror's grandmother Safta Chana, his mother Suad, his sister Sharona, several sisters-in-law, nieces, and his daughters—and listened as their overlapping conversations picked up right where they had dropped off when I entered. Family news and neighborhood updates filled the air as the women shared stories about people and events in their lives. I finished my food and rose to look at the sukkah more closely, newly animated since I last saw it when I helped lay the schach across its top with Dror. As I peered across the sukkah's threshold, Dror looked up from his seat at the head of the small table inside and called me over with a big wave. His brother Ronen pulled up a chair to their table and the conversation began again mid-sentence, as if I had been there all along. As I sat with these four men—Dror; Ronen; their half-brother, Shai; and their uncle, Nissan—in the sukkah for the next three hours, I listened to them exchange Talmudic tales and personal narratives in a way that revealed each one's religious ethics and social creed.

This evening was not unlike the weekly gatherings that the Kahalani siblings organize after Shabbat dinner each Friday night—a coming together for hours of socializing, snacking, and challenging each other's moral code through story swapping and banter. This evening, however, the extended family was also present, which allowed the rare opportunity to have all the men of the family seated around one table, and all the women around another—a separation of the sexes

Fig. 4.16. The Kahalani family extends the eating area out of the sukkah to accommodate all the family guests on the first night of Sukkot. The outside table is largely occupied by the women of the family. Shchunat Hatikva, Israel. 2011.

Fig. 4.17. Inside the sukkah, the men of the Kahalani family sit and discuss morals and themes of the holiday for hours. Shchunat Hatikva, Israel. 2011.

based on preference rather than religious law—which gave rise to discussions with particular content.

When I entered the sukkah, the men were engaged in a debate over how "good" a person could be who did not follow all the commandments of the Torah. Dror and his uncle rapidly exchanged arguments, each one's claim cut off by the other's rebuttal. Dror's position was two-part and resolute: he did not believe in absolute labels such as "good" or "bad," and his commitment to the Torah was preceded by a deeper commitment to his own self. "The Torah says," said Dror, "'*Derech eretz* comes before the Torah.' First of all, be a *mensch* [Yiddish: person of integrity and honor]. After that, use the Torah." Derech eretz literally translates to mean "the way of the land," but it is used metaphorically and commonly to refer to good character and respectable behavior. The line Dror cited was from Midrash Vayikra Rabbah 9:3, a mid-seventh century compilation of commentary on the book of Leviticus, which conveys the message that honorable behavior and upstanding character are prerequisites to living a life of Torah. In contrast to Dror's uncle, who argued that the quality of one's character is measured by her or his literal actualization of the Torah's text, Dror believes that quality of character comes from the self, and only secondarily may be directed and evaluated by the standards of the Torah.

The determined debaters soon tired of each other's arguments and moved to a broader topic—the *tzadik*, or righteous person. The men began by analyzing the character type who should deserve such an exalted title, considering various *tzadikim* (plural) from Jewish history about whom stories circulate for their ability to grant prayers and perform miraculous healings. Dror again asserted a rational view based on life experience, dismissing the judgments of "righteous" or "not righteous" that were flying across the table. He told the others, "History tells many stories that are not always right. It's all relative to what you understand." His brother and uncle immediately rebutted his relativism with two tales of inexplicable medical healings at the hands of revered Jewish spiritual leaders, then began to list the qualities that might characterize such righteous men—such as wisdom, purity, and honesty. Dror interrupted the list and asked the group, "Do you know why they say, *tzadik v'ra lo, rasha v'tov lo* [The righteous suffer and the wicked receive good]? Do you know where this sentence comes from? It's written in the Mishnah, the *Chazal* said this.[14] Moses was punished, therefore, he is a righteous man." His statement silenced the table as the men considered why the righteous would suffer and the wicked prosper. It seemed illogical but the Sages wrote it, Dror repeated, and to clarify his point, he continued: "There are things we do not understand and we will not understand. That's why we don't open up these deep things . . . and this is why we can't measure words like poor, rich, righteous, wicked." Dror's citing of the Torah and Talmud throughout the evening demonstrated his knowledge of these holy texts and enabled him to counter arguments with authoritative references that the group could evaluate together, each according to his own theological beliefs and experience. This was the structure of the conversation: a dynamic dialogue in which personal experiences, social histories, cultural values, and individual theologies were woven together through debate to define singular philosophies.

No sooner did Dror make his point that the righteous suffer and the wicked prosper than his brother-in-law Shai countered with a play on Dror's quote: "Today, it should be *ani v'ra lo, ashir v'tov lo*," he said, smiling. Shai had replaced the words "righteous" and "wicked" with "poor" and "rich" so that the saying now meant, "The poor suffer and the rich receive good." The men all nodded in agreement with Shai's recasting of the saying. Dror then responded: "But now the question is, what is poor?" For the next ten minutes, the men proposed and rejected definitions of the word according to their standards of economic, psychological, social, and cultural capital. Class was on the table, and they examined their socioeconomic realities in light of their Jewish principles in a continued search to make sense of their lives.

As the hours passed, the conversation kept circling the table, broaching topics such as wealth, poverty, religion, materialism, righteousness, selfishness, education, and happiness. The style of discourse was provocative, probing, and improvisational. Conversation was unstructured, and yet these issues were seamlessly threaded together, allowing each of the four speakers to continuously refine and defend his views. With a spectrum of religious affiliation at the table from Dror, the self-declared "traditionalist," to Dror's uncle Nissan, "believing but not practicing," discussion in this sukkah was spurred by varied theologies and life experiences. Here, in this space of improvised self-expression, all could enter and share their system of belief, their dreams, and their disillusionments. Although such conversations can occur in other places at other times, the egalitarian architecture of the sukkah—a modest material structure set apart from the house—and the holiday's resonance with the economic and social realities of life made it a space particularly suited to common dialogue about society and personal faith.

Dror laments modernization because he perceives a diminishing appreciation of the value of labor and collective effort. When Henry Glassie notes that "most deeply vernacular homes are social facts; their primary order is ethical," he highlights the intention behind Dror's method of sukkah construction and his use of its social space (1984, 16). Dror creates a social rather than physical space—a place in which people may sit together and enjoy themselves, valuing human connectedness more than precision of construction. When Dror pointed to the wall in his synagogue that he helped construct and said that it had watched him pray for forty years (chapter 3), and when he builds his sukkah each fall as a space in which to observe his own character and place in the world, he engages with society through physical creation and metaphysical interpretation. He produces knowledge and understanding through hard work, and he works from a perspective that considers conditions greater than his own.

Notes

1. "Selective retrieval" was a concept discussed by a panel of folklorists including Ray Cashman, Henry Glassie, David McDonald, and Pravina Shukla at the American Folklore Society meeting in New Orleans (2012). They variously defined the term as "excellence within tradition" (Glassie), "the best ideas of the past [that] create visions for the future" (McDonald), and "sniffing in the air of the past" (fieldwork collaborators of Glassie).

2. In *Revisioning Ritual: Jewish Traditions in Transition* (2011), Simon Bronner argues for a focus on the contexts of Jewish ritual performance beyond the strictly religious. He remarks that to examine Jewish ritual situationally allows for the expansion of the concept of ritual "from remarkably persistent and stable religious rites to symbolic practices that are contextualized culturally and analysed for their changes" (3). The book's authors thus adopt the perspective of interaction and lived experience to allow their analyses of Jewish ritual to move beyond "the mere bifurcation of *minhag* ["custom"] into biblical and post-biblical custom," and to be "alternatively summarized by their cultural connection to contexts of (1) liturgy and prayer, (2) time and yearly cycle, (3) passage (or life course) and initiation, and (4) performance and practice" (14–15). In a like manner, I emphasize the socioeconomic and cultural contexts of the lives of Sukkot observers in this study to allow for a fuller picture of the motivations for, implications of, and meaning made through Jewish ritual practice.

3. I use the term "Persia" and "Persian Jews" in this dissertation when individuals with whom I spoke referred to Iran and Iranian Jews in these terms. In Israel today, the generally accepted word for Iranian Jews is *Parsim*, or Persians. Persia is the name of the ancient kingdom for which Iran is the legal name. When I use the terms "Iran" and "Iranian" in this writing, I do so to offer the reader the linguistic counterpart commonly used in Western countries today to refer to this same geographic area, but not because those with whom I spoke in Israel referred to it as such.

4. *Bamba* is a peanut butter-flavored puffed corn snack, one of the most popular children's snacks in Israel.

5. The *lira* (plural, *lirot*) was the currency of the British Mandate of Palestine from 1927 until the establishment of the State of Israel in 1948.

6. Lentils are a traditional Jewish mourning food, their circular shape commonly associated with the full life cycle. According to *The Encyclopedia of Jewish Symbols* (1992), "Traditionally, lentils are eaten by Jewish mourners, because 'the lentil has no mouth,' just as the mourner must not speak of ordinary topics but must remain silent in the face of death. Mourning itself is likened to a wheel, round like the lentil, which symbolizes the inexorable cycle of mortality [*Bava Batra 16b; Genesis Rabbah 62:14*]" (Frankel and Teutsch 1992, 95).

7. See Simcha Fishbane's article, "Jewish Mourning Rites—A Process of Resocialization" (1989), for an analysis of such community involvement in the mourning process as a method of re-integrating the mourning individuals into the community.

8. Henry Glassie also observed the effects of modern materials and methods of construction on social relations in Ballymenone, Ireland (2006). Regarding the shift from impermanent thatched roofs to permanent metal roofs, Glassie writes, "Under a tin roof, the householder is not obliged to be a craftsman, or to be connected—as once they were in Ballymenone through trades of aid—with neighbors who are skilled. He lives alone—in isolation, Mr. Nolan would say, in silence—managing without effort or knowledge or skill or social connection" (2006, 192–193).

9. Yoram's description of and participation in the ritual of Sukkot illustrates what Dorothy Noyes conceptualizes as the process of a social imaginary becoming an actuality through performance. Noyes notes that "acting in common makes community," emphasizing that through the features of collective performance—repetition, formalization, and "concensus"—individuals are able to relate to one another in conceptual and bodily ways (1995, 468). "The community exists in its collective performances," writes Noyes; "they are the locus of its imagining in their content, and of its realization in their performance" (469).

10. Dror's daughters help decorate the sukkah and fill the interior with chairs and a table. Dror constructs the sukkah's frame and roof alone because his wife, Smadar, works evening hours and then returns home to cook for the family and clean the house. Dror's siblings are often occupied with their own families. Though a meager distance between his house and the street on which the rest of his family lives, the five-minute drive by car across the four-lane main road makes the difference in casual involvement in each other's lives. Dror did not complain about building the sukkah alone, but he welcomed my help and enjoyed the sociality of working together, explaining why he constructs elements of the sukkah in particular ways to adhere to religious law. Despite our productive work together, Dror made it clear that the construction of the structure is the means to the greater end, which is the construction of a space for socializing, conviviality, and spirituality.

11. Jason Baird Jackson and Hasan El-Shamy recognized that this fragment of Dror Kahalani's narrative echoes a verse in the Koran and also contains a common motif identified in *Motific Constituents of Arab-Islamic Folk Traditions* (El-Shamy 2016). The Koranic verse of relevance concerns the undertaking of trust and responsibility. It reads, "We [God] did indeed offer the trust to the Heavens and the Earth and the Mountains, but they refused to carry it—being afraid thereof; but man carried it. Surely he is unjust and very foolish" (Koran 33:72). The first part of Dror's narrative describes God's offer of the Torah to Christian and the Muslim peoples, who did not trust it without knowing what was written within, and then the offer to the Jewish people, who accepted it without question. The second part of Dror's narrative conveys the obedience of the Jewish people toward God by first acting, and only afterward asking questions. This may be recognized as motif V0008.1, or "Obedience to God (deity): unquestioning compliance with divine commandments" (El-Shamy 2016, 1768).

12. Of note, Dror's comments about cultural change in Hatikva were echoed by many of his generation with whom I spoke in the neighborhood. These first generation Israelis, born in the 1960s and most now in their forties, often remarked on the rapid modernization of Israeli society at the expense of the cultural customs and social practices that their families had brought with them from native countries and cultures. Uriel Zada and Yoram Meshumar also belong to this generation and held similar perspectives on the cultural changes they have already experienced in their lifetimes.

13. While I do not undertake a deep analysis of the notion of "value" in a broader cultural context here, David Graeber's work to formulate an anthropological theory of value (2001) from the perspective of social action rather than material goods would be an appropriate lens through which to investigate Dror's appreciation of value today. Graeber views value as "the

way in which actions become meaningful to the actor by being incorporated in some larger, social totality—even if in many cases the totality in question exists primarily in the actor's imagination" (2001, xii). The performance-centered approach of folkloristic study today would meaningfully intersect with Graeber's theory for their shared focus on process rather than product.

14. *Chazal* is an acronym in Hebrew for *Ḥakhameinu Zikhronam Liv'rakha*, or "Our Sages, may their memory be blessed." It refers to the rabbinic commentators of the Mishnah and Talmud from the time of the Second Temple of Jerusalem to the sixth century CE.

5   *Sukkot* in Jaffa and Jerusalem

In the previous chapter's three case studies, each individual or family built a sukkah as an expression of his or his family's belief system. Each one constructed a ritual dwelling to perpetuate a tradition that has structured his, or their, religious and cultural histories and that continues to structure daily life with personal and social significance. During the week of the holiday, in the space of the sukkah, these families gather together to discuss their faith in God and in one another, the value of the material aspects of life, and the value of belief. In their sukkot, these individuals confront how the various dimensions of their lives—ethnic, class, cultural, social, and religious—intersect, and they reflect on their current circumstances, those from which they came and those toward which they are moving. These considerations define and redefine notions of home and community for each participant each year. The material forms and social performances through which the Sukkot ritual unfolds are animated by the relationship between divine and earthly powers and between individuals and collectives, and it is in these relationships that the hope that sustains them all lies.

Although I conducted the major part of my fieldwork in Shchunat Hatikva, each year in the weeks before and after the holiday, I took several trips to families living outside of Tel Aviv to collect comparative research.[1] I had engaging visits to families celebrating Sukkot in Rehovot, Holon, and Masuot Yitzhak, but the ritual practice of one family from Jaffa and one family from Jerusalem were notable. Each of these families illuminated for me the reasons behind their own ritual customs as well as the ties that bind their own practices to those of the individuals in Hatikva—a community to which they each related for particular reasons. The Jaffa family was of Moroccan-Syrian descent and had friends living in Hatikva at the time that I met them. The family in Jerusalem was of Kurdish descent and had professional connections to the housing demonstrations that took place in Hatikva's park in the summer of 2011. Although limited, these connections were sufficient for each of these families to have firsthand knowledge of the sociopolitical and cultural complexities that define South Tel Aviv, which was often not the case when I spoke of Hatikva to individuals living in other parts of the city or country. These two perspectives are thus valuable for the light they shed on the ritual practices and beliefs of the last chapter's individuals, as well as for the comparisons that they present.

Dreams and Love

Shaul Moyal

I first encountered Shaul Moyal virtually and unintentionally. I had just unloaded a tray of hot lunches for the elderly Iraqi women who played cards in the far corner of the Beit Dani community center's senior program room when Pnina, the director of the program, called me into her office.[2] She had just finished reading an article on Facebook announcing the finalists in an online sukkah competition, the photographs from which had been posted. She clicked on one photograph to enlarge a richly colored image of a bejeweled sukkah with a black-and-white checkered floor and a glittering chandelier hanging from above. The caption below the photograph read that second-place winner, Shaul Moyal, had built this sukkah at his home in Jaffa, the ancient port city and southern half of the Tel Aviv-Jaffa municipality. Pnina and I immediately replied to the author of the post and were soon contacted by Sivan Moyal, one of Shaul's four daughters. Sivan had submitted the photo of her father's sukkah to the contest and was excited to learn of my research, immediately inviting us for a tour of her father's sukkah at their apartment building in Jaffa Dalet, a lower-income section of the city.

As we drove up their street the following day, we could see Shaul's sukkah from a block away. It stood below the concrete overhang of a cream-colored building, in front of a parking lot, surrounded by concrete pillars and a metal fence that enclosed the residential lot. The sukkah's frame was made of brown wood and illuminated by primary-colored lights and hanging decorations. Sivan and her father stood outside the entrance waiting for us. Up close, the decorative details appeared even more elaborate. The sukkah's four walls had images of palm trees, stars, moons, and suns carved out of the walls, as well as the words *succat shalom*, "sukkah of peace," cut into multiple sides. In front of the sukkah, a large plaque hung above the entrance that also read "sukkah of peace" in large engraved letters. Into all the cutout words and images, Shaul had inserted multicolored plexiglass to create the effect of stained glass, and he had placed a clock in the center circle of the cutout sun. The floor was covered with wall-to-wall black-and-white checkered linoleum, on top of which sat a large oblong table that Shaul had built out of wood and decorated with colorful jeweled patterns, filling the length and width of the sukkah. Chandeliers covered in dazzling designs, miniature disco balls, and strands of multicolored crystals dangled from inside the sukkah's roof so densely that it was nearly impossible to see the actual bamboo roofing. Pink-, blue-, and silver-streaked plastic garlands were woven into the trellised interior side of the wooden walls. Several outdoor sconces were affixed to the top interior of the walls, and Shaul had installed both a working wall phone and an intercom to the left inside wall by the sukkah's entrance. He had connected the phone to the telephone wire used by residents of the building, and he set up the intercom to dial directly to his fourth-floor walk-up apartment so that those in the apartment and those sitting in the sukkah could communicate without continuously climbing and descending the four flights of stairs. At the electricity panel installed on the far wall of the sukkah, Shaul showed us with a grin how flipping any of the ten switches up and down would illuminate the sukkah's ceiling and walls with a variety of lighting styles—blinking strings, colored light bulbs, or glowing wall sconces. Outside the sukkah, to the right of the entrance, Shaul had also constructed a stepped platform covered with red cloth upon which they would display a range of sweet homemade Moroccan delights on the first, most festive feast night of Sukkot.

When he welcomed us into his sukkah, Shaul said that he has been using this same structure for many years, its deconstructed pieces stored during the year in a shed on the ground floor of the apartment building. Shaul's sukkah is 4 meters long, 2.5 meters wide, and 2 meters 10 centimeters tall, sized according to the space available on the lower level of the apartment complex. On the first night of Sukkot, however, Shaul has to extend the table outside the sukkah's entrance, doubling its length to accommodate up to thirty dinner guests.

Although the sukkah's structure is reused each year, Shaul has worked to improve the form since its creation. Early on, he found it was too windy inside, and thus decided to replace the cloth walls with wooden walls. One year, when it rained the entire holiday week and flooded the sukkah's interior, he was inspired to build a wooden base on which the table, chairs, and guests now sit. Most recently, in 2009, when trays of sweets and decorative objects were stolen from inside his sukkah, he built doors that bolt shut and installed a camera on the wall of the apartment building to guard the ritual structure when not in use. The sukkah's decoration is also under constant reevaluation as Shaul redesigns the decor to express his latest aesthetic ideas. Shaul built the entire sukkah by hand, drawing and carving the images and words into the wooden walls, constructing the table and dessert platform, and hand-gluing each individual plastic jewel into place on the chandeliers' many octopus arms. "He's an artist," his daughter concluded after he finished giving us the tour, "not in his profession, but in his life."

At last we all sat down together in the sukkah for sweet Moroccan mint tea. Shaul tells us that he began building the sukkah thirty years ago, when his daughter Mia was born; however, he continues, "I had the dream to make this sukkah from the age of ten. We used to make a sukkah in Morocco out of reeds and sticks. Once we finished building it and sat down to eat, the wind would blow and knock it down. It was then that I said, 'That's not enough! It should be strong.' I would

Fig. 5.1. The exterior of Shaul Moyal's sukkah. A carved wooden sign that reads "Sukkah of Peace" hangs above the entrance. Jaffa, Israel. 2011.

Fig. 5.2. Shaul Moyal designs and hand-crafts the bejeweled interior of his sukkah. Jaffa, Israel. 2011.

walk around and visit the sukkot of other people, rich people, who had nice, strong sukkot, and I said to myself, 'We are not rich, but when I'm older, I'm going to try to make a nice sukkah, even more beautiful.'"

Shaul was born in Marrakesh, Morocco, in 1938. He grew up in an area of the city that he described as a "fortress" or "camp," surrounded by a wall that enclosed Jewish shops and homes, and an entrance gate that was guarded by a Muslim Moroccan official. "Only Jews lived inside there," he said. "The Arabs were outside. Arabs could enter only if they had business to conduct inside, and they could not enter at all on Shabbat." This was the *mellah*, or the Jewish quarter that separated Marrakesh's Jews from its Muslims.[3] Shaul lived in the mellah until he was sixteen years old, with strong social and religious routines prescribing his early life there. As he refilled our tea glasses of tea, he recalled two specific memories that marked his childhood. First, he remembered holding his father's hand as they walked to synagogue every Saturday morning. And second, he remembered when his father died, when Shaul was ten years old. After his father's death, a friend of his father heard that Shaul had been skipping school and running around the neighborhood, so he found Shaul and told him that it was time to learn a trade. He brought Shaul to work in his office as a dental technician and launched Shaul's lifetime of self-taught professions. I did not begin my conversation with Shaul by asking him about his early life, but my questions about the structure and design of his sukkah—how he learned to make the chandeliers and wire the complex interior lighting and intercom systems—prompted his description of his informal education.

Shaul was shaped by inspiration and hard work as a boy in Morocco and as a young man in Israel. In response to my query about the extravagant adornment of his sukkah's interior, Shaul recounted the moment in Marrakesh when his eyes were opened to worlds of color and design:

> My mother's sister had her own private house, and I remember my sister got married at her home. My sister was thirteen and her husband, of blessed memory, was forty-five. He was a religious man, a friend of my father. I was a child. Now, when I went to my aunt's house on the wedding day, someone took me away, put me outside. They didn't know who I was. They put me in another house, I remember. Now, why am I telling you this? Because in that house was a one-meter-twenty mosaic, and all kinds of stunning paintings, all over the house. I saw them in every room of the house, on every wall. This two-story house was open in the middle, and you would go up the stairs, with a railing, and in the middle there was a tree. I wondered how the tree got there, in the middle of the square. It was an olive tree. I wondered about these stones, the mosaic. I was a little boy. How did they paste them? They were beautiful and smooth. I touched

them and touched them. How did they do it? From then on, I began to look at the places where the Arabs were praying, and I became concerned with all things that were beautiful.

Shaul remembers this moment as the beginning of his cultivation of an aesthetic sensibility. Thereafter, he said he had an eye for color and design in all the jobs he held, trying to help support his family throughout his young adulthood.

In 1956, as a young teenager, Shaul and his family immigrated to Israel. They arrived by ship to a transit camp for Iraqi and Moroccan immigrants in Rehovot. There was no work for him, his mother, or his younger brother at the camp, so Shaul started to work in a nearby orchard picking oranges and lemons. It was during that time in Rehovot that he also learned about electrical systems, he said. He began to study the field but soon enlisted in the military, and only after working in construction in the army did he again pick up his studies. This education in electrical mechanics has carried him through to this day, and he now says, "I understand all the theories of electricity. What I have trouble with, I ask, and I read books on electrical theory. That's it." Shaul tells us that in the apartment building in which he has now lived for over thirty years, not a single tenant calls in a professional repairman if something breaks. They knock on his door, and he repairs it. His daughter Sivan nods and says that he repairs broken electronics all over the neighborhood. The construction experience he gained in the army grew during his next thirty-five years of work in ceramic flooring, pavement, and tiling. The work was tedious, but he loved it: "I love to do beautiful work. This isn't the work of strength; it's work here [points to his head]. You need exactness, precision." As Shaul finishes his history of labor, he says, "Oh! What I've gone through in my life! I've had enough."

Shaul's life experiences are not unrelated to his ritual practice. His early life in Morocco inspired his visions of the beauty that he would create in his later life, and his experiences in Israel equipped him with the tools to realize them. The simple, unstable sukkah of his childhood that the wind knocked over when he was ten motivated his dream of a sukkah that would stand secure in all its beauty; his struggle to make a living after immigrating to Israel gave him the skills with which he built the sukkah that stands today.

I asked Shaul again about the sukkah of his youth as our conversation returned to my reason for contacting him. He remembered it clearly and began to describe it: "It was just a sheet, a few planks of wood, and sticks that were tied together with string, but across the space, on the opposite wall from where you entered, my mother hung the most beautiful tapestry. For the entire year, you were not allowed to take it out of the house, but on Sukkot, she would take it out and hang it. It was the most beautiful carpet." The picture in his mind of this tapestry was still vivid, and his association of the sukkah's space with rare beauty and value was unmistakable. Shaul's reverence for the sanctity of this space is deeply rooted in his impoverished and precarious past in Morocco and Israel.

Besides the few chairs that fit inside his family's first sukkah, if they had them, Shaul remembered one more feature of the ritual space of his youth—the lighting. "We only had one light, and we had it by renting it from the Arabs. The Arabs rented us the house, and they rented us one light, no more; any more was prohibited. They had electricity in their houses—we had only candles and lanterns. They would pass the wire from one house to the next until we got it. So the landlord rented us the light every day, but if you did not turn it off by ten o'clock at night, he turned it off from his location. That was it." Today, the multitude of lights in Shaul's sukkah are multicolored, large and small, flashing and constant, on strings, in chandeliers, and in wall sconces, on the ceiling and on walls. Shaul controls them with the ten switches on the sukkah's inside wall, and their illumination during the tour of the sukkah is a great moment of pride. Shaul's daughter Sivan chuckled when she heard her father's story about the single light

Fig. 5.3. The panel of light switches that Shaul installed on the interior wall of his sukkah controls the many different styles of lighting that illuminate the interior. Jaffa, Israel. 2010.

Sukkot *in Jaffa and Jerusalem* | 159

Fig. 5.4. Shaul installed in his sukkah an intercom that connects to the Moyal family's fourth-floor apartment and a telephone hooked up to the building's exterior telephone line. Jaffa, Israel. 2010.

in the Moroccan sukkah of his youth and said, "So you've compensated here for what happened in Morocco!" Shaul did not hear her comment as he continued to admire the waves of flashing lights in the sukkah behind us.

For Shaul, his sukkah is a place of dreams, a place where he can create all that he was denied. When I asked Shaul what he thinks about when he sits inside his sukkah, he responded, "I try to think of the best idea yet, how I can make it better next year. I hope that I will get a better idea than this one, for there is no end to beauty." Shaul's sukkah is a place of creativity, a place to dream of the future in spite of the past, and a place of hope.

Sivan Moyal

I met with Shaul's daughter Sivan several times at different cafés around Tel Aviv in the months following my visit to their sukkah. Although we had met because of my interest in her father's sukkah construction and ritual use, I asked Sivan if

I might speak to her as well about her own Sukkot observance and her relationship to the ritual structure. She gladly agreed, and we set a date to meet for coffee.

When we met, I began by telling her that, generally, I was interested in the relationship between people and their surrounding physical environments and how they influence each other. Sivan instantly nodded in understanding: "People build their houses exactly as they build their lives. And what is it to build your life? It's building relationships with people, developing emotions." Today, in modern urban societies where space and time are generally limited, I continued, the sukkah offers an unusual case in which individuals can pause to translate their life experiences and ideals into the design and construction of personal space. She nodded again with a smile, pulled out the paper napkin from under her coffee cup and began to sketch a sukkah, narrating the strokes of her pen:

> The table and everyone around the table—that's your life. Who sits around the table? Although in Jewish tradition strangers also sit around the table, that's still as in life, for there are strangers in life. But who is sitting close to you at the table? Those are the people who are closest to you; this is your family. What is this schach lying over the top of your head? This protects you. What are the decorations in the sukkah? These are the ornaments that decorate your life, the things that make you complete. If Moroccans decide to put beautiful tapestries on the wall, which is cultural, they add cultural content to their lives. It's as if I decide to dress specifically traditional. If I decide to wear a *keffiyeh* [Arab headdress], or if orthodox women wear long skirts—this is like the carpet on the wall of the sukkah. It is the symbol of culture. These ornaments come later, with culture, but the basic structure—the trees, the all-natural materials—those are the connections. These corner poles and the beams on the roof, they are connected with ropes. Those are exactly the ties you have with people in life.

On the napkin, Sivan had sketched the square frame of a sukkah with brush lying on top and a lamp hanging down over a table in the sukkah's center. As she spoke, she drew arrows pointing to three parts of the sukkah and labeled them. At the top left corner of the structure where two beams were tied with rope, she had written *ksharim*, or "ties." Near an arrow pointed at the lamp dangling down in the center, she had scribbled *ruchanit*, or "spirituality." And, next to the arrow pointed at the table, a sideways word read *mishpachtit*, an adjective from the root word for "family." Along the left side of the sukkah unattached to any arrow, she had written *ani + abba*, or "me + father." Sivan's sketch was simple and profound. In the construction of this ritual shelter, Sivan saw the construction of one's social and cultural life, and for her, the construction of a relationship with her father.

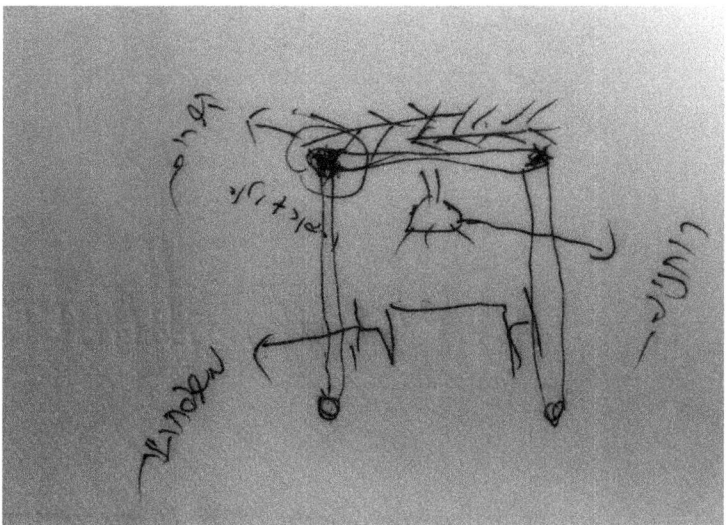

Fig. 5.5. Sivan Moyal's sketched image of a sukkah, annotated with the symbolic meanings of its different physical components: the light in the center is labeled "spirituality," the table and chairs are labeled "family" or "intimacy," the ropes tied around the corners of the beams are labeled "ties," and along the side of the whole sukkah is written "me + father." Tel Aviv, Israel. 2011.

Sivan's relationship to the sukkah is constituted by her social relationships. She continued to explain the significance of the ritual structure in broader terms, recognizing the different meanings it may hold for different people. To do this, Sivan focused on two elements of the physical structure and their symbolic meanings, describing them through the lens of her father's experience. The first element was the material used to build the structure. She said:

> The sukkah has something very primal about it. What is that? It's that it is all natural. It's trees and it's leaves. It's very pure and simple. Anyone can do it. You do not have to be rich to have it; you do not have to be talented to make it. It's as if it is telling you that to be happy, you do not need economic wealth. You do not need the luxury of the modern world; you do not need a big, nice car; you do not need villa; you need the basic. You need to be loved; you need to be guarded, to have strong relationships with people so that when you are sad, someone will soothe you and say that he loves you, and that that is what will make you happy.

The sukkah's modest material nature leads by example: its significance does not lie in its economic worth. The deliberate material simplicity of the sukkah's form

Fig. 5.6. Sivan stands with her father, Shaul, in front of their sukkah. Jaffa, Israel. 2011.

directs attention to the people who make and use it, to their process and their intention.

Sivan emphasized her point by contrasting the sukkah built from modest, natural materials with the manufactured kits that are increasingly available and used. "We live in an instant culture," she said. "Let's put it into percentages. If twenty percent still build sukkot, and eighty percent do not, it tells you that twenty percent still remember what makes them happy and eighty percent think they will find happiness in money. That's why they go and buy a sukkah. What is it to buy a ready-made sukkah? It's modernism. It's metal poles. And these poles reflect today's reality in their emptiness. What is iron? What is this material? It's a cold material. Iron is like a chameleon—its heat comes from the outside. If it's cold outside, so the metal will be cold. If you put it near a fire, so it will be warm. It doesn't have character." In this comparison between wood and metal, Sivan reiterates her point: a sukkah constructed of organic materials is meaningful for what it is (inclusive, natural, warm) and for what it is not (exclusive, manufactured, cold).

At this moment, Sivan stopped and quietly chuckled. "It's funny, though," she said, "because my father's sukkah is not simple at all." Her father begins constructing his sukkah at least five weeks prior to the start of each Sukkot, designing new decorations in an increasingly elaborate process and structure each year. Sivan considered this paradox aloud:

> I think he does this because he has lived his whole life in simplicity. So, this is his dream. He wishes this, and maybe he once thought that if he had lived a financially rich life, he would be happy, so he has created this life in the sukkah. There is a lot of richness in there. Crystals and decorations, all very shiny and glamorous. But there is something still creative and basic about it because it's not as if he went and bought an expensive lamp to hang in there. He built all of it by hand from simple things, so the richness that you see built is based on simple materials. The walls may seem rich to you, but they are built from cork and transparent plastic, the most basic things. Perhaps these were not basic materials to ancient Egyptians or Israelites, but they are basic to our people.

Initially, Sivan had analyzed the sukkah as an isolated form, valuing its simple and natural source. She continued, however, by situating the sukkah in the context of her father's life. This contextualization requires the reconciliation of theory with practice, of what is prescribed in the text of the Torah with what is manifested through experience. Considering the meaning that is made of the sukkah's materiality in this context, Sivan then concluded,

> Materials do not matter because when you look at his sukkah, your eyes open, and you feel happiness, but it is not material happiness, it's emotional bliss. It's art. When you look at the sukkot of any people, you see their lifestyles, what they have experienced, you see them. When you look at my father's sukkah, you see his soul, his inner happiness. And with what means he has, this is what he built. It's his family. If someone makes a modest sukkah, that indicates his modesty. If you see a big structure, it shows up in his big nature—it's the character of the person, especially because they build it by hand, for themselves.

Sivan recognizes the creative process of construction as an expression of self.

The second element of the sukkah that Sivan identified as a source of significance was its temporary nature. Recalling Shaul's immigration experience, Sivan reflected upon the uprooted nature of her father's life:

> Perhaps it was the hard life he lived, maybe the ups and downs of the economy, or of the emotions, these jolts of life, but the portability of the sukkah meant "Do not despair, do not lose hope. It was destroyed? Build it again." As my father said, the sukkah falls down and is rebuilt. There are houses out there like that. I've studied about East Asia and learned that

> Japan is an island, a chain of islands that is constantly subjected to the natural elements. There are storms and tsunamis, and the houses there are temporary. Think about what it means to live in homes that are often destroyed. Think—you're living all your life in an area where nothing is stable. That's why their homes are built of wood and partitions made of rice sheets. Everything seems temporary. So just by looking at someone's house, you can understand the meaning of their lifestyle and culture and the way they live.

Sivan also finds meaning in the sukkah's simultaneous instability and promise of return. The annual recurrence of this shelter teaches hope and perseverance. It evokes the challenges of Sivan's parents' immigration experiences, but it also highlights for Sivan how her life as a first-generation Israeli has determined her personal relationship to this ritual. "My father emigrated from Morocco, and my mother came from Syria, but I am a different generation," she says.

> I have an education, and probably my children will be educated. My parents have no education. I cannot look at my mother and say I want to be like this. My mother all her life cleaned other people's homes. This is what she did. She cleaned the houses of other people. If my parents had been sent to the *ulpan* [Hebrew language program] when they came to Israel, maybe their lives would have looked much better. As you know, my father came by ship from Morocco, and they were thrown into *ma'abarot* [transit camps for refugees and immigrants] in Rehovot. My mother came from Syria through some underground smuggling of Jews and was also discarded in the camps in Rehovot. They had no basis for a productive and healthy future, and true, they had no chance. It's as if their absorption in Israel was beneath contempt. They reached a wasteland, and I succeeded in lifting my head slightly. I'm the bud of a flower trying to grow in this filth, and my children will probably flourish and fulfill themselves as if fully in this world. They will have it a bit easier because they will have some money; they will be able to grow properly, not as I grew up, in poverty. Only then will we be loosened from it. But then these flowers, these lotuses, will probably all purchase sukkot. You will not have anything to do research on. They probably will not make sukkot.

The resonance of the sukkah's characteristics with the life experiences of Sivan's parents is striking, and she admits the absence of this resonance in her own life. When I asked Sivan what meaning she takes from participating in the ritual construction with her father and if she would build a sukkah on her own one day, she said, "My father, he's my twin, my soul mate. He's my life. And if I ever make a sukkah, it will only be for my father, to activate the memory and express my love through this gesture—a tribute. I would not do it for tradition and not for faith. And this just brings us back to the point that it's all connections, it's all people. If I do it, it's just for that—it's me and my father. It's for our own relationship, not for belief in God."

Sivan does not begrudge her father for his strong faith in God, which she says she does not share, but as a thirty-one-year old graphic designer living and working in the center of cosmopolitan Tel Aviv, she realizes that her sense of spirituality is constituted differently. Acknowledging her father's belief in God, she tells me that I will only find his kind of commitment to ritual practice among "people who believe in religion, in tradition." Our lives are now directed by modernism rather than religious tradition, she says and pauses, looking at me in the eye and adding, "And by the way, you and I are the result of modernism." Sivan identifies herself as both "secular" and "believing," and she references "God" as a source of a certain spiritual power, regardless of the form. "Maybe there is a God in each of us," she thinks aloud, "and perhaps this is why people pair off in couples. It's as though you are looking for God in a second person, to cling to him, and lean on him." Sivan searches for and believes in spirituality as it resides within us.

One year after this discussion, I met Sivan again to continue our conversation. We had been in touch throughout the year, but now, a second Sukkot had passed, and sadly, a friend of hers had just taken her own life. These two events, timed not far apart, prompted us to meet that afternoon to talk about death, religion, family, and belief. The fiancé of her friend had informed Sivan about her friend's suicide a few weeks earlier, and the fiancé had taken solace during their conversation in the notion that "God needed her above." Sivan had not been comforted by this thought, however, and she shared her frustration with me: "Religious people have answers for every situation," she said, "and when someone dies, you can just say that God gives and God takes. People who believe in God always have an answer, and therefore they do not need to deal with hard situations." Sivan was critical of the fiancé's reaction because it did not acknowledge the hardships that she knew her friend had faced. Sivan also sought to make sense of the tragedy, but through a different belief system that rose out of particular circumstances rather than universal principles. "Secular people who don't perform mitzvot in order to go to heaven. They have a modern religion," she said, "and that religion is hope. They don't have these automatic answers, so they imagine hope. I don't have a religious God, a Jewish God, but I have a God of hope. Religious people live to go to heaven or to not go to hell. I don't have any heaven or hell. I live to be here." For Sivan, hope is a resource that human beings may create and draw upon, making them responsible for and in control of their lives, as much as she sees that is possible.[4]

Sivan then concluded her thoughts, "It seems to me that in secularism, if there's a very strong love, there's no need to search for answers, in religion or

166 | *Framing Sukkot*

Fig. 5.7. The Moyal family hosts friends for a meal in their sukkah. Jaffa, Israel. 2011.

elsewhere. What is so strong about religion is love, love for God. What is this belief in God? It's love." Love, she said, overwhelms uncertainty and offers the answers for which people seek. Sivan participates in Jewish rituals with her family toward this end: to strengthen the social relationships that sustain her faith in hope and, ultimately, to express her love.

Over the course of the time that I spent with Shaul and Sivan, through two Sukkot, I came to learn about the core principles that guide their ritual practices. Shaul's relationship to his sukkah is built on faith and contextualized by his experiences of immigration and poverty, his uprootedness, and his search for stability. He has built a shelter that he, his family, and his neighbors have come to anticipate, admire, and share. Through the ritual creation, he has cultivated a structure of permanence and beauty that he has sought throughout his life, and with it, he moves into the future. Sivan, solidly grounded in the present day, joins her father in this expression of faith to honor him and strengthen her own belief in hope and love.[5]

Family and Equality

Drori Yehoshua

I met Drori Yehoshua because of the nationwide housing protests that began in the summer of 2011. Drori worked as Rosh Beit Midrash, or Head of House of

Study, at the Jerusalem-based organization Memizrach Shemesh. This organization is "a *Beit Midrash* (House of Study) and Center for Jewish Social Activism and Leadership in Israel" that describes its mission as "inspired by Mizrachi and Sephardi Jewish experience, philosophy and commentaries" and "dedicated to the values of communal responsibility and social action rooted in all Jewish traditions."[6] I had first met Drori's colleague Pazit Adani at meetings held in Shchunat Hatikva's public park when the protests began, and Pazit's experience as a community organizer and educator at Memizrach Shemesh had made her an invaluable contributor to the movement's efforts. Her participation in the protest was motivated by personal as well as professional interests, as she had been born in Kfar Shalem, a neighborhood that abuts Hatikva, where her family still lives. Pazit and I were interested in each other's presence in the park, and we soon befriended each other, sharing our backgrounds and current work. As I became more aware of Pazit's family history in South Tel Aviv and her approach to community outreach using the tools of Jewish religion and culture, I became interested in the intersection of her own religious and social life experiences. Our park conversations were always inevitably interrupted as protest meetings and spontaneous actions demanded attention, so Pazit invited me to her office in Jerusalem, if I were ever passing through, so that we could speak at ease. I used my first free day in September 2011 to board a bus to Jerusalem and visit her, and it was there that I met Drori.

After Pazit and I had reviewed the last week's protest events in Hatikva and discussed how my research was faring, she led me into Drori's office and told me I was about to meet the local expert, a man who studies and teaches Jewish religion, history, and philosophy, and who directs the Jewish education program at Memizrach Shemesh. As soon as we sat down, Drori put his work aside and took interest in my questions about Sukkot, eager to hear about my research in Hatikva. His patience and knowledge fueled our discussion about the religious and social meaning of this holiday for several hours, until at last he announced that he was hungry and it was time for lunch. He invited me into the office kitchen to continue our conversation and insisted, with a smile, that he would be offended if I did not share his meal with him, noting that one does not have to be hungry to join a meal because it is eating together and sharing food that is important, not satiating hunger. Only after people eat together do they ask questions of each other—this is how it works in Mizrahi cultures—he said. Drori takes a short break like this with fellow staff members every day because it is important to sit and eat together, he continued: "This is like what you do in the sukkah, but imagine if every day could be like that. We should try to live that way, for all food is a gift and we have to appreciate it." First comes life as we live it in the tents, then in houses, and then at work, he said, bridging his religious, personal, and professional worldviews. So I accepted his offer and we continued our conversation with another staff member over plates of bread, sardines, salad, tahini, and olives.

After a whole day at his office, I thanked Drori and bid him good-bye. We were in touch several more times in the weeks that followed through early October, when he invited me to visit his family's sukkah at his home in Jerusalem. I accepted his invitation and spent that day in his sukkah witnessing the ideals of Sukkot that we had discussed in his office actualized in the material construction and social exchanges that took place in his sukkah.

Drori's knowledge of Jewish religious and legal texts, his surrounding environment, and his family history all inform his theoretical interpretation of Sukkot ritual and its expression. As with Shaul and Sivan Moyal, Drori interprets the sukkah's form and function through the multifaceted lens of society, culture, politics, and religion.

As we sat inside his sukkah, Drori analyzed the three essential aspects of his sukkah: its structure, decoration, and the use of its space. In his mind, these three elements come together to create the sukkah's most characteristic quality—its ability to equalize those who dwell within it. Drori values the democratic, open space that the sukkah creates for the seven days that it stands, a temporary moment in which people from different worlds may sit together under one roof. Drori first explained how the sukkah's material structure generates a space of equality by the nature of its roof:

> On the one hand, it has to be a roof that offers shade from the sun, and on the other hand, it has to be made of materials from the ground. The main idea of the holiday is, therefore, here in its roof—the idea of equality. The roof brings together heaven and earth, but also, we're talking about just cutting down branches to make it, so it can't be that you have the materials and I don't have them . . . The idea is for everyone to have the same thing, to make similar sukkot from plant materials, not from stone, and to create a situation of more equality.

In both the poetic function and the practical construction of the organic roof covering, balance is built into form.

Within Judaism, the notion that architecture may communicate social values such as equality is not exclusive to the sukkah, however, and Drori offered a parallel example to illustrate this point:

> There's a discussion in the Talmud about housing in the second century AD, when people used to live together around a community yard, their houses one against the other to make a wall . . . the discussion in the Mishnah is, if we have the surrounding wall and now we want to add a gate but there is one person who doesn't want the gate, can the rest of us force that one to have the gate? It's not just a question of common property—it's a discussion of values, and it says that every time someone comes and says,

"I want to have this gate," we are supposed to be on his side to make this happen. Why? Because there is a unique problem of voyeurism. But then they realize that this is problematic, and they explain it with a story. There was once a man, a real *hasid* [member of Jewish mystical sect committed to strict observance of ritual law], someone that God really loves, and he met Elijah the Prophet. When he put the gate in his wall, however, Elijah came no more. Why? Because when you put in a gate, the poor person doesn't come anymore. So now there are two issues: first, I want to avoid voyeurism, but second, I want to have my place be a place where people can step in and show their faces, and give me the opportunity to show my real face. It's a whole discussion in the Talmud, and they give several solutions about how you can do this, hold those two values at the same time . . . So when you say that Sukkot also has to do with architecture, this is like what I described here, the classic material from [year] one BCE until six or seven hundred AD—it's very important. There's a whole Mishnah about how to build the sukkah, and it is all about how we're going to function together as a community.

Talmudic debates over the details of sukkah construction reveal how physical actions express metaphysical conditions. Viewing architectural plans as designs of value, Drori understands the aesthetics and construction of a place as a personal expression of the self. He equates closed doors with closed minds, open spaces with open hearts, and the character of the physical material with the character of the builder and the meaning of the space. His interpretation of the design of his own sukkah further elucidates this idea.

Drori builds his sukkah in the backyard of his house, its metal frame six meters wide, three meters long, and two meters tall. The frame is a standard size, he said, according to the size of the manufactured poles, even though he has pieced poles together from different frames that once belonged to his grandfather and brother. The walls of his sukkah are where Drori dwells in description, weaving together his current life story and his family history to explain the sukkah's design. "These [he points to the fabric walls of the sukkah] are the *parochot* from the *aron hakodesh* of two Kurdish synagogues here in Jerusalem—Barashi and Bamedi—which represent two villages in Kurdistan.[7] In Kurdish, you say *Barash*. My father would pray in Barashi, where I pray today. My mother would pray in Bamedi. They stand opposite each other. There is no difference in the prayers— maybe in the music, but only people who pay attention would be able to tell." The parochot that Drori points to are beautifully woven tapestries made of maroon velvet and golden thread; green, red, and yellow bouquets of flowers embroidered with gold Hebrew words; filigree patterns; Jewish stars; and crowns, surrounded by the Decalogues. They are old and visibly used. Drori's younger son entered the sukkah as we examined the parochot, and pointing his finger at the curtain facing us, he announced, "This one was hanging behind Grandma and Grandpa when they got married!" Drori smiles and nods: "They married in Israel, a Kurdish wedding." He then draws close to us a framed black-and-white photograph that stands upright on the table. With one hand pointing to the blurred backdrop behind the young wedding couple in the photograph and the other hand pointing to the curtain that his son had just identified, Drori says with a smile, "That's the same curtain! That's their wedding, and there they are standing in front of it."

Drori's father, Moshe, immigrated to Israel from Kurdistan with his family in 1952. He came with his parents, three brothers, and one sister after three other brothers died in Kurdistan. Drori's mother, Margolit, was born in Israel, her family having emigrated from Kurdistan in 1928. Both sides of his family had settled in the Old City of Jerusalem, where Moshe and Margolit met and then married in 1963. I looked again at the black-and-white photograph of their wedding day as Drori continued to share his family history with us:

> The family name was Ajami, which in Arabic means "stranger." Why? Because Kurdistan is located on the border of several nations—Turkey to the north, Syria to the west, Iraq and Persia to the south and east—and my grandfather and father came from the Persian border, so they identified him with a different accent. They were like Bedouins, moving back and forth. They had a Kurdish-Iraqi identity when they arrived here in Israel, and because they lived in a Kurdish neighborhood in Jerusalem, their Kurdish identity remained strong. There was a general atmosphere in Israeli society then, a melting pot of Ashkenazi identity, which they didn't talk to me about, but I understood it. It was possible to look upon them [the Ashkenazim] as *adonei haaretz* (Rulers of the Land). My mother used to clean houses of middle-class Ashkenazi, and my father used to work in places like Super-sal [Israel's largest supermarket chain]. My father, Moshe, was killed in 1973 in the Yom Kippur War, and my mother raised us, me and my five siblings.

Drori closes his narrative there and, after a moment of quiet, returns to our discussion of the sukkah. We look up again at the waving tapestry walls of his sukkah and, in particular, at the one that his parents were married in front of, not three feet from us. "So how do you have these parochot?" I asked, and he replied:

> I borrow them from the synagogues and explain to them what I want to do with them. First of all, I am a man who contributes to the synagogue—I blow the shofar for them, and I am the *chazzan* [cantor]. And second of all, these parochot are interesting because the older they are, the less frequently they are taken out of storage, and this one [he pointed to one

hanging behind us] hasn't been out for fifteen years. In my opinion, it is one of the most beautiful. This one also doesn't get taken out. This is a problem. So I take these out for Sukkot and hang them, use them, and sometimes if I see a tear, I sew it or clean it. These are very, very important. Most times, parochot are made in memory of someone. If it's old, there's only a small chance that the children are still in the synagogue; if it's new, it's a sign that they are definitely still there, and on the *yahrzeit* [death anniversary] they will take it out.

Drori's relationship with these Kurdish synagogues and their prayer communities is symbiotic, each one serving the other. He serves as the community's cantor and is given use of the parochot during Sukkot. Drori's relationship with his surrounding community is bound with these materials of memory and devotion.

All walls of Drori's sukkah are created with these parochot, four that he borrowed from his father's synagogue and four that he borrowed from his mother's synagogue. He has chosen to equally represent the two sides of his family in this way. The parochot not only track his parents' roots, but they anchor Drori in his past and present life as well. "In my house, I have things I bought from IKEA, from here and there, and maybe I have a coffee pot from Kurdistan, but it's a little hard to tell who I am from just that. When I go outside my house, there are possibilities in the sukkah to create a home design that says who I am. So I hang the parochot. This is my father, and this is my mother," he says, looking back and forth between the two sides of his sukkah. "What more does a man need to say than where his father and his mother are from? It's a kind of identity." For Drori, the space of the sukkah is a space of intense identification.

In addition to being tangible expressions of his identity, the parochot also contribute to the atmosphere within Drori's sukkah, which he described as "one of holiness, like a small synagogue." The kind of synagogue to which he refers, however, Drori clarified, is "the wider definition of synagogue—the synagogue as a home space." These parochot represent his Kurdish roots, but they were made and used in Israel. Drori thus connects various "homes" through use of these parochot during Sukkot: the Israelites' temporary shelter evoked through the sukkah's construction, the house in Jerusalem behind which he builds this sukkah, the sense of home that is embodied in the memories of his parents, and the two Kurdish synagogues that bridge the communities from which his family emigrated with the Kurdish communities in Jerusalem into which he was born and where he continues to live. Through the construction and decoration of his sukkah, Drori consolidates all of these notions of home for an annual, ephemeral experience of belonging.

Drori paused to heat up more water for the strong black coffee that we drink from his tall brass Kurdish coffee pot. He returned with a small plate of cookies

Fig. 5.8. Drori Yehoshua builds his sukkah with a metal pole frame, fabric walls, and gathered brush for the roof. Jerusalem, Israel. 2011.

Fig. 5.9. Interior view of Drori Yehoshua's sukkah. Each Sukkot, Drori borrows eight *parochot* (the curtains that cover the Holy Ark in a synagogue) from local Kurdish Jewish synagogues to adorn the interior walls of his sukkah. A framed picture of his parents on their wedding day stands at the far end of the table. Jerusalem, Israel. 2011.

and a full pot. We were ready to move on now from the sukkah's material reality to the spirit of its space. I began by asking Drori generally how he understands the space within the sukkah that exists for the one week that it stands. He thought for a moment and then began again from the top, the roof:

> Maybe the idea behind having this kind of roof is to allow people who are pure and impure to be together. I'm reaching back to ideas from when the Temple was around. There are ideas about purity and impurity, so that if I touch someone who is dead, for example, I'm impure, and if then I sit with you, who are pure, under the same roof, I make you impure. So causing each other to share this impure situation has to do with the roof we share. But if we have the sukkah, we have a space during this pilgrimage festival when there is now a time that we don't have to have a problem being together. I can't go up to the Temple if I'm impure, but in the sukkah, we can sit here and eat together without a problem.

The ritual space of the sukkah creates a unique time and space in which past actions and judgments are temporarily suspended for the greater purpose of social togetherness. The space that is created within the sukkah's walls is one that allows difference to be transcended for a moment of unity and equality.

Drori's interpretation of this ritual space not only applies to the Temple Periods, however. He explains its continued relevance today through the custom of hospitality that is central to the Sukkot ritual. During Sukkot, he said, "People are requested to not be in their homes, which is a very interesting request, and then they are also requested to be either a visitor or a host—the idea of ushpizin. There's something very interesting about creating this place where I'm either a visitor or a host, but not in someone's house." Drori considered the difference between sitting together in a house and sitting together in a sukkah, again, through the lens of equality. "When I'm in your sukkah, I feel more comfortable than when I'm in your house, because it's similar to my sukkah," he said. "This enables conversation and shared experience." He used our meeting in his sukkah right then to emphasize his point:

> Before you came, of course, I cleaned a little. When you visit me, you examine me—how did I place the vase, what did I put where . . . that's how we are. Your culture will examine my culture. That's not a simple situation to be in, and especially not if we're speaking of hierarchies. Most simply, we can say that you come from a culture that is higher than mine in the world—you come from an imperial culture, America. In any situation when you meet someone, when I come to your home or you come to mine, there are two cultures—how will you feel comfortable if you feel you need to change the surroundings or you have to apologize all the time? This is

what's interesting about what the holiday—what is it really about . . . During Sukkot everyone is located under God's sukkah, so that we understand how people feel when they're in the center of equality. There is a lot of serious wisdom in making people feel equal but different.

The power of this temporary space in which social difference and social equality may coexist is due to its neutral ground outside the house.

That the sukkah is a space of equality by virtue of its physical construction and placement constitutes the first half of its significance for Drori. The second half lies in the intention of the sukkah's space. This intention, Drori said, emerges from the narrative of the holiday—the journey through the desert. "How do people go on a long journey in the desert and arrive in a new land together where they all live as one society? The sukkah is supposed to be a way to be together now, in solidarity and partnership, before the arrival," he says. "This is, therefore, a space of meeting." Here, the significance of the sukkah's space comes not from its materiality, but from its temporality—from the moment of potential that it represents and creates anew each year. He continues:

> The second before entering Canaan, we say, "Come, let's protect for a moment the previous place we have been." How do we create a conversation so that at the end of it all, we will have a future together that will be more than dictated from the outside, saying, "You are of the same group"? Before defining our outside borders together, let's define our own inner borders—the ability to talk to each other, to help each other. I am more comfortable visiting you in your sukkah than in your house because it is this minute before we enter the house. To be defined from the outside without any effort is much easier than from the inside.

Before entering Canaan, individuals may think critically about who they are and how they behave. Sukkot creates the time and space for thinking in this way and the chance to define oneself for oneself and then for others.

During the week of Sukkot, while still on the metaphoric journey, individuals may meet together in the sukkah and shape a vision for their future in a new land. "Conversations between cultures are very important," Drori explains. "The question asked on this holiday is, 'Now that we are on this journey for forty years in the desert, how do we walk together?'" Drori's question grows out of the Israelites' circumstance in the Sinai Desert, but it remains relevant today for all peoples who must learn how to peacefully coexist. He continues:

> I don't believe that there is any culture not influenced by other cultures . . . Sometimes, someone decides, "No, I reject that," and then fundamentalism is created because you don't have give and take. My rabbi used to say,

"Whoever goes to sleep at night thinking the truth is in his pocket will wake up tomorrow a fundamentalist." To what extent can you express your culture loud and clear in a pleasant way, and on the other hand, to what extent are you ready to engage your foe? For me, this is the sukkah—a place to speak between cultures. There's power in this holiday to awaken ideas of pluralism, or for discussion and bridges between cultures, to enable cultural connections, to make space to think about borders between people.

From Drori's perspective, at the core of this site of social and cultural exchange for a more enlightened future is the cultivation of a self-conscious awareness of personal values and collective action.

Although Drori has considered these issues throughout his life, one thought returns to him each year during Sukkot. "For me," he says, "most importantly, the sukkah is a place to host people." Hospitality is not only a core principle of Sukkot observance but of Drori's worldview as well, and he reiterated to me from a personal (as well as religious) perspective how this element of Sukkot ritual performance enables the social and cultural exchange that for him is the reason for observing the holiday. "It's not the idea of *v'ahavta l'reaacha camocha* [Love your neighbor as yourself], which is very important in and of itself," he says. "The point is, how is a cultural environment of different groups created?" Drori admits that what he refers to as HaMifgash (the meeting)—the cultural exchange that occurs through the ritual of gathering together in the sukkah—can occur elsewhere too, such as in people's homes, on park benches, and in coffeehouses; however, it is harder to feel equal in these public settings without an enclosed space into which one may welcome others. "To find yourself entering someone else's house, or to invite them into your own house—this place, in the heart, is not a simple place," he says quietly as our conversation comes to a close. To open oneself to others is to bring them into one's heart, into one's home. Drori recognizes the hierarchies of social, cultural, and economic power that undermine individuals' abilities to trust and understand each other today, but he sees the sukkah as resource for possibility and progress. On the neutral and fertile ground of the sukkah, for a limited but reliable moment of time, individuals may sit together in order to learn how to walk together.

Drori adheres to the religious laws of sukkah construction but engages in an ongoing analysis of the voices of authority documented in Jewish texts throughout history. As he interprets past discourses in the context of his current life, he situates himself in his religious and social worlds. He views the temporary structure as a physical manifestation of equality, a material shelter whose goal is social, and an independent space that nurtures togetherness. Through the construction of his sukkah and interpretation of the space within, Drori makes visible the history of his family, makes audible the conditions of his life, and makes active

Fig. 5.10. Drori Yehoshua sits with his two sons for lunch inside his sukkah. Jerusalem, Israel. 2011.

the stalled dynamics within Israeli society that thwart social progress. Above all, however, Drori's belief in the power of the sukkah as a place of unity celebrates being in the world by being in the world together.

Notes

1. On several occasions, I visited a family for a meal in their sukkah during the week of Sukkot itself, when invitations to visits sukkot in Hatikva did not conflict.

2. A basic but meaningful sketch of the scene in the senior program room at Beit Dani takes the following form: approximately fifty elderly women from the Hatikva neighborhood arrive each day at noon and informally arrange themselves at the long tables according to their ethnic origin—the Yemenites, Iraqis, Egyptians, Iranians, and Moroccans each sitting with their friends of shared ethnic background. They are all neighbors, having lived among each other in Hatikva for most of their immigrated lives, but in this room, they voluntarily choose to group themselves by their countries of birth through seat arrangement.

3. See Shlomo Deshen's classic study *The Mellah Society: Jewish Community Life in Sherifian Morocco* (University of Chicago Press, 1989) on Moroccan Jewish history and culture.

4. Sivan's relationship to Jewish religion evokes such philosophies on the relationship between the individual and society as Émile Durkheim's notion of "anomie"—a term used to describe the incongruity of an individual's standards with a group's standards, or a difference in the individual's and group's social ethics. In his books *Suicide* (1897) and *The Elementary*

Forms of the Religious Life (1912), Durkheim considers the reconciliation of the forces of social integration with moral regulation and the effects on individuals engaged in that process. Sivan's interest in redefining the "Jewish God"—and reinvesting Jewish ritual with particular meaning that she draws from the present context of her life—demonstrates her active negotiation between the particular and the universal, the past and the present, and the individual and the society.

5. Robert Plant Armstrong's humanistic anthropology sheds light on Shaul's and Sivan's interpretations of their sukkah. Combining theories of aesthetics and anthropology to understand the relationship between the individual and material creation, Armstrong describes the objects that he studies as "special kinds of things ('works') which have significances not primarily conceptual (they are 'affecting'), and which own certain characteristics that cause them to be treated more like persons than like things ('presence')" (1981, 5). Within these "works of affecting presence," he distinguishes two classes and describes their features:

> Works of the first class tend rather clearly to be of the nature of persons. They have both social role and status. Further, they manifest some of the same needs as a person—must be fed, bathed, and often clothed. This is the aesthetic of invocation.
>
> The works of the other class of presence are not dedicated to the management of the energies of the world, but only to the management of the energies of their own internal systems—their conflicts, harmonies, resolutions, and balances . . . They are not presences of persons (whether these be the incarnations of gods or of ancestors or of cosmic power), but rather presences of qualities and internal significances. This is the aesthetic of virtuosity. (10)

The work of invocation is communal, metaphysical, externally invested with meaning, and time-sensitive, whereas the work of virtuosity is individual, psychological, internally contained, and constantly active. Armstrong observes that these two classes are distinct yet inextricably connected: "The invoked work owns, at the very least, virtuosity of the ability to cause, and the work of virtuosity owns the power to move one's sensibilities. Both invocation and virtuosity are means to power . . . which yields presence" (14). In the construction of their sukkah, Shaul and Sivan manifest both a work of invocation and a work of virtuosity. Shaul's devotion to the achievement of excellence, both through the structural integrity and decorative creativity of his sukkah, is an effort to affect those who sit in his elaborate creation. Sivan's commitment to the ritual process is an effort to order her universe and define the structures of her life. In her symbolic interpretation of the physical components of the sukkah, she imbues the structure with social and spiritual components as well, epitomized by her closing statement about her father's sukkah: "It's his family." Together, through acts of invocation and virtuosity, Shaul and Sivan project their histories and desires onto a world of impoverished physical and social conditions to create a work of affecting presence as an expression of believing.

6. Memizrach Shemesh, accessed May 16, 2016: http://mizrach.org.il/en/.

7. *Parochot*: the ornamental curtains that hang in front of the Torah ark in a synagogue. *Aron hakodesh*: the Torah ark in the synagogue that contains the Torah's scrolls.

6   The Right to House and Home

A RESIDENT OF SHCHUNAT Hatikva once recounted to me a brief history of housing in his neighborhood. He said Hatikva used to be covered with orchards, among which Jews and Arabs lived together in peace, but during the War of Independence in 1947, the Arabs fled and the Jews moved into their homes. In the decades that followed, waves of Jews from Middle Eastern and African countries immigrated to Israel; they lived in tents in refugee camps before building makeshift structures by themselves or renting apartments from public housing companies in cities such as Tel Aviv. A decline in public housing construction in the 1960s created high demand and low availability across Israel as struggling Jewish immigrants and, later, non-Jewish migrants continued to settle in low-income areas, such as South Tel Aviv. As a transitional home for migratory and working-class populations, this section of the city is overpopulated and underserved. This simplified history provides a framework for understanding Hatikva residents' relationships to housing and the concept of home.

For the residents of Shchunat Hatikva, building and enacting rituals in the sukkah marks the convergence of the religious, social, cultural, and political circumstances of their lives. The narrative of Sukkot is recalled, the experiences reenacted, and the messages reinscribed each year. However, from late July of 2011 through December of 2011, representatives from the disadvantaged neighborhoods of South Tel Aviv, Jaffa, Bat Yam, and Holon met in Hatikva's public park to demand public housing reforms, making clear that homelessness not only characterized the Israelites on their biblical journeys through the desert but also contemporary Jews living in the Promised Land today.

The connection between historical and current experiences crystallized for me one evening in Gan Hatikva. At ten o'clock at night on August 9, 2011, beneath tall, florescent park lights, representatives of the Peripheria Forum gathered for the first time to discuss their specific situations and common mission. The Peripheria Forum was a coalition of South Tel Aviv neighborhoods that had been established during the summer months of 2011 in an effort by the lower-income communities in Israel's "periphery" to gain fair representation on the national protest stage. Populated by lower-income Jews of Middle Eastern and African origin and Arab Israelis, these peripheral communities spoke for the strata of society not represented on Rothschild Boulevard, where middle-class university students had first raised tents to demonstrate against the rising costs of living and where the media had found its center of gravity. In these early weeks of protest, these peripheral populations had already become frustrated that their basic need for shelter was being overshadowed by student objections to increasing rents in the center of Tel Aviv. Fear of invisibility in this struggle caused representatives from South Tel Aviv to begin communicating with one another about their common plight, and ultimately it led to the formation of this united alliance, the Perpheria Forum.[1] Prior to this meeting on August 9, the developing protest camps in South Tel Aviv's disadvantaged neighborhoods of Bat Yam, Jaffa, and Holon were receiving word of each other's formation and sending representatives to visit neighboring sites. These visits were symbolic and practical gestures that helped to further solidarity.

During the discussion in the park, individuals from each community took turns describing their distresses. With each impassioned story, the group's facilitator interrupted, "But what is the priority! What is your top demand?" Housing, everyone immediately replied. Late in the night, after hours of productive exchanges, the meeting adjourned. As the group dispersed, I approached a man who had traveled from Jesse Cohen, a neglected neighborhood in Holon, to speak on behalf of his recently established encampment. During the group discussion, he had described a desperate need for food, water, and clothing for the homeless families in his community, resources that he said were being donated daily to the student protesters on Rothschild Boulevard but not reaching the peripheral populations in the direst need. Now, one-on-one, I asked him for more information on the homeless situation in his neighborhood. He crossed his arms, looked me in the eye, and spoke with an intensity that communicated as forcefully as did his words:

> My name is Rafi and I live in Jesse Cohen. I've told this several times to all the reporters in many places . . . This is no reality show. This is no joke. Today at our site, and from what I see here [in Hatikva] today, people are really suffering. This is not North Tel Aviv . . . here people can't pay even one thousand shekels . . . We left Egypt, Moses took us out, so we wouldn't be slaves, and today we're slaves to the mortgage. It's exactly like that! If Bibi Netanyahu doesn't wake up . . . we're not a party, we're not political. It hurts me to see people go to sleep and wake up in tents. One hundred and thirty families in Jesse Cohen now are homeless, with two and three kids. It hurts me to see children in tents. How will they go to school in three weeks? How will they shower? What kind of education are they receiving? As I said, we left Egypt so we wouldn't be slaves and here we are, slaves to the mortgage.

Rafi's message was echoed in various speeches at the protests organized by the Peripheria Forum in the weeks to follow. Speakers repeatedly made connections between the suffering of the Israelites and the suffering of Israeli citizens today. Jewish suffering in the Jewish State was especially distressing, they said, for the Promised Land had become a nation marked by political corruption and economic inequality.

As Sukkot approached nearly two months after the first Peripheria Forum meeting in the park took place, a barrage of announcements about demonstrations during the week of Sukkot were distributed via Facebook, email, and posters. Spokespersons for the student contingent on Rothschild Boulevard, led by undergraduate film student Daphni Leef, sent messages to over five thousand people via Facebook to announce a widespread weeklong march entitled "Building Sukkot of Social Justice—which will change the face of Israel." In an effort to connect their sociopolitical circumstances with those of the greater Jewish population, they crafted the invitation to their Sukkot demonstration in October in powerfully written prose:

> Date: Saturday, October 8 at 6:00 p.m.—October 19 at 6:00 p.m.
> Location: Every avenue, street, and square across the country
>
> At the end of Yom Kippur 2011, we will all, tens of thousands of Israelis, go to squares and boulevards in towns and villages in Israel and build sukkot. Sukkot of justice. Sukkot of sharing, of solidarity. Sukkot to remind us that we will not give up, we started marching and we will not stop. No dysfunctional committees nor polished speeches will quiet us. Until we have here a country and society that respects every citizen and every person. Until we have here a country where health, education and social welfare are not commodities but basic rights in a country that is a guarantor for the old, the sick, and the homeless. A country where citizens can converse with each other rather than fight and squabble over crumbs left by tycoons.
>
> At the end of Yom Kippur, we will start building the sukkot. Every evening until the start of the holiday, we will go out to the streets with the children, parents, and grandparents and prepare decorations for the sukkah and invite the ushpizin, and then on the holiday, we will go out in the sukkot. "And you shall celebrate Sukkot for seven days as you harvest your fields and vineyards" (Leviticus 23:13). "You and your son and your daughter and your servant and handmaid Hagar and Halevi and the orphan and the widow within your gates shall be joyous on the holiday" (Leviticus 23:14).
>
> Two thousand years ago, the people of Israel moved out of slavery to freedom, slept in sukkot, crossed the desert confused for forty years, made

themselves a golden calf, smashed it, received the stone tablets, and arrived in the Promised Land.

Sixty years ago, the children of Israel moved out of slavery to freedom and lived in encampments and established a state that imprinted on its flag the justice and welfare of all its citizens—a state that beyond being the national home, was also an attempt to establish a new and rightful society.

Last summer, we understood that we were slaves. We understood that something went deeply wrong here. All of its assets, our assets, the State sold to a handful of tycoons counting that money, and we sat desperate and sad in front of the television. Not anymore. This summer we started to march. Shattering (well, still breaking) the golden calf. Now, incredible timing, Sukkot has arrived again. But this time it will be a different Sukkot. Sukkot 2011 will be a Sukkot we will not forget, it will be a Sukkot that will change the face of Israel.

"On Sukkot you will sit for seven days, every citizen in Israel will sit in the sukkah" (Leviticus 23:42–43).

Their message was laden with allusions to biblical circumstance and the historic struggle for freedom and security. In the previous months' demonstrations, images of both material greed and spiritual belief had been deployed through the use of protest props—a gold, paper-mâché calf and nylon tents that the crowds had thrust high into the air as they chanted warnings about corruption and demands for a more just society.

This invitation called out to citizens across the country to journey together to Jerusalem, to the Israeli Knesset (government center), during the seven days of Sukkot. Accompanying the invitation, the students had created an online interactive map on which supporters of the protest could mark the locations of their individually built sukkot as sites of refuge for protesters along their route—ritual "homes" where they would be ceremoniously welcomed inside to eat, drink, and rest. The student hosts had imagined the biblically prescribed pilgrimage to Jerusalem, an original element of Sukkot observance during the Temple periods, to be revived in Israel in 2011. Now, however, the Temple would be replaced by the government center as the destination of the pilgrimage, and sacrifices would be made daily as expressions of social injustice, rather than ritually as offerings of gratitude and devotion.

Imbuing Jewish ritual practice with contemporary significance is as old as the Jewish holidays themselves.[2] The coincidental occurrence of Sukkot in 2011 with the protests against inadequate housing conditions across the nation and the world, however, created heightened meaning of this ritual. The public demonstrators seized the holiday as an opportunity for political dialogue, its observance as a tool for political action, and the sukkah as a symbol through which to simultaneously communicate their message on several fronts—religious, social, cultural, political, and economic.

Although the convergence of crises in all these dimensions of Israeli life during Sukkot was exceptional, residents of Shchunat Hatikva have capitalized on the political potential of Sukkot ritual practice on smaller scales since the earliest waves of immigrants settled in the neighborhood. For example, I was told by several residents about a clever tactic for adding needed rooms to small homes in the early years of the State. At this time, the process of obtaining municipal approval for building construction was complicated and protracted in the Mizrahi-populated neighborhoods of South Tel Aviv, which were not served like the Ashkenazi neighborhoods of North Tel Aviv. Residents would build sukkot for the holiday, but instead of dismantling them after the holiday ended, they would leave them standing year-round. With the sukkah's walls concealing developing projects inside, permanent add-ons could be built inside the space of the sukkah. Residents recounted this strategy with humor to convey the irony of the situation, but also with admiration for these builders who succeeded in attaining their needed spaces despite the obstruction of the government. A friend from Hatikva showed me a tattered sukkah on top of a roof and told me it had been standing there for years. He smiled with pride and amazement at this remnant of clandestine construction, which proclaimed the ongoing need for attention to housing deficits in neighborhoods such as Hatikva.

Whether expressed by masking additions to homes or by demanding housing reform, the persistent repurposing of Sukkot ritual practice for essential needs holds at its core the issue of the "right to housing." An announcement distributed in September 2011 by the Peripheria Forum appealed for protestors to gather in front of the home of the Minister of Housing of Jerusalem to assert this right. It read:

> The Peripheria Forum demands the recognition of guaranteed and independent shelter as a fundamental right and urges you to participate in a protest vigil outside the home of the Minister of Housing. Together we will demand housing solutions for everyone and an immediate end to all evictions and demolitions until there are just and adequate housing solutions. Shelter is a civil right—it is not given by grace. Shelter is a fundamental right that requires renewal and public housing policy changes, including thawing of the frozen Public Housing Law through legal arrangements and accelerated construction of public housing to catch up on the needs of tens of thousands of eligible people waiting for housing . . . Do not throw families from their homes without adequate housing solutions in the communities in which they live. Evacuation will be by agreement only and shelter provided or an alternative equivalent immediately . . . Public housing is a

civil right. We demand the updating and adjusting of the eligibility criteria for public housing, eliminating discrimination and demanding public housing construction in all sectors and communities.

My conversations with residents of South Tel Aviv neighborhoods helped me understand what constitutes this right to housing and what is lost by its denial. Although the discourse of the Peripheria Forum centered on policy, my conversations with individuals were philosophical and psychological in nature, residents emphasizing the deeply personal as well as socioeconomic implications of permanent shelter. Individuals described to me an array of affective thoughts and behaviors as being fundamentally related to and influenced by one's living conditions, such as self-consciousness, self-confidence, and hope. Understanding what a permanent home provides illuminates what is denied, beyond a physical roof, when individuals are deprived of it.

Pazit was one person with whom I spoke about the effect of Hatikva's housing history on its residents. Born and raised in Kfar Shalem, a neighborhood that borders Hatikva, Pazit helped facilitate dialogues in Hatikva's park during the summer months of protest. When I asked her about the public housing situation in the neighborhood, she explained that the problem reached beyond a shortage of housing units. The populations living in Hatikva have never had a *ba'al bayit* feeling, a feeling of home ownership, she said, since their arrival to Israel. These populations immigrated to Israel and moved straight into refugee tents, then into makeshift huts, and finally into public housing, if possible; but now they are back in tents again in Hatikva's public park, reexperiencing the impermanence of shelter. "What is the consequence of never having the feeling of ba'al bayit?" she asked me, and then answered with the words of French philosopher Emanuel Levinas. "Levinas said that man is nothing without a home, for only in a state of 'at-homeness' may one give and share with others. How can you do that if you do not have a home yourself?" Generations in Hatikva have lived like this, said Pazit, and as a result of being deprived of this "at-homeness," they now lack cultural power and cannot participate as equals in Israeli society. Pazit explained that although younger Mizrahi generations may be increasingly reappropriating traditional Mizrahi cultural forms—predominantly music—and transforming what was once cultural shame into cultural pride on a national scale, Hatikva's cultural roots are still weak on a local level.[3]

The point is not that all individuals without permanent physical shelter lack cultural power. Residents of a desert tent, a makeshift hut, or a rented apartment may all have the feeling of "at-homeness" to which Pazit refers. Rather, it is a sense of sovereignty over self, having "the right to housing," regardless of the kind of housing, that Pazit believes is lacking in Hatikva. This deep psychological deprivation due to the lack of physical shelter, puts into stark relief the ritual of

Sukkot, in which shelter is temporarily available to all, regardless of socioeconomic background. For the week that it stands, the sukkah provides the feeling of ba'al bayit to those who build and sit within its walls, empowering individuals as equals as they host and are hosted in these ritual dwellings. As seventy-four-year old David Zada (who emigrated from Persia to Israel and has lived in Shchunat Hatikva for almost fifty years) had said, "The sukkah is similar to a house, but the house is temporary—it comes and goes, while the sukkah is forever . . . it is of the world to come." Although the narrative of impermanent shelter at the core of the Sukkot experience is challenged by the reality of impermanent shelter that has undermined the lives of Hatikva's residents, the transcendent permanence of the sukkah offers respite from the uncertainty of physical shelter through an annual opportunity to create and identify with home.

Building Sukkot in the Park

The association of the narrative of Sukkot with the conditions of the protesters remained in the consciousness of the public throughout September of 2011, but it was during the actual week of the holiday in mid-October that I observed the full integration of religion and politics, when Sukkot ritual and daily events coexisted in undeniable symbiosis. On Wednesday, October 12, 2011, I biked to Gan Hatikva to see if any protesters would be celebrating the holiday. I wondered how the practice of building a temporary ritual shelter might be reconciled with the raising of these protest tent communities.

As I neared the main camp in the late afternoon, I could see from the edge of the park three men hammering a wooden frame surrounded by several small silver protest tents. Itzik Amsalem, one of two representatives of the Hatikva encampment, was heading the project. "You're building a sukkah!" I called as I rode up, surprised to see the flurry of activity just hours before the sun was to set on the eve of the holiday. According to halakha (Jewish religious law), one is required to hammer the first nail into the sukkah's frame (or, more often today, knock into place the first leg of a prefabricated metal frame) as the sun sets on Yom Kippur, four days prior to the start of Sukkot. Although not all abide by this rule, beginning to construct one's sukkah several hours before the eve of Sukkot pushes the process to the limit of its allotted time. "Of course I'm building a sukkah!" said Itzik, "but it's last minute because I returned from the Peripheria conference this morning and we had no time to get supplies until this afternoon." In the four-day break between Yom Kippur and Sukkot, the Peripheria Forum had organized a conference for representatives from the participating communities across the country to discuss the situation in their encampments and clarify their goals. Time was of the essence in these fall weeks as the weather cooled and the momentum of the social demonstrations was starting to wane. Itzik had traveled two hours north by bus to Haifa to represent Shchunat Hatikva at the conference, and he had only just now returned.

Back in the park at last, Itzik and his two friends Yaakov and Moshe were working quickly to nail two-by-four-inch planks of wood together across the base of one of the sukkah's walls, making sure to secure them according to halachic standards. As Itzik hammered the corner of a maroon bedsheet to the top of a wooden beam to create one of the sukkah's walls, he told me that he had worked in construction all his life. He grew up in poverty, he said, and that is how he learned to build. I asked him if he constructs a sukkah every year, and he said of course, whenever he had a place to build it. I then asked what he thought about when he sat inside the sukkah. He looked at me in shock and said, "It's a holy space. You don't think, you *feel*. It's all about feeling. I don't understand how anyone could not feel the energy of a sukkah."

I stood back and watched the three men work together to decide where palm branches should be attached to create the most aesthetically pleasing archway over the sukkah's entrance and what color sheets to use for the remaining walls. In the weeks prior to Sukkot, I had grown accustomed to seeing these men organize and carry out demonstrations—driving through the neighborhood, rallying residents, painting signs, chanting into megaphones in front of marching crowds,

Fig. 6.1. Itzik (left) and Yaakov (right) stand in front of the community sukkah that they built in Gan Hatikva just hours before the holiday begins. Tents erected in protest of unfair housing conditions surround them. Shchunat Hatikva, Israel. 2011.

and reporting back, late at night, the day's stories of protest and arrest. I was not used to seeing them quarrel over the aesthetics of a palm-arched doorway as they were now so adamantly doing. These hours of construction, though rushed and tiring, provided a welcome break from the political activities of recent months.

Although the material composition of the sukkah resembled many of the makeshift protest shelters that had stood in the park for months (wooden frame, cloth or tarp walls, furniture inside), the ritual time period and the intention with which the sukkah was built imbued it with distinct meaning. This construction reached out to eras and geographies beyond the park's encampment. I left Gan Hatikva as the sun set over the finished sukkah, palm branches secured into a sweeping arch over the doorway and a string of shiny tinsel stars dangling from the roof.

The Last Night

One week later, on the last night of Sukkot, I returned to the park for a gathering and discussion about the meaning of the holiday inside the sukkah that I had watched Itzik, Yaakov, and Moshe build. Social events and study sessions about aspects of Jewish religion, law, and practice are common in Hatikva, particularly on holidays. After work, residents regularly attend lessons in synagogues and community centers to study that week's portion of the Torah or analyze a topical news story from a religious perspective. Especially on holidays, when work is suspended, group prayer and Torah study take place in a more intensive rotation, beginning early in the morning and lasting through the night. On Sukkot, evening learning commonly takes place in the sukkah rather than in the synagogue, the sukkah being a holy space of prayer. The notable element of this meeting in the park on the last night of Sukkot, however, was not the setting but the guest list.

Earlier that week, neighborhood activists and residents had informed me that Reuven Abergel, a founder of the Israeli Black Panther Movement of the early 1970s, had been invited to this last evening's gathering. The Israeli Black Panthers were an Israeli protest movement of second-generation Mizrahi Jews that formed in Jerusalem in the early 1970s. Saadia Marciano, one of the founding members of the Israeli Black Panthers, had met Angela Davis of the African American Black Panther movement when she visited Israel in 1971, and then adopted the name for the new Mizrahi movement. The Israeli Black Panthers were "the first to make the connection between the concepts of 'class' and 'ethnicity.' They claimed very clearly and directly that a state in which Mizrahim (and Arabs) are so economically unequal has no right to exist" (von Oston, 2012). They protested largely against the problems of unequal housing conditions and segregation of space, challenging the notion of Israel as a project of European Zionism. Although the movement did not last, it offered an unprecedented exposé of ethnic discrimination within the State.⁴ In 1973, Black Panther demonstrations against the treatment of the Mizrahi Jews as second-class citizens in Israel were cut short by the Yom Kippur War, national security taking precedence over civil unrest, as routinely happened in Israel. Abergel's public reappearance as a featured speaker on behalf of lower-income Mizrahim in the 2011 social protests, therefore, revived the spirit of the Black Panther's social struggle, which had been dormant for decades. He soon become a central figure in the Periphera coalition's efforts, enfolding the history of Israel's discrimination of lower-income Mizrahi Jews, against which he had fought decades earlier, into the current struggle against Israel's economic and social inequality.

Along with Abergel, Rabbi Chaim Amsalem had also been invited to the sukkah that evening. Rabbi Amsalem was a former Knesset member and now the founder of the nascent Whole Nation party. Born in French Algeria, he immigrated to Israel in 1970 and had been a member of the ultra-orthodox Sephardic political party, Shas, until 2010, when he was expelled for critiquing rising unemployment, a lack of secular educational opportunities for children, *yeshiva* (Jewish educational institutions that focus on the study of Jewish religious texts) students' evasion of national army service in Israel, and the party's restrictions against conversion. He had retained his seat in the Knesset, however, and five months later he established the Whole Nation Party, a new social movement named for his surname, Am Shalem (Whole Nation). Rabbi Amsalem founded the Whole Nation Party as "a unifying, tolerant Jewish approach" to political leadership, for which he had called upon "those who aren't destined to be great Torah scholars and who have families to work for" (Mandel 2010; 2011). Rabbi Amsalem's moderate position, which reconciled the realities of the working-class poor with religious practice and politics, addressed the difficulties of the group gathered in the sukkah that night—disadvantaged Mizrahim whose religious practices and beliefs were influenced by economic and social restrictions as well as by Jewish tradition. His presence acknowledged the dual religious and political purpose of the evening's gathering.

By bringing into their sukkah two political figures such as Reuven Abergel and Rabbi Amsalem to discuss the meaning of Sukkot, South Tel Aviv's residents had intentionally created an opportunity for reinterpretation of the holiday within the context of civil resistance, integrating the political and ritual within the space of the sukkah.

"Without Aravah, Nothing Is Equal"

The *kippah* (skullcap worn by observant Jewish men) atop Rabbi Amsalem's head brushed against the schach that hung down from the sukkah's roof as he stood to face the group seated in front of him. "What can the *aravah* bring me?" he began, rhetorically, referring to one of the Four Species of plants that are bound together for prayer during Sukkot; "It has no smell, no taste, and no beauty." The aravah, like each of the Four Species, has a distinct and necessary place in Sukkot ritual. Common interpretation of the Four Species likens them to four parts of the human body. The *etrog* (citron) symbolizes the heart, the *lulav* (palm branch) the spine, the *hadas* (myrtle branch) the eyes, and the *aravah* (willow branch) the lips. The plants resemble the body parts in physical shape, but the comparisons also give each plant its significance: the heart powers the body, the spine holds the body upright, the eyes enable sight, and lips enable speech. Together, these four plants, like these four parts of the body, comprise a whole expression of the self.

A second interpretation relates the ritual plants to the human mind as well as the body, each plant symbolizing a different "kind" of Jew who, together, make up a single nation. The etrog symbolizes those who both learn Torah and perform good deeds; the lulav—those who study Torah but do not perform good deeds; the hadas—those who perform good deeds but do not study Torah; and the aravah—those who neither study Torah nor perform good deeds. This analogy stems from observation of the plants' biology: the etrog possesses both smell and taste; the lulav only taste; the hadas only smell; and the aravah, neither taste nor smell. This sensory evaluation sets up analogies that place the plants—as well as the parts of the body and mind that they represent—in hierarchical relation to each other.

When Rabbi Amsalem asks what the aravah can bring him as it offers neither smell, taste, nor beauty, he speaks about the plant's physical form to inquire about its deeper purpose for being. "If you have the lulav, the hadas, and the etrog, but no aravah," he continued, "you have nothing. You can't pray. What's the aravah? It's the least expensive material, but you can't do anything without it." According to Jewish law, the ritual bundle used for prayer during Sukkot must contain all four of the ritual plants tied together with care and in particular order. Although the plants individually hold distinct values, they are equally valueless until bound together as one to create the ritual bundle.

After noting the need for the modest but invaluable aravah, Rabbi Amsalem paused and began a new topic, one that he knew his audience was waiting to discuss. "This summer was a summer of social demonstration," he began. "They talked and talked, and the train left the station, but there were people still left on the platform. Our duty, especially on Sukkot, is not to forget about the people left behind . . . If there's no good will, if there is no togetherness between us, if we don't work with each other, if we don't try to be in someone else's situation, if we don't help those who were not given equal opportunities . . . If those who are really on the bottom stay on the bottom, then what have we accomplished? Without the aravah, nothing is equal." The unity of a people, like the unity of the

Four Species, said Rabbi Amsalem, fulfills a potential immeasurably greater than that of anyone who stands alone.

The sukkah in which we all sat was two meters wide and four meters long, constructed of wooden beams, scrap plywood, and recycled bed sheets. Inside, two long tables wobbled on the uneven ground to form a T-shape around which were placed assorted hard plastic chairs. Paper plates filled with pretzels, chocolate cookies, and nuts decorated the tables, and tall liters of soda variously obscured lines of vision. To the right of the sukkah's entranceway stood a small square coffee table on top of which sat a large, boxy television reaching beyond the table's edges. A white microwave was balanced on top of the television, and extension cords dangled down the side of this tower of machinery. Rabbi Amsalem stood opposite the sukkah's open entranceway, which offered a view of the makeshift outdoor "kitchen" set up in a trailer about thirty feet away, around which children without shirts or shoes were running in the dark. The sukkah itself was now the topic of discussion. Why did we build this temporary rough shelter in the middle of the tent encampment in Gan Hatikva, and why did we gather here each night?

"What does the sukkah symbolize?" asked Rabbi Amsalem. "That everyone is equal. Everyone builds a sukkah. Everyone leaves their regular circumstances, their warmth, their poverty. The Torah says, 'Don't forget that once you too were a foreigner in Egypt, that once you too had no house, that once you too were in the desert.' And what was in that desert? Sukkot. Don't forget where you came from." We build the sukkah, said Rabbi Amsalem, to recall a history that may guide us into the future with reason, respect, and an awareness of ourselves. These are the intentions nurtured by this holiday's observance and the messages that the Rabbi imparted throughout the night. By nurturing self-awareness, he instilled in his listeners an awareness of others.

"There's a story about King David," Rabbi Amsalem continued halfway through his talk. "After he became king, he had a little room that he wouldn't let anyone enter. No one could enter. One day, someone said, 'Open it! Open it! What's in the room? Open it!' King David said, 'No! No!" But this man begged, 'Open it, we want to see what's inside!' He thought, 'Who knows what treasures might be found in the king's room?' So King David opened the door and what did he find inside? He found a stick, a backpack, and a canvas sack. 'The stick is in case I see a disaster. The backpack is to put my bread in, and the canvas sack is what I use at night because I don't have a blanket. I don't forget where I came from.' The wisdom is not in being a king, but in remembering where you came from." This is the most important message of this holiday, concluded Rabbi Amsalem: when you want to be happy and celebrate, you must also think of those who are lacking.

Aware of the circumstances of the population whom he faced, Rabbi Amsalem acknowledged that although the ritual sukkah was not the appropriate place in which to speak about politics, he recognized the correlation between the holiday's themes and the community's current distress. "After forty years in sukkot, where did we go? We went to permanent homes, and our hope today is that everyone is able to move to a permanent home from which he will get respect and in which he can educate his children, and that he will get equal opportunities and not return to this same situation each year." That dialogue would be continued another time, he said, after the holiday ended, and outside this ritual space.

Reuven Abergel next stood to speak. His face was solemn and his shoulders softly slumped from seeming exhaustion, but his voice was resolute: "We are all temporary in this world. All of us. We come in without free will and leave without free will. We are temporary. The sukkah symbolizes the transient nature of our existence. We as humans are a walking sukkah. We need to remember morning and night that we are a walking sukkah so that we protect it, beautify it, care about it, guard its inner beauty, and decorate its outside despite the thunderstorms that might knock it down while we are sitting inside." While Rabbi Amsalem had spoken of the sukkah as an ideal realm in which to experience equality and empathy, Reuven Abergel saw it as an expression of ordinary life—a vulnerable structure at the mercy of unknowable life forces. In the ephemeral nature of this structure, Reuven Abergel located the beauty, power, and courage that had sustained a struggle for recognition throughout his life.

After sharing these words, Reuven Abergel sat down and a woman seated in front row immediately raised her hand to ask a question: "Why must you take the sukkah apart at the close of the holiday when on Passover, you may continue to eat *matzoh* after the holiday ends?" A man seated behind her burst out, "If you take the sukkot down, people will have nowhere to go! Where will they go?" To reassure them, Rabbi Amsalem clarified the religious law: "You may take down just one part of the sukkah, the schach, for example, and put on a nylon tarp, and it's no longer a sukkah . . . you may turn it into your house this way . . . You want to stay in the sukkah—I understand, I know," he said, looking at the woman for an extended moment. The woman looked back and responded, her voice slightly raised: "This is a country where, from the establishment of the State, a large number of people were neglected—Yemenites, Moroccans . . ." Rabbi Amsalem interrupted her politely and agreed, but said he did not want to open a discussion about historic injustice here. The sukkah was a place for spirituality and joy, and he wanted to maintain that atmosphere on this last night of the holiday. He spoke slowly and seriously:

> Mistakes were made when the State was established. I don't even want to say it was done intentionally with a bad heart, but there were the "Dear Sons," and there was the "Second Israel." Unfortunately, those who came after continue to be with us in this position. We have to prohibit that sort

of discrimination. What does the Torah command us to do? Pay attention to the foreigners, the orphans, the widows, the deprived, to the ones who cry in their hearts even if you don't see their tears. You have to pay attention, take an interest in them, and ask, "What bothers you? What hurts you? Where's your problem?" Or else we will be egoistic and say, "Myself and no one else. I worry about myself." On this holiday, that is exactly the point: the mitzvah is to go to other people and show interest in them. I came to embrace you, to sympathize, to help you. I know what the issues are. I know about the protests this summer.

And with that, he thanked the group, began to sing, and shook hands as he walked out of the sukkah. Even briefly, the residents of South Tel Aviv had addressed the political within the framework of tradition.

Within days, the sukkah in which Rabbi Amsalem and Reuven Abergel had sat with the community had been converted into a control center for the Gan Hatikva protesters. The ritual, organic roofing through which you could see the stars had been replaced with a strong weatherproof nylon tarp and a weatherproof zip-up fabric doorway was draped over the palm-branch-framed entranceway. A laptop was set up inside to spread word of upcoming protests and communicate with other Peripheria representatives via Facebook, and a better lighting system

Fig. 6.2. Rabbi Amsalem speaks with members of the Gan Hatikva encampment in their sukkah on the last evening of the holiday. Shchunat Hatikva, Israel. 2011.

had been installed inside the structure so that meetings around the table could be held late into the night. Other sukkot in Gan Hatikva that had been erected out of scrap wood and sheets were similarly reinforced for the coming winter, and although no major changes in the appearance of the encampment were visible between the week of Sukkot and the weeks that followed, the ritual shelters had been transformed into ordinary dwellings overnight.

Representatives of the South Tel Aviv's disadvantaged neighborhoods, Jaffa, Bat Yam, and Holon continued to meet in the Hatikva encampment from late July through December of 2011, attesting to the fact that the desperation and uncertainty of the biblical exodus and desert journey described the daily conditions of their current existence. The week of Sukkot, however, gave Israelis a particularly vivid occasion to call for housing reform and *tzedek chevrati,* or social justice—the cry that rang across the country.

Occupy Sukkot

The wave of global protests against economic inequality between 2010 and 2011 dramatized the fact that that the biblical narrative that had produced a ritual of reflection on materiality and home for two thousand years was as much a reality today as it was when the holiday began. The journey of survival and reflection that Sukkot commemorates, continues. During the period of my research, peoples across the world were rising up against their governments to protest political and economic inequality and oppression. The Arab Spring of 2010 shocked Tunisia and Egypt and swept across the Middle East, followed by the Spanish "Indignant" Protest Movement of 2011 and the Occupy Wall Street Movement that fomented demonstrations in over one hundred cities across the United States. The "Declaration of the Occupation of New York City," accepted by the New York City General Assembly on September 29, 2011, declared that "corporations, which place profit over people, self-interest over justice, and oppression over equality, run our governments . . ."[5] Years later, the word "occupy" is now synonymous with civil resistance all over the world and has become part of the language of protest in place names ("Occupy Philadelphia," "Occupy Nigeria," "Occupy Europe"), for environmental causes ("Occupy Earth," "Occupy Food Safety," "Occupy Animal Rights"), and for holidays ("Occupy Christmas," "Occupy New Year's Eve," "Occupy Memorial Day").[6] The word galvanizes political, economic, and social action and energizes the struggle for equality and justice.

In 2011, the identification of the ancient Sukkot ritual with the contemporary protest was unmistakable. "Occupy Judaism" and "Occupy Sukkot" became widespread slogans as protesters erected sukkot in tent encampments all over the United States during the weeklong holiday. The story and significance of Sukkot reverberated throughout the Occupy Movement's proclamations and demands.

In Zuccotti Park in lower Manhattan, Dan Sieradski, organizer of Occupy Judaism NYC, commented, "There is no better place to celebrate the festival of Sukkot this year than right here at Occupy Wall Street. We stand in solidarity with all those who are challenging the inequitable distribution of resources in our country, who dare to dream of a more just and compassionate society." (Fleischman 2011). The word "occupy" itself embodied the fundamental intention of the holiday and protest. The biblical prescription for Sukkot requires one to "dwell" in the sukkah to reflect upon values such as materiality, spirituality, and equality. Similarly, to "occupy," in the protest movement's rhetoric, is to inhabit a space for the purpose of generating reflection and change. In the historic period of global uprisings, the meaning of "dwelling" in a temporary shelter expanded so greatly that it encompassed a park, a city, a country, an economic and political system, a religion, a concept, a value system, and an ideal.

In "Protest Camps: an Emerging Field of Social Movement Research" (2014), sociologists Anna Feigenbaum, Fabian Frenzel, and Patrick McCurdy declared the crucial need and current lack of research into the protest camp as the locus of organizational and symbolic power within a movement. Describing the international waves of social protests in 2011, the authors declared protest camps to be sites of "'contested space,' representational space, home space and convergence space"—all new contexts of "alternative" or "transformational" democracy in the world (Frenzel, Feigenbaum, and McCurdy 2014, 463). Their analysis of the social and symbolic power of the protest camp accurately depicts both the Israeli protest encampments and the space of the sukkah in 2011.

This discussion of the sukkah as ritual shelter in light of the housing protests reveals a tension: the ritual celebration of being sheltered and the lived experience of lacking shelter. In the midst of political uprisings, individuals used the physical, social, and historical space created by the construction of the sukkah to express current social and economic distresses that echoed the holiday's religious messages. As protesters reinterpreted Sukkot to highlight neglected housing needs in Israeli society, they harnessed the holiday as a powerful tool of protest and change. They reversed the values for which Sukkot is commonly known by relating it to a current-day expression of the narrative: the lack of home as a positive reminder of human equality became the lack of home as a negative reminder of material disadvantage. The ephemeral sukkah became the stable, reliable shelter. As the physical locus of a dynamic tradition that invites annual reinterpretation, the flexible space and structure of the sukkah gain value with each new context of use.

Speaking of houses, Henry Glassie has observed, "Since social order cannot be disjoined from economic aspiration and ideas of the sacred, then houses cannot be understood outside of their economic, political, and religious contexts." (1984, 17). In 2011, at a moment when economic inequalities were being vividly projected around the world, the fundamental concept of Sukkot, the lack of and search for a permanent home, gained renewed relevance. Changing conditions around the world demonstrated the responsive nature of this traditional practice. Reconstructing sukkot in protest encampments in 2011 not only commemorated the Israelites' shelters as they journeyed through the Sinai Desert, it cast bright light on the journeys being undertaken to cross the deserts of today.

Notes

1. The Peripheria Forum authored and circulated their mission statement as follows:

    What is the Peripheria Forum? We are the backyard of Israeli society. Our troubles were not born yesterday. The solution lies not in a policy decision one way or another, nor a one-time allocation of resources, but in a fundamental change of policy and in repair activities for social structure and power relations in society and the State. However, we focus initially on immediate action to achieve urgent needs and strengthen the Periphery while preparing for a long-term change in Israeli society and repairing past injustices that impose marginality and weakness. We, representatives of encampments in weakened neighborhoods in towns and villages in the social periphery of Israel, including Mizrahi and Arab populations, social activists struggling in different arenas for social justice and equality, hereby declare the establishment of a mutual alliance for the common struggle for fundamental and profound social change for the future of all citizens of Israel.

2. The reinvestment of religious ritual with contemporary relevance is evident outside of Judaism as well. Wayne Ashley provides a meaningful case of the intersection of urban distress with religious rites in "The Stations of the Cross: Christ, Politics, and Processions on New York City's Lower East Side" in *Gods of the City: Religion and the American Urban Landscape* (1999).

3. Pazit provided examples of popular figures of Mizrahi heritage who have successfully moved into the Israeli mainstream. She mentioned the acclaimed author Dudu Bosi, who speaks and writes about the shame of being born and raised in the stigmatized Hatikva neighborhood, marked by neglect and desperation; and, the Iraqi-Yemenite musician Dudu Tasa, who is known for reproducing the traditional Iraqi music of his grandfather and reviving formerly dismissed Iraqi musical styles in new form. While Bosi speaks for the continued cultural disempowerment of Hatikva's Mizrahi Jews, Tasa represents a more recent turn to reclaim cultural power by the third generation of Israel's Mizrahim.

4. Marion von Oston. 2012. "Israeli Black Panthers," March 5. Accessed May 16, 2016. http://www.transculturalmodernism.org/article/125.

5. #Occupy Wall Street NYC General Assembly website, accessed May 16, 2016. http://www.nycga.net/resources/documents/declaration.

6. Each of these examples has an official website with information on their efforts and membership.

7 Transcending Architecture: *Sukkot* in Brooklyn, New York

EACH OF THE stories of sukkah builders and users that has been presented illuminates a guiding principle of contemporary Sukkot practice: the search for shelter and the Promised Land, creativity and self-expression, compassion and social cohesion, and equality and hope. Three years after Occupy Wall Street and Occupy Sukkot rallied the disadvantaged and their supporters, I was back in the United States for the holiday in the fall of 2014. The city of New York, home to the second-largest urban Jewish population in the world after Tel Aviv, is the final setting for this study of the sukkah. This last example, from the heart of Hasidic Brooklyn, contributes yet another fundamental purpose of Sukkot practice: faith. Like the vignette from Bloomington, Indiana, that opened this book, this New York vignette closes it by expanding even further the diverse and unfolding practice of contemporary Sukkot observance.

Given the range of religious beliefs and practices among Jews in New York, from the ultra-Orthodox to the fully secular, with multiple nuanced denominations in between, this last case study will not attempt to provide a comprehensive overview. Instead, I focus on one particular Orthodox Jewish community in Brooklyn. Similarities and differences connect this community with those in Bloomington, Indiana, and South Tel Aviv, Israel: it is a community located in an ethnically diverse urban environment; a community with a strong sense of history, identity, and neighborhood borders; and a population negotiating past traditions with present living conditions through its particular expression of Jewish faith and culture. However, it is the only Ashkenazi Orthodox community represented in this book, the only community that emigrated from one country to another en masse to follow a spiritual leader, and, significantly, the only one in which the custom of *not* decorating the sukkah has become standard accepted practice.

Describing his childhood memories of Sukkot in Crown Heights, Brooklyn, in the 1970s, Joseph Piekarski remembered, "The Rebbe once said 'You should dance so much that you feel the street dancing with you.' That's how much you have to dance." The Rebbe whom Joseph referred to is the spiritual leader of Lubavitch Judaism, this Orthodox Hasidic Jewish movement founded in the late eighteenth century in Lyubavichi (Lubavitch), Russia and whose home today is based in this neighborhood of central Brooklyn.[1] In 1940, the sixth Lubavitcher Rebbe, Yosef Yitzchak Schneerson (referred to as "the Previous Rebbe"), escaped the Holocaust in Poland and immigrated to the United States. He purchased 770 Eastern Parkway, a former medical clinic at the corner of Kingston Avenue and Eastern Parkway in Crown Heights, and declared this building his movement's new home and the community's center (Mintz 1992, 139). Lubavitcher Jews followed. As in other Hasidic dynasties, the Rebbe's leadership is transferred to successors, usually within the family. Inherited by his son-in-law and successor Rebbe Menachem Mendel Schneerson in 1951, 770 Eastern Parkway continues to be the worldwide spiritual center of the Lubavitch community.[2]

The Lubavitcher population continues to grow because of a high birth rate—between five and eight children per family—compared with the United States' average of under two per family, and it is considered the largest and fastest-growing Hasidic Jewish community in the world.

Fig. 7.1. Front façade of 770 Eastern Parkway, the worldwide headquarters of the Lubavitch Jewish movement. Crown Heights, Brooklyn, New York. 2015.

Transcending Architecture: Sukkot *in Brooklyn, New York* | 197

Joseph Piekarski

Joseph Piekarski was born in 1971 in Crown Heights. He learned Yiddish as a first language and spoke it with friends and family at home, in school, and on the streets, gradually learning English as he grew older. He studied Torah and Talmud in yeshivas from childhood until his early twenties, training to become a rabbi, which is the common path for men to take in this Orthodox community. Today, over twenty years later, he lives in Manhattan instead of Crown Heights, but regularly visits family and friends in his former home neighborhood. For the past year, he has begun to meet with his father, a rabbi and former principal of the main yeshiva in Crown Heights, every Wednesday evening at his father's home for a weekly Talmudic discussion. This is a time for a father and his grown son to continue learning together and from each other.

When I asked Joseph about Sukkot observance in his youth, he painted for me a picture of Crown Heights during the ritual week: "Can you imagine as a kid, a holiday for a full eight days—first of all, there's no school. Everything shuts down, everybody makes a sukkah. Every house has a hut in front and back. You have these beautiful meals, you sing songs. Even when I was really young and I wasn't able to stay up late, the sukkah was underneath my window and I would hear the men singing all night. I'd hear my father giving lessons and people telling jokes . . . it was a beautiful atmosphere." Side streets in Crown Heights are lined with historic row houses, mostly one-, two-, or three-story residences with stoops and porches, and oftentimes with small courtyard-like areas behind the residences. Rectangular, empty porches and courtyards are transformed during Sukkot, enclosed with wooden-sided or prefabricated sukkah constructions. When porches and courtyards are unavailable for use, second-floor terraces are lined with sukkot, and oftentimes, tall steel-framed platforms that reach from the sidewalk up to second-floor apartments are constructed especially for use during Sukkot, when the ritual shelters occupy these barren stands. Narrow spaces on sidewalks and streets are also reapportioned as the numerous synagogues in the neighborhood build community sukkot, usually much larger than those at family residences.

Reflecting upon the value of the material structure itself, Joseph Piekarski remembered:

> *Succos* [Yiddish: Sukkot] for me wasn't about the actual hut, but the hut represented the beautiful circus . . . You could go into anyone's sukkah—if you heard singing, you'd go into that sukkah and listen until two o'clock in the morning, and then go to Kingston Avenue and dance if you wanted, and during the weekdays they have a whole band, live music in the street . . . It was the best time of the year. The sukkah was nothing really; it was the intensity, the *farbrengens* [Yiddish: Hasidic gathering],

the intense conversations. That's also when the Rebbe was alive, and every night he'd give a little talk so we'd run to 770 at eight o'clock to listen. And also there's ushpizin, and there's particular Hasidic ushpizin, and we'd talk every night about what you learn from each one. There was so much going on in this period—music and dancing and spiritual intensity. It was a spiritual festival.

Today, more than twenty years after the Rebbe passed away (1994) without a successor, and more than thirty years after Joseph's early memories of the neighborhood, Sukkot in Crown Heights is remarkably similar. The ritual structures begin to populate the neighborhood at the close of Yom Kippur and in the four days preceding the start of the holiday, streets are packed with vendors selling raw materials for sukkah construction, manufactured decorations, and plastic furniture to use inside the structure. Hasidic bands set up stages in the middle of Kingston and Montgomery Avenues to play melodies long into the night for new generations of children, young adults, and veteran residents who live outdoors in these temporary shelters for eight days, learning, singing, and dancing until the street dances with them.

Rabbi Chaim Halberstam

Stepping out from the number 3 subway station at Kingston Avenue and Eastern Parkway in Crown Heights, one's eyes immediately fall upon 770 Eastern Parkway just across the street, the Lubavitch worldwide headquarters. Inside this building, which is the Previous Rebbe's home and office and now a pilgrimage site for Lubavitcher Jews from around the world, Rabbi Chaim Halberstam established and runs the Lubavitch Communication Center. When you enter the building and walk straight down a narrow hallway, you reach small room with an illuminated sign above the door that reads, "WLCC," the initials of "Worldwide Lubavitch Communication Center." This is the control room where all of the Rebbe's sermons and teachings were recorded and from where they are now disseminated.

Rabbi Chaim Halberstam was born in Israel and immigrated to New York in 1966. His father, originally from Poland, had worked for a grand rabbi of another Jewish community in Israel, which he had helped to build. When Rabbi Halberstam was fourteen years old, his father sent him to a new yeshiva run by Lubavitch Jews so that he might learn from a different perspective. Halberstam vividly remembers the move: "Once you go into the Chabad world and discover the way of thinking and the way of living here, and everything has a different meaning . . . my whole life changed for me, and I stuck with it," he said. "Chabad is unique even within the Hasidim. It's a different way of thinking, a different way of behaving, a different way of life altogether. In Chabad, every individual is an individual thinker." And so, in 1966 as a young man inspired to join the Lubavitch Jewish movement at its center, Halberstam immigrated to Crown Heights, and began studying at a local yeshiva. He became close to the Rebbe's family, and soon after his arrival, was offered this small room in the back of 770 Eastern Parkway as a temporary place to sleep. The Rebbe's wife slept on the second floor of the building, and the family preferred that she not be alone in the building when the others were away, so the arrangement benefited all. Halberstam moved in and lived there for several years.

In 1970, the Rebbe decided to record a broadcast for the first time and needed a room with a view of the main sanctuary space so that he could see the immediate community to whom he was speaking. The room with this view was Halberstam's small bedroom, so within several months, this room was transformed into the broadcasting space. Halberstam was given the task of developing the technology to broadcast the Rebbe's speeches, first on one phone line, then on eight lines, then on twenty-eight lines, and then on hundreds of lines that connected Lubavitcher Jews all over the world to the Rebbe's word through a custom-made switchboard that Halberstam designed. He taught himself basic electronics, or in his own words, "I learned from actually doing," and he read books to understand the complexities of the communications systems he was building as he was constructing them.

Today, Halberstam lives several blocks from 770 Eastern Parkway on a quiet street lined with old trees and brick townhouses, fronted by terraces and stoops. When I visited him the day before Sukkot, he walked me down the side alley to the back of his house, where he builds his sukkah out of plywood and repurposed metal poles. "If you look at my makeshift sukkah," he proudly observed, "people wonder how it's held up. The whole sukkah is held with eight bolts." Halberstam has painted large numbers on the interior wooden panel walls to remind himself of the order in which to assemble the structure, and the roof covering is an assortment of bamboo mats that he reuses each year. The structure is bare but for a florescent light hanging from the roof inside. When I asked him what else was still to be accomplished before the start of the holiday, he said, "It's done,"—nothing is to be added but a table and chairs. "You know Chabad doesn't have any decorations," he said. "Chabad is different than the whole world in two ways. First, no decorations. And second, when it rains, the whole world goes into the house to eat. Chabad will stay in the sukkah and eat in the rain. Once, I started eating a soup and I kept eating and eating and never finished because it kept raining," he said with a smile. When I asked Halberstam how the custom of remaining in the sukkah when it rains is reconciled with the verse that states that one should not perform a mitzvah if it causes discomfort, he replied, "If the mitzvah causes pain, you're not obligated, but to me, not doing the mitzvah is a bigger pain!"[3]

Fig. 7.2. Rabbi Halberstam stands with his wife, Mindy, in front of the sukkah that they built behind their house. He constructs the sukkah out of metal poles and plywood panels, all held together with eight bolts. Crown Heights, Brooklyn, New York. 2015.

Fig. 7.3. Rabbi Halberstam paints large white numbers on each plywood panel so that he knows the order in which to construct the frame. No decorations adorn the interior, as is customary in Lubavitch Sukkot observance, but a table, chairs, and a lamp will furnish the inside. Crown Heights, Brooklyn, New York. 2015.

Transcending Architecture: Sukkot in Brooklyn, New York

Fig. 7.4. Rabbi Halberstam creates a *schach* made out of bamboo mats. Crown Heights, Brooklyn, New York. 2015.

Rather than decorations, the material that deserved attention, said Halberstam, was the schach. The Talmudic interpretation decreeing that the roof covering should not exceed a height of approximately thirty feet, he told me, is derived from the need to see the schach when you enter the sukkah. "The schach has to be noticed," says Halberstam. "Your attention should be on the schach, not on all the beautiful drawings and decorations. Our custom is that when you make the special *brachah* (prayer) for the sukkah—*L'shev b'sukkah* (to sit in the sukkah)—we look up at the schach. We should feel the sukkah." The schach, revealing the stars of the night sky and providing shade from the hot day's sun with its weave, is religiously interpreted as the "Clouds of Glory" with which God surrounded the Israelites to protect and comfort them in the wilderness (Rubenstein 1994).

Mayer Preger

Two days later, at lunch in the sukkah of another Lubavitch family a few blocks down from Halberstam, I watched as the men of the family raised their eyes to the woven brush while reciting the prayer before we began our meal. This sukkah belonged to the family of Mayer Preger, who was born and raised in Crown Heights and now lives with his family in the Five Towns region of Long Island. Many of his relatives still live throughout Crown Heights, and he spends his Sukkot, among other holidays, at his father-in-law's home in the middle of the neighborhood. Today, Mayer runs a large home appliance store in Brooklyn called Drimmers Appliances—where several other family members also work—and I met him both in his family's sukkah and in his office to learn about his interpretation of the Lubavitch customs related to sukkah construction and use. Beginning with memories of his youth in Crown Heights, Mayer echoes what Joseph had recalled: "The energy in 770—people would ask what it was like and I can't explain it, that energy—it was truly beautiful, it was unmatched. Succos was an extremely festive, happy time, especially as a kid—to have off eight days off was incredible." Mayer's memory of the neighborhood's atmosphere throughout the ritual week is characterized by the intensity of singing, dancing, and spiritual enlightenment.

Regarding the custom of not decorating the sukkah, to which Mayer adheres, he explained,

> There's something about customs that's very important—there's an appreciation that it's a custom. No one took out the decorations, or said don't focus on it because they didn't appreciate it. The decorations are really nice, and that's the problem. You're making it very beautiful and then appreciating just the beauty of it, getting distracted by the superficiality of it. Chabad philosophy as a whole is that we try to not be distracted by the superficiality of it, not because it's not beautiful—on the contrary, we appreciate its beauty—but because it shouldn't be what controls us. The more you're distracted and thinking about the mundane physicality of it, the more you will, by nature, end up losing the main point. So do I appreciate decorations? Yes. When I go into someone's sukkah that's decorated, do I like it? Of course! But I also appreciate what our custom is trying to do.

Mayer continued by singling out the schach as the most significant material of construction but did not dwell on details of the structure's materiality. Rather, he focused on the symbolic meaning of the whole architecture by sharing a story of the Baal Shem Tov, the mystical eighteenth-century rabbi who is considered the founder of Hasidic Judaism.

> One year, the Baal Shem Tov called all the rabbis of the town to come eat in his sukkah. They all looked at his sukkah and said, "Is this kosher?" And they all debated it because he had built a sukkah that had so many issues that it was a real question whether it was kosher or not. The story goes, he

had to hang a paper from above saying that it was kosher. So what was the point of the sukkah? Why did he have to make a sukkah that was maybe not kosher? Why not just make a simple sukkah? One of the Baal Shem Tov's main things was about accepting and loving everyone but keeping to your core beliefs. He wanted to build a sukkah that would bring everybody in, so he made a sukkah that was so questionably kosher, to get that person who was so out there . . . He wanted a sukkah to represent that person. I found that story amazing, the concept that the walls themselves, the whole structure, is a message of inclusion, that the Baal Shem Tov made himself this crazy sukkah just to make a statement to everyone. That was his point—that it's not about my sukkah, it's about making a message about other people.

Mayer appreciated custom, and he appreciated intention. "The whole point is that our physical life and our spiritual life should not be two separate lives, they should be one," he concluded. In Mayer's practice, the sukkah is a physical structure that reflects, communicates, and nurtures the value of inclusion through its spiritual purpose and use.

Rabbi Ephraim Piekarski

Rabbi Ephraim Piekarski is Joseph's father and the former headmaster at Educational Institute Oholei Torah, the main yeshiva in Crown Heights. He is a well-known and well-respected leader in the community. Rabbi Piekarski grew up in Crown Heights in the 1950s in what he describes as a tenement apartment building across the street from 770 Eastern Parkway. Although the building was demolished and replaced by a hotel, he still remembers the kitchen windows of the apartments in that building that opened out into an interior courtyard where, he recalled, "My father, may he rest in peace, would bang together doors, those old doors with glass in them. He'd take one piece of wood and use it to bang four or five doors all together to make a wall," which he used to build their sukkah each year. His family's close proximity to the Rebbe's home and office in 770 Eastern Parkway was not insignificant, and Rabbi Piekarski summarized the relationship between the physical and spiritual landscapes of his youth with an anecdote:

> In the fifties, the Cold War was very cold, and in school they would tell us about air raids and what to do—put your head between your knees—and if the sirens go off, what to do. One day I realized, and I asked the teacher to make sure, "Wait a second, how much time between when the siren rings and the bombs actually hit?" And she said, three or four minutes. So

I said, "I have no problem. I live right across from 770. As soon as I hear the sirens, I'll run to 770 and I will be safe. I'll have no problem. The Rebbe is there, and I'm protected." I really believed it. I really believed it then. I don't think I have that naiveté or faith now, but then I really believed it as a child. And I'm happy that I believed like that then—it served me well.

The faith with which Rabbi Piekarski was raised has changed form but not strength over the course of his life. Although he may not believe that the spiritual power of his Rebbe can shield him from the ravages of war, he does believe that spirituality can have affective power. He explained this by interpreting the schach as having such spiritual power. To describe it, he first distinguished between two concepts in Lubavitch Jewish thought—immanence and transcendence:

> We can understand in theology or philosophy that there's a certain aspect that's immanent in the sense that it's penetrating to you, that it goes into you; and there's a certain feeling that is transcendent, encompassing, something that is too big for a person to take it in or have it permeate him because the experience is too great. It's the difference between listening to a lecture and going to a concert. Listening to a lecture, if you don't understand what the lecturer is saying, you're not going to go away with anything. But if you go to a concert . . . you don't have to know what the lyrics are, it's not important at all—it's the beat, the music, and the atmosphere. And it's the same thing with spirituality. There's a certain part of spirituality that a person can attain by learning, by praying, but then there's a certain other kind of experience—an outer worldly experience that you attain just by being in a certain environment. The reason we can't take it in is because the revelation or spirituality is much greater than we can attain, we can't really internalize it, but we're affected by it. Let's say we meet a great person: it's not what he's saying that's always important, it's his aura, it's what he gives over, but you really can't say what effect it has on you. What did he tell you? It's not important what he told you. I was in the presence of greatness. We call this a transcendent feeling.
>
> Now, the sukkah is called a sukkah because of the main aspect, the schach, which encompasses us, it's over our head. It encompasses all of us—a baby, a child, an adult, a sage, we all fit into the same sukkah; we all do the same mitzvah. How could that be? When a child prays and an adult prays, it's a different kind of affair. We observe with different depths, different meanings, different kinds of intellect. But here you're saying, "No, the sukkah is the same for all, the sukkah encompasses everybody and everybody takes from the sukkah whatever they're going to take."

> The holiness of the sukkah is manifested by the schach, the covering, which symbolizes something that is transcendent. As opposed to something that is immanent. This is such a great and powerful holiness, so great for us that we are afraid to sleep in it. That's what one of the rebbes said, that he's afraid to sleep in such a place because it's too holy of a place to sleep in. He's afraid of the revelations . . . I guess it's somewhat mystical, or more than somewhat, and not explainable.

From this explanation, Rabbi Piekarski identifies three basic concepts that shape his ritual practice. First, he distinguishes two forms of spiritual experience—one that may penetrate one's being and one that transcends it. He understands the two as halves of a whole spiritual self. Second, he recognizes the roof covering of the sukkah as an instrument of transcendence, an affective element of the structure that allows ineffable understanding to take place. Third, he recognizes the power of intensely spiritual experience by noting that Lubavitcher Jews choose not to sleep in the sukkah, "not because we are less observant or we don't care about it," he says, but because "where's there's transcendence, you cannot sleep. You cannot afford to sleep there. This has been our mantra. We were taught by our leaders throughout the generations that we do not sleep in a sukkah." There is a respect for the custom and a respect for the spiritual power.

When I asked Rabbi Piekarski about the lack of decoration of the sukkah in the Lubavitch community, he said, "We strike out for the decorations, but it has to be put into context." Two explanations, one practical and one philosophical, explain the custom. The practical explanation is rooted in the Lubavitch community's country of origin, Russia, which Rabbi Piekarski compared to the native countries of other neighboring Orthodox communities in Brooklyn:

> The Chabad community is a Russian community as opposed to other communities, like the Borough Park community or the Williamsburg community. They grew up in Poland, Hungary, and we grew up in Russia under the tsar. Even before communism but certainly after communism came, after 1917 or those years, the economic situation was much worse in Russia than it was in other countries and I think that people were really just happy to get together some boards and some straw and make a sukkah. They were just happy to do that, because they couldn't afford it. While in the Hungarian, Polish, even Lithuanian communities, the economic situation was better than it was in Russia. Therefore, no jokes, there was no money to buy *tchotchkes* (Yiddish: knickknacks).

This explanation related religious custom to the economic conditions of life in late eighteenth-century Russia, and it acknowledged the adaptability of Jewish ritual to the constraints of actual circumstances.

Rabbi Piekarski's second explanation addressed the philosophical reasons for the absence of decorations in the Lubavitch sukkah:

> Let's talk about only Orthodox Jews for a second here. Now, Orthodox Jews know that there's a God, and He gave us the Torah on Sinai, and we have to do all the commandments in the Torah because if we do, *HaShem* [God] will give us everything that we want: a wife, children, money, the world to come, we'll go to heaven, and we'll have the most blissful life in the world. I could say that, to a great extent, today in America, Orthodox Jews are getting rewarded in full spades—they really have a good life. And that if you don't observe the Torah, you're going to have this calamity and that calamity and HaShem will punish you and eventually you're going to hell. Fine, end of story. That's what I call Classical Judaism—the notion that doing a mitzvah is a good thing, that I'm doing what God wants and it's a good feeling, and that if we observe the holiday properly He'll take care of us. It's a warm and fuzzy feeling. We want to show our appreciation by doing the mitzvah as beautifully as possible. Okay? Here's an example. When a person buys an *estrog* (Yiddish: etrog), you could buy a twenty-dollar or thirty-dollar estrog, but anybody with a few dollars in his pocket will not pay less than four hundred dollars for an estrog because that's not a way to do it. Two hundred dollars was the going price for an estrog last year but if you have extra dollars you will pay five hundred dollars for an estrog.
>
> We don't look at Judaism exactly the same way though. Everything Classical Judaism is saying is true—we do what God wants, and God is going to reward us or not—but I want to ask you a question. Let's take the archetypal grown child and parent: should he respect his parents? One-hundred percent. Why should he respect his parents? Should there be a "why"? And an answer? Or should there be no question? There should be no question. You wouldn't want there to be a "why" because for every "why" there is a "because." And once there is a "because," then you're not respecting that person, you're respecting the "because." If we're doing the mitzvah because HaShem is giving us a reward, we only care about the reward. That's how we see it. If you're doing mitzvahs because of the reward or because of fear of punishment, then we're not connecting to the parent, you're connecting to the "because."
>
> By us, a mitzvah isn't fuzzy; it's a way of saying we're connecting to HaShem. It should be a sort of losing oneself and giving oneself over to HaShem and not trying to make oneself feel good so I can check off the list that I'm doing a good thing today. It shouldn't be that type of worship. It should be more of a transcendent worship—that it's not about me, it's about HaShem, it's about me subjugating myself, about me giving myself over. That's important to get.

Transcending Architecture: Sukkot *in Brooklyn, New York* | 207

Rabbi Piekarski distinguishes Lubavitch Judaism from Classical Judaism by focusing on the intention behind religious practice, and specifically on the centrality of HaShem and not the ego. He summarizes this by invoking the words of Jewish philosopher Martin Buber, explaining: "You know there are Hasids and *Misnagdim*, or non-Hasids. And also, the word for God in Hasidism or mysticism is *Ein Sof* [no end]. So, Martin Buber said, 'The *misnaged* wants to find himself in the Ein Sof, and the Hasid wants to lose himself in the Ein Sof.' I think that answers all the questions. That's the key of the game." In order to connect with God in a pure and complete way, he says, one must let go of an awareness of the self and external conditions. Rabbi Piekarski then connected this principle to the decoration of the sukkah:

> The beauty of all sitting together and the unity and everything that's beautiful about Succos, it's true, but there's something much deeper. There's no mitzvah in the beautification of the sukkah per se—the mitzvah itself is the schach. So get good schach, schach that's fresh, schach that doesn't fall into your soup, and that's good. The commandment of the sukkah has nothing to do with decoration—the rules are very clear. There are three or four walls and the schach on top, and that's it. In fact, we're told that the schach has to be something that is not a fruit, just the leftover hay so to speak. After you harvest all your grain and everything else, all the leftover stuff is what the schach has to be made of. Therefore, we feel that it's not appropriate. The plainness of the sukkah is what shows us the plainness of the relationship. Sometimes, when something is sophisticated, it loses the intrinsic, basic feeling of the people.

The purity of the structure and the attention to the schach nurture a direct connection to God. They dismiss the possibility of distraction or of focus on the materiality of the structure. Eyes gaze up toward the roof and up toward God as Lubavitch Jews transcend their physical world through the spirit of the schach.

In her study of a weekly Sabbath tea ritual at a Jewish retirement home in Toronto, Canada, Jillian Gould realized that despite the elderly residents' appreciation of formal table settings and fine dishware in their private home spaces, the shared public space of the Sabbath tea engendered contrasting attitudes. She observed that "the 'existing value' of the tea and table settings are not the material objects and consumer products, but rather the creation of home through hospitality . . . the domestic ideal is not material, but rather social" (2013, 203–4). Gould witnessed residents create "home" in a public space each week through social engagement and visibility, rather than through object arrangement and décor. Her observations may apply to Lubavitch Jewish Sukkot observance as well: while private homes are filled with Judaica and holy texts, the home space of the sukkah remains bare, a testament to the primacy of the transcendent relationship rather than the material that defines this spiritual domesticity.

Notes

1. The Lubavitch movement is otherwise known as *Chabad*, a transliterated acronym from the Hebrew words for wisdom *chokhmah*, understanding (*binah*) and knowledge *da'at*, concepts upon which the movement is founded. While I refer to the community as "Lubavitch" for consistency, several community members used "Chabad" interchangeably in our conversations and I present their words as they spoke them.

2. Many ethnographies of the Lubavitch community in Crown Heights, and of Hasidic communities in the United States more broadly, provide detailed context for the vignettes presented here. See Belcove-Shalin, Janet S. 1995. *New World Hasidim: Ethnographic Studies of Hasidic Jews in America*. Albany, NY; Fishkoff, Sue. 2003. *The Rebbe's Army: Inside the World of Chabad-Lubavitch*. New York; Goldschmidt, Henry. 2006. *Race and Religion among the Chosen Peoples of Crown Heights*. New Brunswick, NJ; Mintz, Jerome R. 1992. *Hasidic People: A Place in the New World*. Cambridge, MA.

3. Mishnah Sukkah 2:4 describes the occasions when one is obligated to perform a mitzvah or not, specifically with regard to Sukkot observance.

Conclusion

In their individual, creative interpretations of the sukkah, the American and Israeli Jews described in this book confront essential paradoxes that the sukkah embodies between religious values and life circumstances, between an unfulfilled present and an ideal of the future. Under its ritual roof, the sukkah unites materiality and spirituality, wilderness and domestication, transience and permanence, friend and stranger, reality and dream.

From Bloomington to South Tel Aviv to Brooklyn, the builders and users who encounter these contradictions span the full range of spiritual belief, from secular to traditional to Orthodox Judaism, creating an endless variety of material expression. Sukkot are erected beside swimming pools and in parking lots, elaborate interiors sparkle with chandeliers and tinsel streamers, and bare walls are illuminated by single light bulbs.

All these builders and users define a fundamental philosophy—a conviction—that guides their Sukkot observance. These principles, together with the potential for innovation in the sukkah, nourish a tradition that has sustained holiday observance for over three thousand years. For those who observe the holiday, the sukkah expresses personal ideals of self, community, home, and the future with renewed relevance each year. Whether it is experienced as an ephemeral ritual architecture, a home space along a journey of migration, or a permanent shelter, the sukkah is a source of self-realization and social cohesion for its builders and users.

The varied examples presented in this book offer several insights into the implications of contemporary Sukkot observance whose significance extends beyond the holiday's original religious purpose. By relating holiday practice to current conditions, needs, and desires, builders and users draw upon an ancient ritual as a valuable resource for contemporary life. The following five implications of Sukkot observance enrich our understanding of the builders' and users' intentions and of the role that the sukkah plays in the realization of self and society.

Objects and their Reach

The study of material things in folklore, anthropology, and related disciplines has flourished in recent decades, expanding into its own field of material culture studies. Scholars now find meaning not only in the physical investigation of an object and how it is made, but in how it circulates through different lives, how it is used in one way and reused in another, and the value it accrues and loses depending on the material objects and cultural beliefs that surround it—in other words, the focus has widened to appreciate the "social life" of the object as much as the object itself.[1] As material things, the sukkot in this book may be considered as aesthetically rich creations whose physical structure and ornamentation present information about their builders' and users' interior worlds; these material objects embedded in social contexts reveal the relationships that their builders and users cultivate through their creation.

In Bloomington, Indiana, Bakol Geller and Yonit Kosovske each built a sukkah that reflected the intersection of several identities. The materials with which Yonit constructed the frame of her sukkah evoked her past experiences and communicated her current values. She connects to Judaism by connecting with the environment, building her sukkah out of gathered tree branches and brush, and camping on Jewish holidays "to bring the divine energy that's outside into our hectic lives and into Judaism, and not just have it be something in the synagogue." Similarly, the objects that embellished the interiors of both Yonit's and Bakol's sukkot—Israeli symbols, embroidered textiles, family heirlooms—connected them to the places they once lived, such as Israel, Spain, California, and to aspects of their personalities like artist, naturalist, mother, and Jew, which this holiday enables them to express. Selecting materials that thread their past and present together, they invoke the people and places that narrate their personal histories. Both women observe Sukkot because they can tailor it to their individual understandings of the Jewish aspects of their lives that are shaped by belonging to a Jewish minority in a largely Christian Midwestern American community.

Beyond the meaning of personal objects that are exhibited, the entire sukkah as an object is on display in Shaul Moyal's life, mediating relationships between history and the present. Growing up in a poor Jewish quarter of Morocco, Shaul dreamed of the stability and beauty that he would one day build into his sukkah. Today, the carved wooden walls, bejeweled interior, and glittering lights of his ritual structure represent a permanent home and a place to continue imagining the future. "There is no end to beauty," says Shaul finding abiding refuge in his sukkah as a place of possibility, artistry, and hope. Complementing her father's view, Sivan recognizes the resilience built into the sukkah's ephemeral form: "The portability of the sukkah meant do not despair, do not lose hope. It was destroyed? So build it again." Constructing the sukkah with her father is a ritual of perseverance and an expression of love—the foundation of her Jewish practice. The construction of the material form is a manifestation of potential for both Shaul and Sivan—the potential of beauty and the potential of love.

The objects that adorn the sukkah's walls, as well as the whole sukkah itself, are forms of communication, signs that signal the people, the places, and the values that ground us in our home space.

Equality

James Clifford has reflected upon changing conceptions of self and other in an era of displacement and replacement. Particularly in the context of Diaspora studies, he warns that "theories and discourses that diasporize or internationalize 'minorities' can deflect attention from long-standing, structured inequalities of class and race" (1994, 313). He recognizes that deep structures of sociopolitical power perpetuate discrimination while being masked by claims of "progress," and mobility. Expanding Clifford's argument, this book illustrates how the minority status of individuals is defined in the contexts of migration and immigration, and how the possibility of full equality is imagined through the ritual of Sukkot. It demonstrates how individuals affirm selfhood and build community through expressive cultural practices like Sukkot observance in spite of social, economic, and political limitations that impede their attainment of full equality.

Drori Yehoshua views the structure of the sukkah as an architecture of equality, or what he calls "a space of meeting," a form built on neutral ground that unites heaven and earth, stranger and friend, rich and poor. During the holiday week, when the lines between host and guest are blurred, he considers how to establish a just society from the ground up, an ideal that challenges the reality of the social and economic hierarchies of power that structure Israeli society—ones that shaped his parents' lives as new immigrants and his own as a first-generation Kurdish Israeli. "There's power in this holiday to awaken ideas of pluralism, or for discussion and bridges between cultures, to enable cultural connections, to make space to think about borders between people," he said. In the metaphoric moment before arriving in the Promised Land, Drori immerses himself in a space that cultivates ties to his family and connections to strangers, enacting his belief that social difference and social equality can coexist.

Through the decoration of his sukkah, Drori also articulates how historic discrimination against Jews of Middle Eastern and North African descent in Israel has shaped his sense of self and his interpretation of Sukkot rituals. Drori borrows the aged tapestries that hang over the holy arks in his mother's and father's Kurdish synagogues in Jerusalem to adorn the walls of his sukkah. His material construction is a personal reconstruction of the Kurdish heritage that he strives to assert in the wake of the social struggles that his parents faced as Kurdish Jews. As he gazes upon the embroidered fabrics, he says, "What more does a man need to say than where his father and his mother are from? It's a kind of identity." Drori's sukkah provides a space in which he may embrace his Kurdish identity on neutral ground through its material display, as well as through his reflections on ethnic equality throughout the holiday week.

Dror Kahalani, raised with limited economic resources in Shchunat Hatikva, also views the world through constellations of experience that have challenged his faith in justice and equality. Sitting with his family in the sukkah that he builds by himself each year, he tries to reconcile what he considers to be Jewish values of humility, contentment, generosity, and love with the socioeconomic struggles that continually shake his experience of fairness and equality in strife-ridden South Tel Aviv. In his ritual practice and religious worldview, Dror depended on the value of individual labor and a relativistic perspective on his place in life to sustain his faith and tradition in a fractured social world. "You can't believe in God if you don't believe in yourself first," said Dror. "God doesn't just give me a sukkah if I pray for it. I have to cut down the branches, build it myself... first of all, I have to believe in myself!" Dror believed in himself because his life experiences had taught him not to expect anything that he did not earn, but social equality is not guaranteed through hard work. Drawing upon the symbolic potential of the sukkah to equalize difference for one week each year, however, Dror and his family bridge their disillusionments and dreams as they celebrate Sukkot.

Ephemerality

The sukkah's symbolic potential is endless, but its material form is fleeting. The experience of building and inhabiting the sukkah endures while the physical structure itself appears and disappears, paradoxically ensuring a lasting architectural form. Through reinvested reading and recurring performance, the architecture is renewed. How does the sukkah's material transience influence the meaning that builders and users make of its structure and space?

In her study of ephemeral vernacular responses to the September 11, 2001, attacks on New York's World Trade Center, such as street shrines and memorials, Kay Turner identified the importance of recognizing ephemeral expression in folklore studies, a discipline centered on issues of temporality, "the mother of tradition" (Turner 2009, 158). The study of ephemerality deepens our awareness of the passing of time through its impermanence: "Ephemerality humanizes time by referring us to the exigencies of our mortality," says Turner (159). In the ritual of sukkah construction and use, the performance of self and the awareness of the present are heightened as notions of the eternal, as well as of life and death, invest the evanescent experience with meaning.

The individuals in this book who reflected upon the temporary nature of the Sukkot ritual were acutely aware of what is lasting in life. Material ephemerality made them consider spiritual permanence, the awareness of each illuminating the other. In Shchunat Hatikva, David Zada from Persia recognized the permanent shelter of his impermanent ritual dwelling. The distinction he made between the permanence of his sukkah and the impermanence of his actual house was framed by a lifetime of displacement and economic struggle: material things are mutable while the sukkah is a recurrent shelter, temporally and metaphorically. "The sukkah is similar to a house, but the house is temporary—it comes and goes—while the sukkah is forever," he declared. "In the Talmud, it is written that the sukkah is a metaphor for what is eternal." The sukkah "humanizes time" by awakening us not only to the exigencies of our mortality, as Turner observes, but also to the possibilities of immortality.

In the Lubavitch community of Brooklyn, the intensity of a religious community's faith and practice is evident. Communion with God is all-encompassing in the sukkah and decoration is deemed a distraction—a striking contrast to the practices demonstrated in Bloomington and South Tel Aviv. Endowing the sukkah with ritual qualities, the sukkah's impermanence provides these observers with a time out of time and a place out of place. For Lubavitcher Jews, the sukkah is a place to transcend the material and ascend toward the spiritual to which their lives are devoted. In the sukkah, individuals temporarily immerse their entire physical selves in transcendent holiness. Sukkah construction is a temporary material means to an infinite spiritual end.

Despite its disappearance when the holiday ends the sukkah continues to signify shelter throughout the year by virtue of its ability to reliably reappear, a reminder of the limited lifespan of our physical worlds.

The Right to House and Home

Personal histories of migration shape conceptions of home for people throughout the world. The annual holiday of Sukkot provides an ideal framework within which to examine notions of home because its narrative and observance commemorate an historic migration. In reenacting this journey for a full week, observers of the holiday are allowed time for reflection on dislocation and space for social performance regarding that experience. Through this reenactment, the experience of change and the ideal of home are expressed through material creation, social action, and interpretive discourse.

In her study of folk dwellings in Southwestern North Carolina (1991), Michael Ann Williams pioneered a new approach: rather than document only architectural artifacts, she collected oral testimony from the inhabitants about how they used their houses and the meaning they invested in them. The value of these oral narratives, she observed, lies in the fact that "they are not memories of artifacts once removed from the real thing; they constitute direct evidence in and of themselves," and in fact, "The homeplace . . . is often 'preserved' through narrative rather than through the physical rehabilitation of the structure itself" (20). Williams proposed that these narratives do not reconstruct physical sites but fulfill a wholly different purpose—they "preserve" the site through the recounting of intangible, ineffable aspects of its place, aspects not evident in the physical structure alone. The process of recounting these narratives may be likened to the process of building a sukkah: both are expressive forms that recreate home, but not with the goal of achieving the physical likeness of a former structure—rather, of conveying new information about that "homeplace" that reflects its use and significance to the builder and user. In this way, each narrative and each sukkah is a recreation and original performance at once, bridging historical precedents and contemporary realities.

The examples of sukkah construction described in this book illustrate not only the reconstruction of a symbolic house in physical form, but the construction of a home through interpretation and use. Williams noted about her interviews, "Most people did not remember a house; they remembered a home" (4). Similarly, in their constructions, sukkah builders and users transformed their symbolic houses into homes through their association with meaningful people, places, spiritual beliefs, or political ideals, communicated through intentional aesthetic design and narrative interpretation.

In Shchunat Hatikva, rather than leave the neighborhood they called home because of the dangers surrounding them, David and Edna Zada and their son, Uriel, turned inward and created a safe space through faith and family. By placing God at their center and strengthening their belief in Jewish custom and law, they secured themselves in this world and the next amid unpredictability and change. They built a sukkah that sheltered them from their everyday environment, a spiritual home that unfailingly grounded and protected them.

Conversely, Yoram Meshumar and his family honor a Jewish practice that is outward-facing. Through Yoram's belief in the values of hospitality and generosity—his motto being "Never close the door to the world"—and their intensified expression in his sukkah, Yoram creates home through community. By enacting his core values of gratitude and grace during this ritual week, he incorporates himself into society and incorporates others into his sukkah—his home.

Beyond these individual examples of family observance, the ritual of Sukkot as a recreation of house and home were publically reimagined en masse during the worldwide economic crisis of 2011 as the Occupy Movement took force across the globe. The absence of fair housing due to glaring socioeconomic inequalities converged with the holiday's commemoration of shelter, protection, equality, and community. Protesters reclaimed the sukkah as an instrument of political empowerment, a tradition whose narrative expressed the ongoing struggle for equality and justice. As Pazit said of the residents of Shchunat Hatikva who had built and inhabited sukkot next to their protest tents in the park, they had never had a ba'al bayit feeling—a feeling of home ownership, since their families' immigration to Israel. And as Emmanuel Levinas said, recalled by Pazit, "Man is nothing without a home, for only in a state of 'at-homeness' may one give and share with others." The right to fair housing was also the right to sovereignty over self, the right to home.

In all of these examples, the sukkah is a tangible representation of an intangible ideal. Physical shelter becomes a metaphor for shelter from social, cultural, and political strife. The rebuilding of the sukkah each year is the ongoing creation of a place to call home, and a reclamation of the right to own it.

Memory and Modernity

During Sukkot of 2010 and 2011, Baruch Rada of Rehovot, Israel, showed me into the worn, prefabricated metal sukkah that his neighbors shared each night of the holiday. Baruch and his family immigrated to Israel in 1984 via Operation Moses after walking from Ethiopia to Sudan, where they had lived in refugee camps for over a year. More than thirty generations of his family in Ethiopia had dreamed of seeing Jerusalem, which they had invoked in their prayers throughout their lives. And all of those generations had built sukkot in Ethiopia every year, entirely woven of tree branches and brush. When I asked Baruch why he did not build his sukkah out of natural materials in Israel, he paused with surprise and said, "Why would I do that? I'm in a modern state now!" The opportunity to change the materials of construction in a new setting invites individuals to reassess their relationship to tradition and make design and decoration choices that reflect a changed identity and status.

Baruch and his wife, Meital, live in a low-income apartment complex in a neighborhood of Rehovot populated by Ethiopian Jews. Meital comes home exhausted from cleaning houses every day, but when I asked her if she missed Ethiopia, she said, "Miss it? What's there to miss? There's nothing there!" Her neighbor Lea Chekol, however, who cleans offices and bathrooms eight hours a day, seven days a week, responded differently. In Israel, she said, she and her Ethiopian neighbors work so hard that much of the time they cannot socialize with each other as they did in Ethiopia. "Many neighbors and friends cannot be with us in the sukkah in the evening because they're at work," Lea lamented.

Fig. 8.1. Baruch Rada demonstrates how he built a sukkah in Ethiopia before he immigrated to Israel. He holds a branch between two pieces of wood to show how leaves were woven to create the structure's frame. Rehovot, Israel. 2010.

In Ethiopia, they would take the whole week of Sukkot off from work and sit together in the sukkah every night with home-roasted coffee, home-brewed beer, and roasted wheat berries, among other delicacies. Lea immigrated to Israel in 1994 after Christian Ethiopians began burning the homes of Ethiopian Jews, declaring that they did not belong. Nevertheless, she said missed the space and rhythm of rural life in Ethiopia that had been supplanted by the economic pressure and speed of urban Israeli life.

During the week of Sukkot, however, all of Lea's neighbors who were home in the evening descended from the apartment building where they lived, bringing chairs, a radio, home-brewed beer and coffee, a gas burner, and pots of food to share in the sukkah. Hosting responsibilities rotated to a different neighbor each night, as they did in Ethiopia, and the group sat for hours in a circle inside the bare structure with brush hanging down, listening to music on the radio,

Fig. 8.2. From the outside during the day, the prefabricated sukkah that the Ethiopian Jewish residents of this building share appears empty and unused. Each evening of the holiday, however, neighbors gather together inside with food and drink, filling it with celebration and warmth. Rehovot, Israel. 2010.

Fig. 8.3. Neighbors in this Ethiopian Jewish community sit together in their shared sukkah each night of the holiday, rotating hosting responsibilities as they did in Ethiopia. They bring chairs, music, and homemade food and drink. Rehovot, Israel. 2010.

laughing, talking, eating, drinking, and re-creating the social experience they lost in migration. The sukkah's atmosphere makes it special, said Lea, and the people, not the structure, create that atmosphere.

While Baruch and Meital struggled to meet the demands of work, during Sukkot they gratefully connected themselves to Israel through the sukkah's prefabricated frame, a physical, visual proof of modernity. Lea, however, longed for the human connection and social space of her past life in Ethiopia, and she rediscovered herself and her community in homemade Ethiopian food and drink and the gathering rituals of Sukkot. Celebrating material and social aspects of Sukkot rituals empowers these individuals to feel at home in altered surroundings and to create stability in the face of change. Nostalgic remembrance of ritual performance enables them to move forward with tradition toward new goals, inspiring themselves and their community to persevere.

In all the Sukkot narratives that were shared with me, people recalled the sukkot of their childhood when their families built these ritual structures out of different materials, in different places, and different times. Tender memories, like Shaul Moyal's recollection of the fragility of his childhood sukkah in Morocco, represent a past intentionally left behind but memorialized as a foundation to be continually built upon. Poignant memories—like Dror Kahalani's depiction of his extended family taking turns eating in his grandmother's narrow sukkah—that everyone was nourished despite their meager living conditions, serve to recall a former period of cohesion and harmony created together. Joyful memories, like Yoram Meshumar's recollection of the happy hours of communal sukkah construction with his entire family, celebrate the strength of community despite a dearth of social and material comfort. Although Shchunat Hatikva's history in the 1970s and 1980s was indisputably troubled by crime, poverty, and neglect, memories of the neighborhood that individuals shared recalled a place where people knew and visited one another, where hard work was needed and valued, where there was more time, more patience, and more respect. Their memories are filled with longing.

In his ethnographic study of the material culture of a Northern Irish community, Ray Cashman asserts the positive function of nostalgic reminiscence prompted by the collections of antique domestic objects and farm equipment that he observed in peoples' homes, yards, and community spaces. Countering over a century of change, nostalgic practices serve as "a reclamation of individual agency" that enable people to participate in modernity's changes with more or less willingness (2006, 146). The process of sukkah construction demonstrates how Cashman's observation is put into practice through material means; however, because of its temporary and recurring qualities, the sukkah distinctly allows for continual reorientation to change through opportunities to refashion the structure each year. The materials with which people choose to build and decorate their sukkot signal the extent to which they wish to integrate the changes of modernity into their lives and the extent to which their memories motivate their practice.

* * *

Sukkot provides a ritual week in which to reevaluate histories; select the memories, morals, and messages that shelter people in the present; and imagine a home in the future. Constructing and decorating the sukkah nourishes people's deepest sense of self and place. The exceptional diversity of ornamentation and individualized interpretation that exist in contemporary Sukkot observance testifies to generations of religious and cultural tradition in the North American, Middle Eastern, North African, and Central Asian birthplaces of the sukkah builders and users whom I visited. The sukkah materializes belief, questions permanence, and projects hope. Within it, individuals are neither disadvantaged nor unequal for it is an idealized home, a space where dreams of political, economic, and social equality may be imagined and enacted, if only for one week. Barbara Myerhoff has observed that because rituals are intentionally constructed, they are "opportunities to write history as it should be or should have been, demonstrating a culture's notion of propriety and sense" (1992, 234). The sukkah is a challenge to what has come before and a declaration of what is still yet to come.

The week before I left Shchunat Hatikva, sixteen months of fieldwork after I had arrived, I made my rounds in the neighborhood to say good-bye to all my friends and research collaborators. Everyone urged me to come back soon and to come back straight to their houses when I stepped off the airplane in Israel. "Why rent an apartment when you can sleep in this room?" they would declare, pointing to side rooms used for storage or guests. Many of them said they appreciated the fact that I had experienced the neighborhood as it really is, as a family, and that I had learned from "the school of life."

Today, as physical distances give way to virtual travel, and as individuals increasingly migrate around the world, the search for housing and the yearning for home persist. This book has been an examination of the meaning of house and home for individuals still in the midst of change, either from a single family's resettlement or from generations of migration. Sukkot, a ritual of physical and social placement, offers annual respite from the ongoing search for settlement. It is a ritual of religious origin in which principles about how to live each day in peace are embedded. An active and changing resource, this Jewish ritual empowers individuals to imagine and manifest their ideal states of being. Family, community, equality, relativism, possibility, gratitude, grace, and love all reside within the symbolic space of the sukkah, annually renewing hope for their permanent dwelling in the everyday spaces of our lives. Each year, Drori Yehoshua sits in his sukkah and asks himself: *Now that we are on this journey for forty years in the desert, how do we walk together?* The sukkah creates a place to pause and contemplate how to enter a Promised Land. It is a time to look inward and reach outward to know who we are individually, and who we want to be together.

Notes

1. See, Appadurai 1988; Glassie 1999; Miller 2010; Jackson 2016.

Appendix: Materials Chart and Sukkot Floor Plans

Sukkah Materials Chart

	Year	Size	Location	Structure	Schach (roof)	Furnishings	Decorations
Uriel Zada	2010	L: 13' W: 13' 6" H: 6'8"	Backyard (Shchunat Hatikva)	Frame: prefabricated metal poles reinforced with horizontally placed spare wooden doors and bookcases (to ensure *halakhic* legitimacy) Walls: nylon tarps and white lace sheets	Wooden beams and prefabricated bamboo mats	White plastic table and chairs, twin bed mattresses, rolling desk chair, wall fan, florescent lights, radio, small plastic chair designated as "Elijah's Chair," rugs on ground	Handmade paper chains and drawings of religious icons, photographs of respected rabbis and laminated texts from the Torah, palm branches with bunches of fresh dates
Edna and David Zada	2010	L: 10'5" W: 8'3" H: 7'8"	Second floor terrace (Shchunat Hatikva)	Frame: prefabricated metal poles, bottom half of structure composed of concrete terrace walls Walls: nylon sheets printed with names of *ushpizin* and images of sukkot and Seven Species	Wooden beams and prefabricated bamboo mats	Wooden table and chairs, twin bed mattresses, standing fan, florescent light	Hanging tinsel decorations and garlands, photographs of respected rabbis and laminated texts from the Torah, hanging fresh fruit (etrogs and pomegranates from their own backyard trees)

(Continued)

Sukkah Materials Chart

	Year	Size	Location	Structure	Schach (roof)	Furnishings	Decorations
Yoram Meshumar	2010	L: 13'1" W: 13'1" H: 7'8"	Dirt parking lot across the street from his father's house (Shchunat Hatikva)	Frame: prefabricated metal poles Walls: nylon sheets printed with names of *ushpizin* and images of sukkot, Jerusalem, Seven Species, vertical zipper opens/closes to create a threshold in front wall	Wooden beams and prefabricated bamboo mats	Folding wooden tables and white plastic chairs, twin bed mattresses, wall fan, florescent light, wooden bench, side table for altar, small chair designated as "Elijah's Chair," AstroTurf on ground	Hanging tinsel decorations and garlands, posters of the Temple and texts about Sukkot from the Torah, miniature bottles of liquor hang down from *schach*, palm fronds arch over the doorway and tinsel decorations stand high above the roof, large Star of David made of silver tinsel garlands pinned to the right of the doorway on the sukkah's exterior
Dror Kahalani	2010	L: 11'5" W: 8'2" H: 6'9"	Backyard (Yad Eliyahu)	Frame: prefabricated metal poles Walls: plastic tarps and white sheets	Wooden beams and palm branches cut from nearby trees	Plastic table and chairs, florescent light	Handmade paper chains, lanterns, and paper-cut decorations, drawings of flowers and butterflies made by his daughters
Shaul and Sivan Moyal	2010	L: 15'5" W: 8'2" H: 6'9"	Open plaza below their apartment building, which is built on concrete stilts (Jaffa Dalet)	Frame and walls: eleven wooden walls (two of which serve as doors), screwed together; all but back wall and front doors made of wooden trellis structures with	Wooden beam structure and prefabricated bamboo mats	Handmade and decorated oval table, metal chairs with black- and- white leopard print seats, wall telephone and intercom, fan, clock built into back	Colorful tinsel garlands, plastic Jewels, jewel-covered chandeliers, metallic balls hanging from *schach*, palm trees, suns, and *"succat shalom"* carved into back wall and filled

(Continued)

Appendix | 223

Sukkah Materials Chart

			colorful plastic inserted into empty squares, back wall solid wood with hand-carved designs, filled with colorful plastic, window in right side wall with wooden shutter doors		wall, wall sconces with blue, red lights, hanging, standing chandeliers, fluorescent lights, black-and-white linoleum checkered floor	with green, red, and blue plastic
Drori Yehoshua	2011	L: 19'6" W: 9'8" H: 6'5"	Backyard (Jerusalem)	Frame: prefabricated metal poles passed down from family members Walls: *parochot* (curtain that hangs in front of *aron hakodesh* in the synagogue) from his mother's and father's Kurdish synagogues, backed by white cotton and nylon sheets	Wooden beams and palm branches cut from nearby trees	Two folding tables and white plastic chairs, standing fan	Handmade paper chains and lanterns, holiday cards attached to walls, on table, a framed photograph of his parents on their wedding day standing in front of the holy ark curtain that hangs in his sukkah, quilted mat and flower vase on table

The first image provides a bird's-eye view of the sukkah. The second (left) offers a view of the sukkah from its front, and the third (right) presents a bird's-eye view of the sukkah's schach, or roof covering.

Keys for the floor plans:

¼ inch	= 1 foot
~~	= Fabric sheet or curtain used to make a wall
↓|↓|	= Wooden beam or metal pole (see Sukkah Materials Chart to find out the specific material used for each sukkah)
■	= Adjoining point on prefabricated metal frames where one metal pole locks into another
####	= Prefabricated bamboo mat used for *schach*
(Palm frond)	= Palm branches cut from tree and used for *schach*
"Elijah's Chair"	= a chair left empty or covered with decorative cloths and holy Hebrew texts. This chair is an invitation and space holder for holy guests that visit the sukkah, including Elijah and the seven *ushpizin*.

Appendix | 225

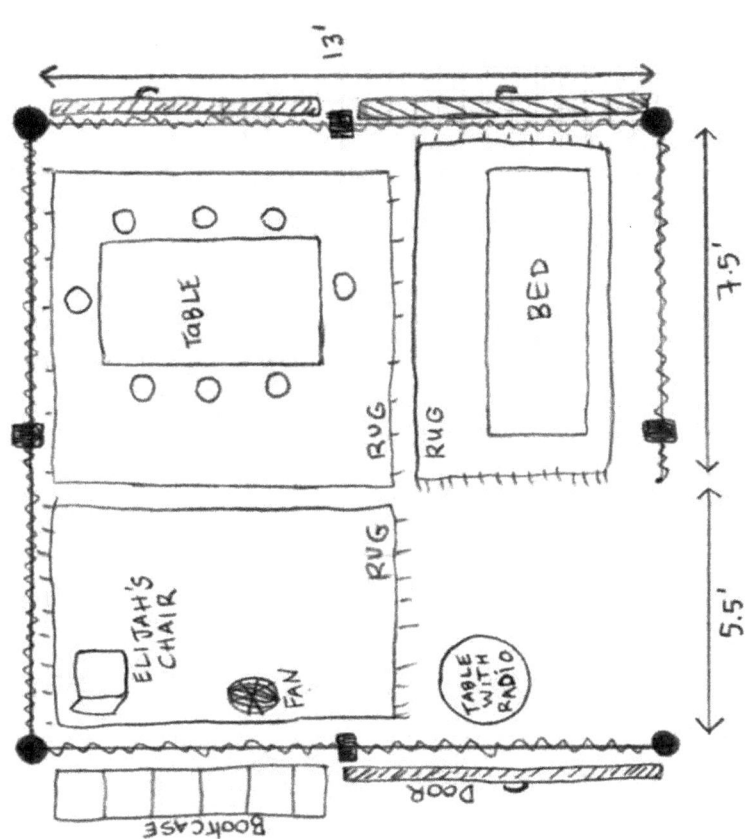

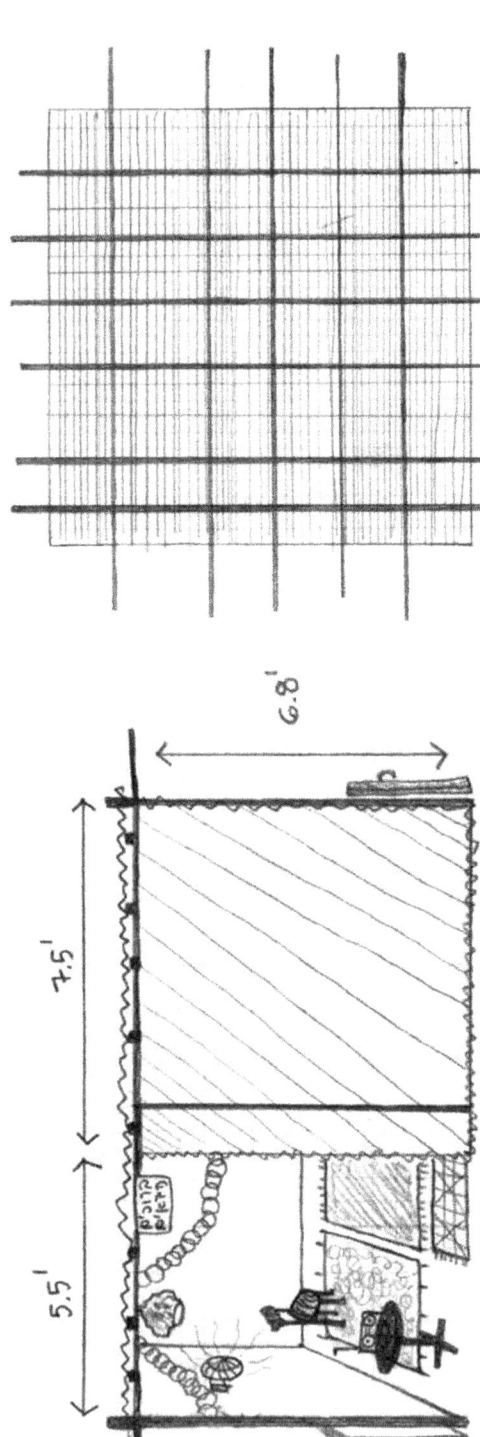

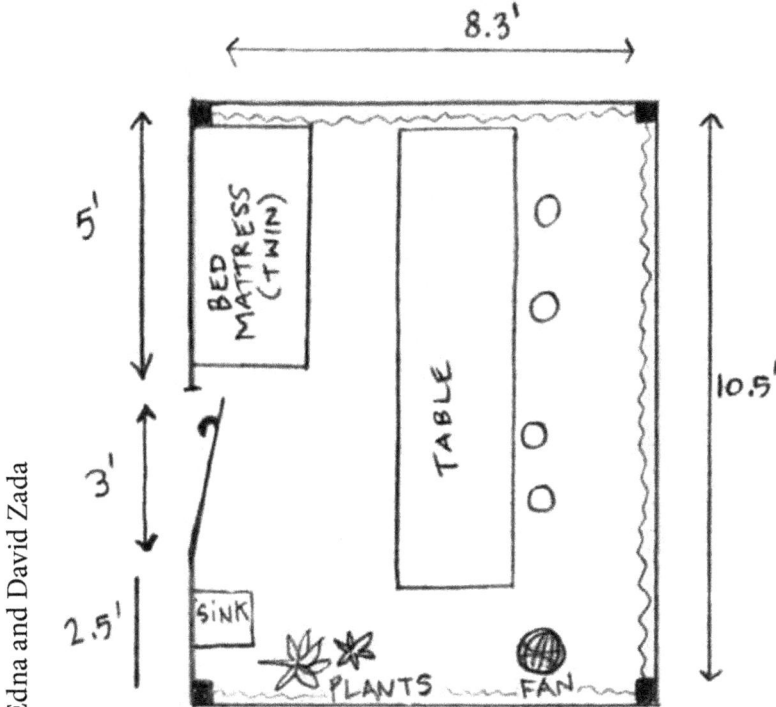

Edna and David Zada

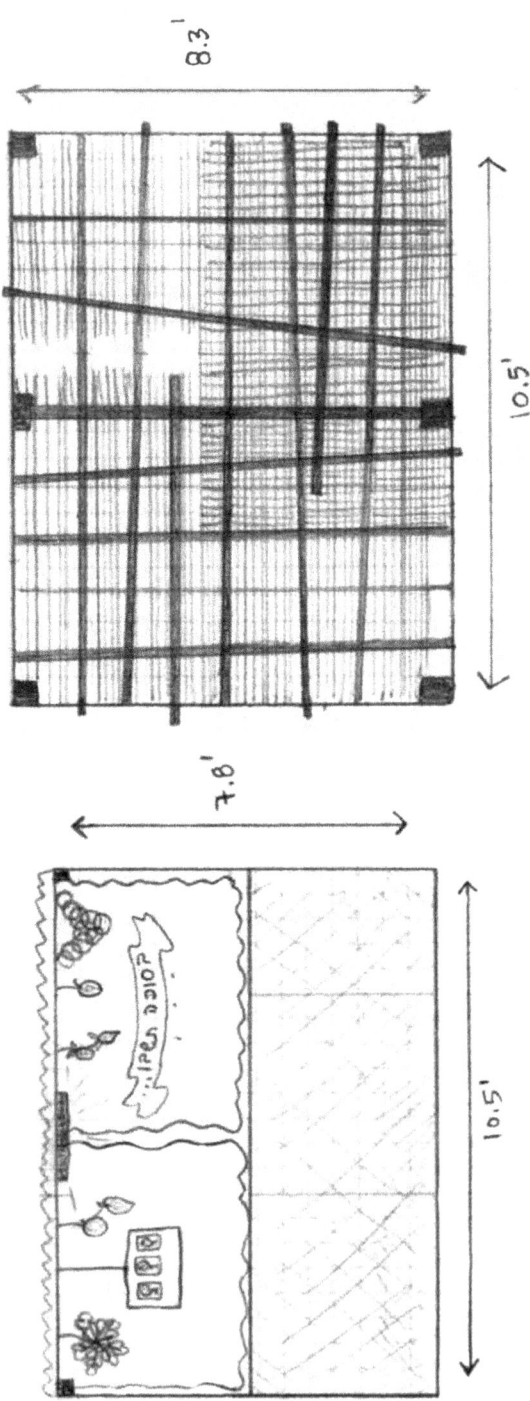

Appendix | 229

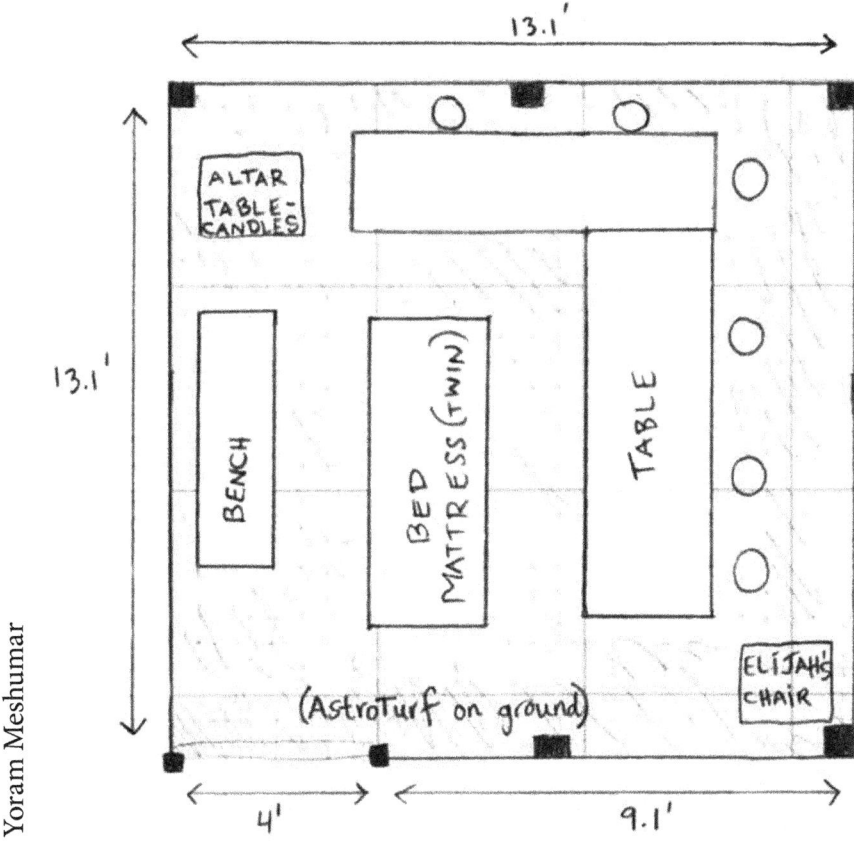

Yoram Meshumar

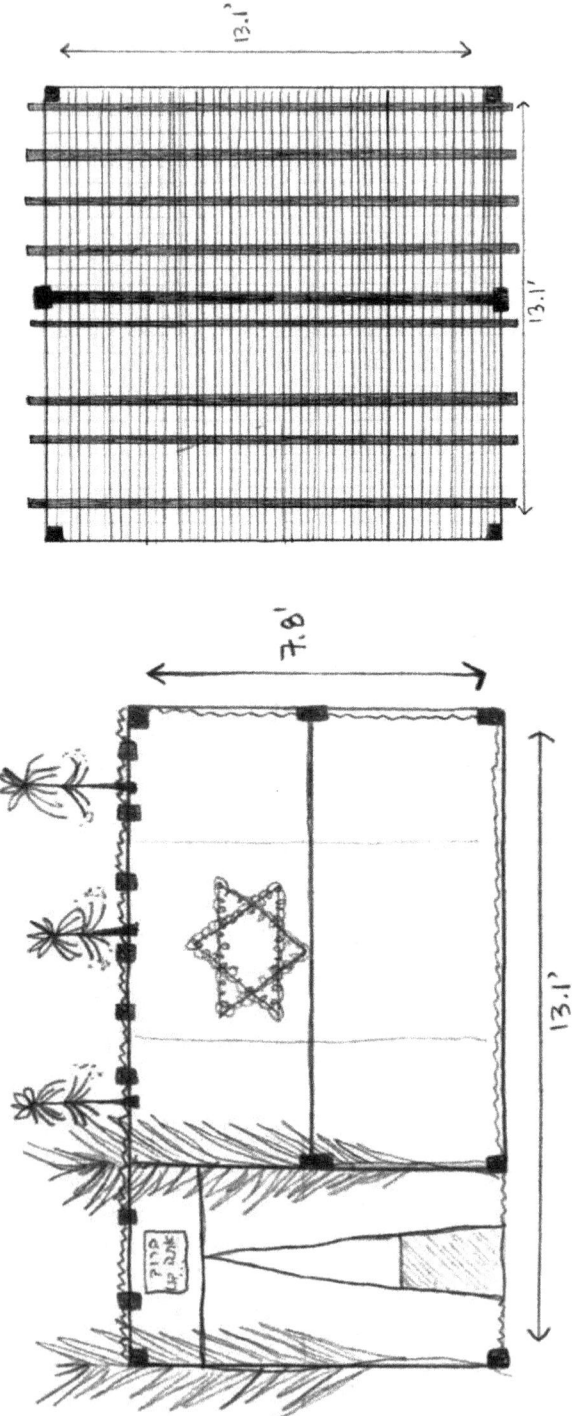

Appendix | 231

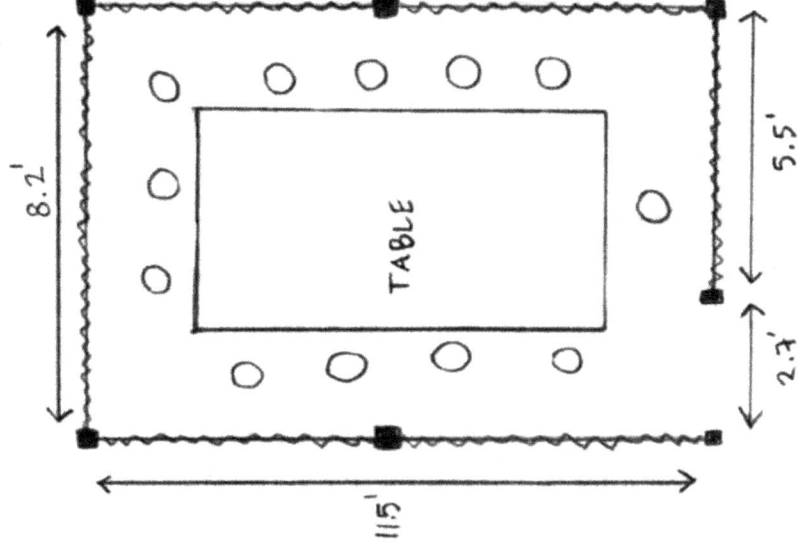

Appendix

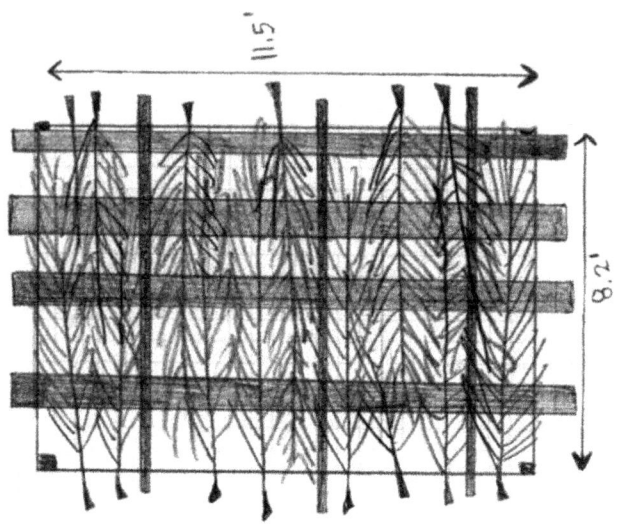

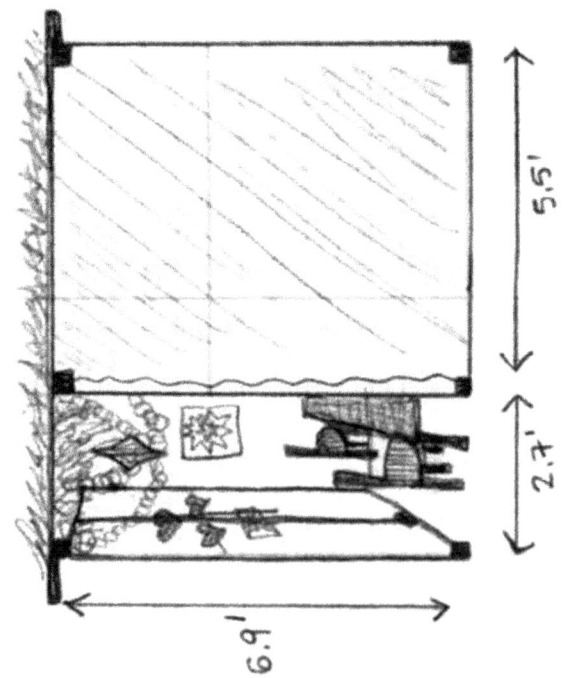

Appendix | 233

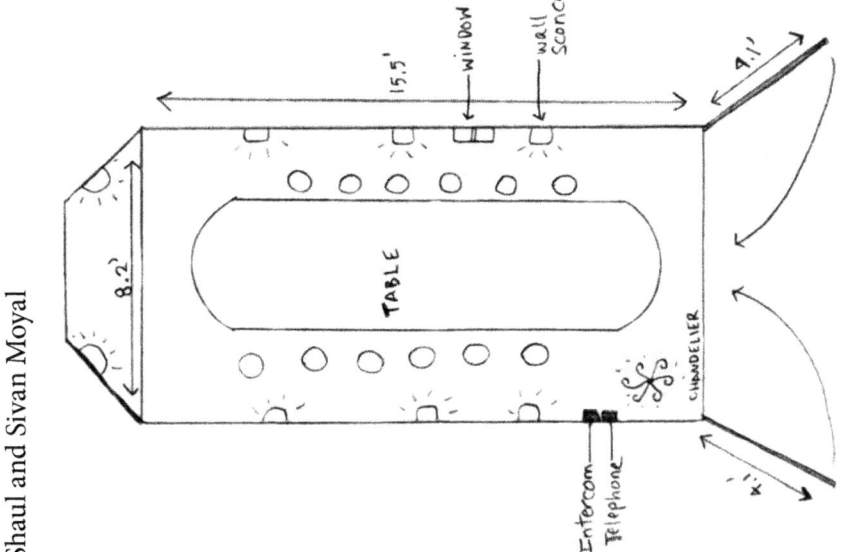

Shaul and Sivan Moyal

234 | *Appendix*

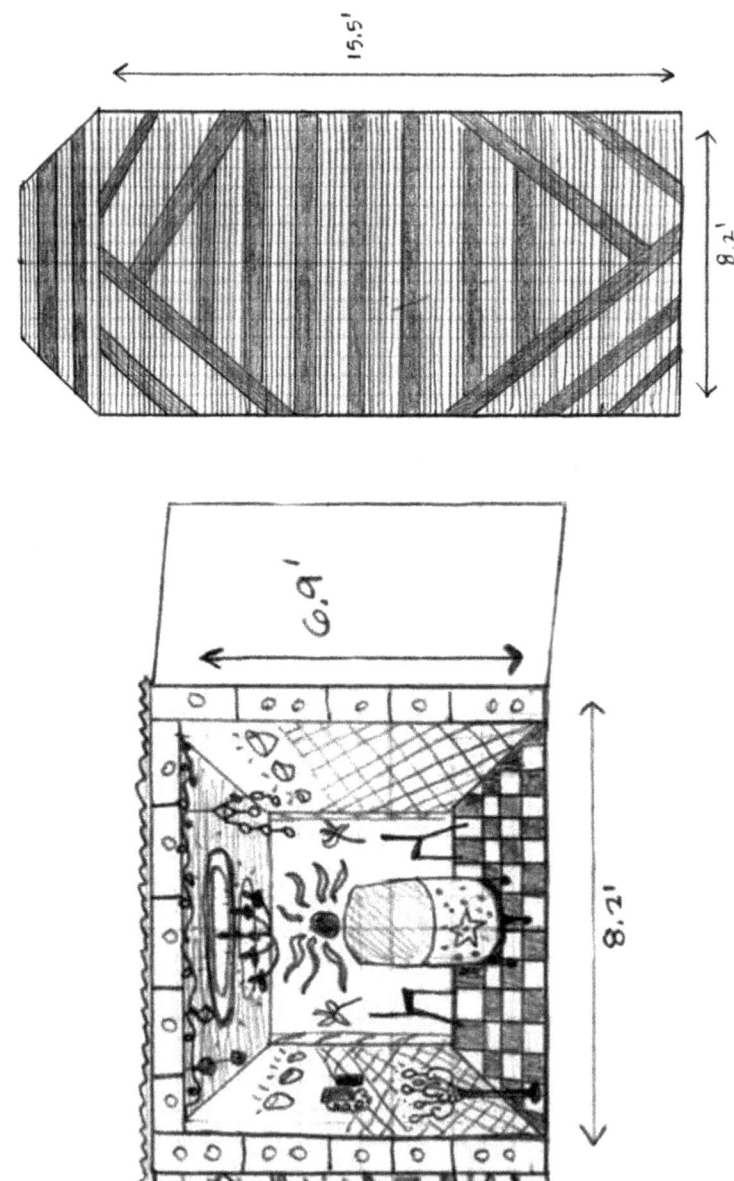

Drori Yehoshua

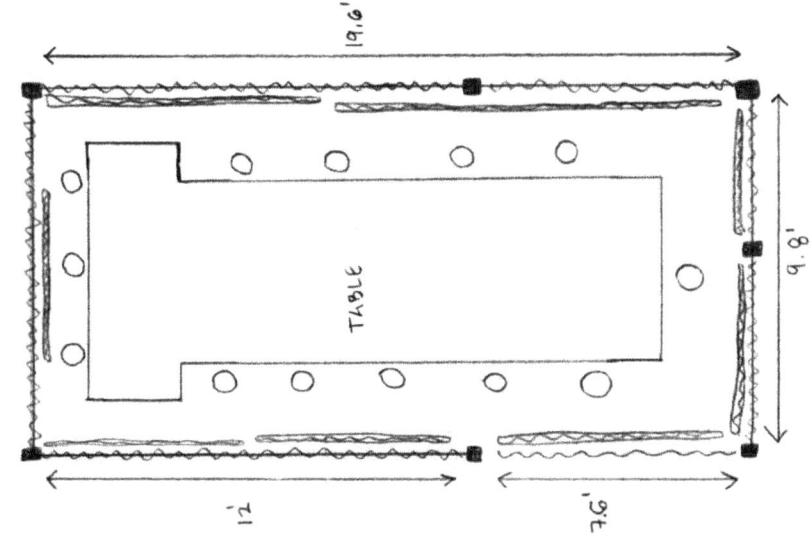

Appendix

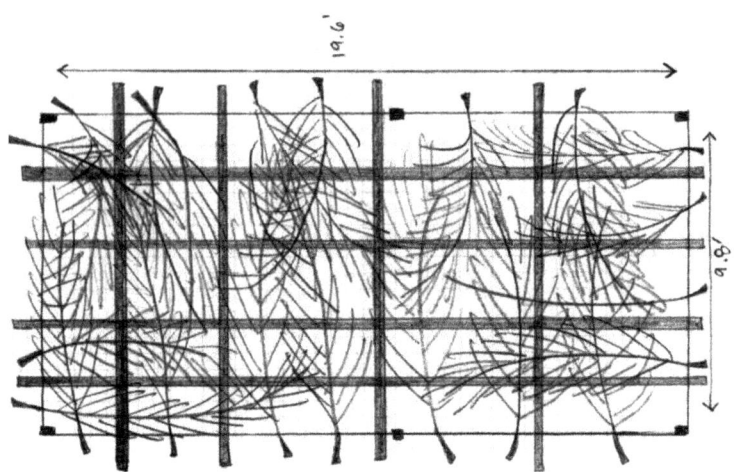

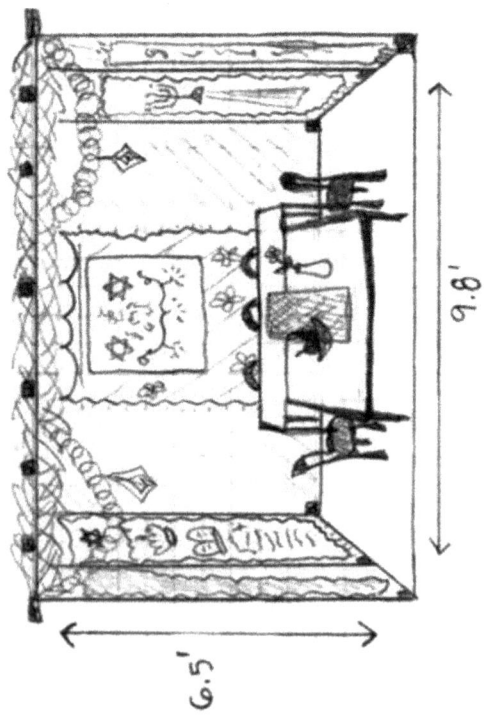

Bibliography

Abrahams, Roger D. 2003. "Identity." In *Eight Words for the Study of Expressive Culture*, edited by Burt Feintuch, 198–222. Urbana: University of Illinois Press.
Appadurai, Arjun. 1988. *The Social Life of Things: Commodities in Cultural Perspective*. New York: Cambridge University Press.
Armstrong, Robert Plant. 1971. *The Affecting Presence: An Essay in Humanistic Anthropology*. Urbana: University of Illinois Press.
Ashley, Wayne. 1999. "The Stations of the Cross: Christ, Politics, and Processions on New York City's Lower East Side." In *Gods of the City: Religion and the American Urban Landscape*, edited by Robert Orsi, 341–366. Bloomington: Indiana University Press.
Bachelard, Gaston. (1958) 1994. *The Poetics of Space*. Translated by Maria Jolas. Boston: Beacon Press.
Bahloul, Joëlle. 1983. *Le Culte de la Table Dressée: Rites et Traditions de la Table Juive Algérienne*. Paris: A.-M. Métailié.
Bar-Yitzhak, Haya. 2005. *Israeli Folk Narratives: Settlement, Immigration, Ethnicity*. Detroit, MI: Wayne State University Press.
Baron, Salo W. 1940. "Jewish Social Studies, 1938–39: A Selected Bibliography," *Jewish Social Studies* (2) 3: 305–388.
Bauman, Richard. 2001. "Tradition, Anthropology of." In *International Encyclopedia of the Social and Behavioral Sciences*, edited by Neil Smelser and Paul Baltes. New York: Elsevier.
———2004. *World of Others' Words: Cross-Cultural Perspectives on Intertextuality*. Malden, MA: Blackwell Publishing.
Bauman, Richard, and Charles Briggs. 2003. *Voices of Modernity: Language Ideologies and the Politics of Inequality*. New York: Cambridge University Press.
Bendix, Regina. 1997. *In Search of Authenticity: The Formation of Folklore Studies*. Madison: University of Wisconsin Press.
Bernstein, Deborah S. 2012. "South of Tel-Aviv and North of Jaffa—The Frontier Zone of 'In Between.'" In *Tel-Aviv, the First Century: Visions, Designs, Actualities*, edited by Maoz Azaryahu and S. Ilan Troen, 115–137. Bloomington: Indiana University Press.
Blier, Suzanne Preston. 2006. "Vernacular Architecture." In *Handbook of Material Culture*, edited by Webb Keane, Susanne Kuchler, Michael Rowlands, Patricia Spyer, and Christopher Tilley, 23–45. London; Thousand Oaks, CA: Sage.
Briggs, Charles. 1996. "The Politics of Discursive Authority in Research on the 'Invention of Tradition.'" *Cultural Anthropology* 11 (4): 435–469.
Bronner, Simon J. 2006. "Building Tradition: Control and Authority in Vernacular Architecture." In *Vernacular Architecture in the Twenty-First Century: Theory,*

Education and Practice, edited by Lindsay Asquith and Marcel Vellinga, 23–45. London; New York: Taylor and Francis.
———2011. *Revisioning Ritual: Jewish Traditions in Transition*. Edited by Simon Bronner. Portland, OR: Littman Library of Jewish Civilization.
Burke, Kenneth. 1973. *The Philosophy of Literary Form: Studies in Symbolic Action*. Berkeley: University of California Press.
Carter, Thomas. 2015. *Building Zion: The Material World of Mormon Settlement*. Minneapolis: University of Minnesota Press.
Carter, Thomas, and Elizabeth Collins Cromley. 2005. *Invitation to Vernacular Architecture: A Guide to the Study of Ordinary Buildings and Landscapes*. Knoxville: University of Tennessee Press.
Cashman, Ray. 2006. "Critical Nostalgia and Material Culture in Northern Ireland." *Journal of American Folklore* 119 (472): 137–160.
Clifford, James 1994. "Diasporas." *Cultural Anthropology* 9 (3): 302–338.
Deshen, Shlomo. 1989. *The Mellah Society: Jewish Community Life in Sherifian Morocco*. Chicago: University of Chicago Press.
El-Shamy, Hasan M. 2016. *Motific Constituents of Arab-Islamic Folk Traditions*. Bloomington: Indiana University Press.
Fabricant, Isaac Nathan. 1958. *Guide to Succoth*. London: Jewish Chronicle Publications.
Feigenbaum, Anna, Fabian Frenzel, and Patrick McCurdy. 2014. "Protest Camps: an emerging field of social movement research." *The Sociological Review* 62 (3): 457–474.
Fishbane, Simcha. 1989. "Jewish Mourning Rites—A Process of Resocialization." *Anthropologica* 31 (1): 65–84.
Fleischman, Danielle. 2011. "Occupy Wall Street Protesters Have a Sukkah." *Jewish Telegraphic Agency*, October 12. Accessed July 5, 2013. http://www.jta.org/2011/10/12/news-opinion/united-states/occupy-wall-street-protesters-have-a-sukkah.
Frankel, Ellen, and Betsy Patkin Teutsch. 1992. *The Encyclopedia of Jewish Symbols*. Lanham, MD: Rowman and Littlefield.
Ginsburg, Rebecca. 2011. *At Home with Apartheid: The Hidden Landscapes of Domestic Service in Johannesburg*. Charlottesville: University of Virginia Press.
Glassie, Henry. 1975. *Folk Housing in Middle Virginia: A Structural Analysis of Historic Artifacts*. Knoxville: University of Tennessee Press.
———1982. *Passing the Time in Ballymenone: Culture and History of an Ulster Community*. Philadelphia: University of Pennsylvania Press.
———1984. "Vernacular Architecture and Society." *Material Culture* 16 (1): 4–24.
———1993. *Turkish Traditional Art Today*. Bloomington: Indiana University Press.
———1999. *Material Culture*. Bloomington: Indiana University Press.
———2000. *Vernacular Architecture*. Bloomington: Indiana University Press.
———2003. "Tradition." In *Eight Words for the Study of Expressive Culture*, edited by Burt Feintuch, 176–197. Urbana: University of Illinois Press.
———2006. *The Stars of Ballymenone*. Bloomington: Indiana University Press.
Goodman, Philip. 1973. *The Sukkot and Simhat Torah Anthology*. Philadelphia, PA: Jewish Publication Society of America.

Goffman, Erving. 1959. *The Presentation of Self in Everyday Life*. Garden City, NY: Doubleday.
———. 1968. *Stigma: Notes on the Management of Spoiled Identity*. Harmondsworth: Penguin.
Gould, Jillian. 2013. "A Nice Piece of Cake and a Kibitz: Reinventing Sabbath Hospitality in an Institutional Home." *Home Cultures* 10 (2): 189–206.
Graeber, David. 2001. *Toward an Anthropological Theory of Value: The False Coin of Our Own Dreams*. New York: Palgrave Macmillan.
Hasan-Rokem, Galit. 2012. "Material Mobility Versus Concentric Cosmology in the Sukkah." In *Things: Religion and the Question of Materiality*, edited by Dick Houtman and Brigit Meyer, 153–179. New York: Fordham University Press.
Heath, Kingston. 2001. *The Patina of Place: The Cultural Weathering of a New England Industrial Landscape*. Knoxville: University of Tennessee Press.
Heilman, Samuel C. 1998. *Synagogue Life: A Study in Symbolic Interaction*. New Brunswick, NJ: Transaction Publishers.
Hercbergs, Dana. 2010. *Narratives in a Divided City: Childhood and Memory in Jerusalem, 1948–2008*. PhD dissertation, University of Pennsylvania.
Hirsch, Dafna. 2011. "'Hummus is best when it is fresh and made by Arabs:' The Gourmetization of Hummus in Israel and the Return of the Repressed Arab." *American Ethnologist* 38 (4): 617–630.
Hobsbawm, Eric, and Terence Ranger. 1983. *The Invention of Tradition*. New York: Cambridge University Press.
Horowitz, Amy. 2010. *Mediterranean Israeli Music and the Politics of the Aesthetic*. Detroit, MI: Wayne State University Press.
Israeli Authority on Population and Immigration. 2013. "Report on Foreigners in Israel." Last accessed 2013. http://www.piba.gov.il/PublicationAndTender/Foreign WorkersStat/Documents/foreign_stat_032013.pdf.
Jackson, Jason Baird. 1997. "Yuchi." In *Encyclopedia of Vernacular Architecture of the World*, edited by Paul Oliver, 1895. New York: Cambridge University Press.
———2003. *Yuchi Ceremonial Life: Performance, Meaning, and Tradition in a Contemporary American Indian Community*. Lincoln: University of Nebraska Press.
———2006. "Diaspora." In *The Greenwood Encyclopedia of World Folklore and Folklife*, edited by Thomas A. Green and William M. Clements, 18–22. Westport, CT: Greenwood Press.
———2008. "Traditionalization in Ceremonial Ground Oratory: Native American Speechmaking in Eastern Oklahoma." *Midwestern Folklore* 34 (2): 3–16.
———2016. *Material Vernaculars*. Edited by Jason Baird Jackson. Bloomington: Indiana University Press.
Joselit, Jenna, and Susan Braunstein. 1990. *Getting Comfortable in New York: The American Jewish home, 1880–1950*. New York: The Jewish Museum.
Joselit, Jenna Weissman. 1994. *The Wonders of America: Reinventing Jewish Culture 1880–1950*. New York: Hill and Wang.
Kershner, Isabel. 2012. "Crackdown on Migrants Tugs at Souls of Israelis." *New York Times*, June 18.

Khazzoom, Aziza. 2003. "The Great Chain of Orientalism: Jewish Identity, Stigma Management, and Ethnic Exclusion in Israel," *American Sociological Review* 68:4, 481–510.

Kirshenblatt, Mayer, and Barbara Kirshenblatt-Gimblett. 2007. *They Called Me Mayer July: Painted Memories of a Jewish Childhood in Poland Before the Holocaust.* Berkeley: University of California Press.

Kirshenblatt-Gimblett, Barbara. 1982. "The Cut That Binds: The Western Ashkenazic Torah Binder as Nexus between Circumcision and Torah." In *Celebration, Studies in Festivity and Ritual*, edited by Victor Turner, 136–146. Washington: Smithsonian Institution Press.

———1985. "American Jewish Life: Ethnographic Approaches to Collection, Presentation, and Interpretation in Museums." *Jewish Folklore and Ethnology Newsletter* 7 (1–4): 4–13.

———1987. "The Folk Culture of Jewish Immigrant Communities: Research Paradigms and Directions." In *The Jews of North America*, edited by Moses Rischin, 70–94. Detroit, MI: Wayne State University Press.

———1990. "Problems in the Early History of Jewish Folkloristics." In *Proceedings of the Tenth World Congress of Jewish Studies, August 16–24, 1989*: Division D, Vol II, Art, Folklore and Music. Jerusalem: World Union of Jewish Studies.

———2004. "Intangible Heritage as Metacultural Production." *Museum International* 56 (1–2): 52–64.

Kitchener, Amy. 1994. *The Holiday Yards of Florencio Morales: "El Hombre De Las Banderas."* Jackson: University Press of Mississippi.

Kodish, Debora. 2011. "Envisioning Folklore Activism." *Journal of American Folklore* 124 (491): 31–60.

Kosharek, Noah. 2010. "New Hatikva Trail Seeks to Take TA Neighborhood the Way of Neve Tzedek." *Haaretz*, January 25.

Lapid, Yair. 2010. "This Is Not Racism: Demonstrations Against Illegal Migrants Have Nothing To Do With Their Skin Color." *YNetNews.com*, December 22. Accessed April 4, 2013. http://www.ynetnews.com/articles/0,7340,L-4002934,00.html.

Lehman, Marjorie. 2010. "Reimagining Home, Rethinking Sukkah: Rabbinic Discourse and Its Contemporary Implications." In *Jews at Home: The Domestication of Identity*, edited by Simon Bronner, 107–139. Portland, OR: The Littman Library of Jewish Civilization.

Levine, Charley J. 1979. "Using Streets as Housing Sites: Proposed Prefabricated Housing for Hatikva Neighborhood of Tel Aviv, Architect Israel Goodovitch." *AIA Journal* 68 (14): 44–46.

Lipis, Mimi Levy. 2011. *Symbolic Houses in Judaism: How Objects and Metaphors Construct Hybrid Places of Belonging.* Burlington, VT: Ashgate Publishing.

Mandel, Jonah. 2010. "Amsalem Defies Ovadia Yosef's Order to Quit Knesset." *Jerusalem Post*, November 24. Accessed February 5, 2012. http://www.jpost.com/NationalNews/Article.aspx?id=196523.

———2011. "Amsalem Launches Alternative to Shas." *Jerusalem Post*, April 15. Accessed February 5, 2012. http://www.jpost.com/DiplomacyAndPolitics/Article.aspx?id=216757.

Mann, Barbara E. 2012. *Space and Place in Jewish Studies.* New Brunswick, NJ: Rutgers University Press.

Marom, Nathan. 2009. *City of Concept: Planning Tel-Aviv*. Tel Aviv, Israel: Babel Press.
Martins, Bruno Oliveira. 2009. "Paper 81: Undocumented Migrants, Asylum Seekers and Refugees in Israel." Beer-Sheva, Israel: Centre for the Study of European Politics and Society, Ben-Gurion University. Accessed March 2013. http://www.euromesco.net/index.php?option=com_content&task=view&id=1162&Itemid=48.
Marx, Emanuel. 1982. "Rehabilitation of Slums? The Case of Hatikva Quarter." *Jerusalem Quarterly* 22 (Winter): 38–44.
———. 1980. "Mayors of NYC and Tel Aviv Launch $100 Million Project Renewal for Neighborhoods in Both Cities." *Jewish Telegraphic Agency*.
Massad, Joseph. 1996. "Zionism's Internal Others: Israel and the Oriental Jews," *Journal of Palestine Studies* 25:4, 53–68.
Miller, Daniel. 2001. *The Dialectics of Shopping*. Chicago: University of Chicago Press.
———2010. *Stuff*. Malden, MA: Polity Press.
Mintz, Jerome R. 1992. *Hasidic People: A Place in the World*. Cambridge: Harvard University Press.
Myerhoff, Barbara. 1980. *Number Our Days: A Triumph of Continuity and Culture Among Jewish Old People in an Urban Ghetto*. New York: Touchstone.
———1992. *Remembered Lives: The Work of Ritual, Storytelling, and Growing Older*. Ann Arbor: University of Michigan Press.
Noyes, Dorothy. 1995. "Group." *The Journal of American Folklore* 108 (430): 449–478.
———2006. "The Judgment of Solomon: Global Protections for Tradition and the Problem of Community Ownership." *Cultural Analysis* 5: 27–56.
Ochs, Vanessa L. 1999. "What Makes a Jewish Home Jewish?" *Cross Currents* (Winter 2000), 49 (4).
———2007. *Inventing Jewish Ritual*. Philadelphia: Jewish Publication Society.
Oliver, Paul. 1997. *Encyclopedia of Vernacular Architecture of the World*. New York: Cambridge University Press.
Park, Robert E., and Ernest W. Burgess. 1925. *The City: Suggestions for Investigation of Human Behavior in the Urban Environment*. Chicago, IL: University of Chicago Press.
Pocius, Gerald. 1991. *A Place to Belong: Community Order and Everyday Space in Calvert, Newfoundland*. Athens: University of Georgia Press.
Primiano, Leonard Norman. 1995. "Vernacular Religion and the Search for Method in Religious Folklife." *Western Folklore* 54 (1): 37–56.
Ravid, Barak. 2010. "Netanyahu Warns Israelis: Violence Against Minorities Won't Be Tolerated." *Haaretz Daily Newspaper*, December 22. Accessed December 22, 2010. http://www.haaretz.com/news/national/netanyahu-warns-israelis-violence-against-minorities-won-t-be-tolerated-1.332204.
Regev, Motti, and Edwin Seroussi. 2004. *Popular Music and National Culture in Israel*. Berkeley: University of California Press.
Rotbard, Sharon. 2015. *White City, Black City: Architecture and War in Tel Aviv and Jaffa*. Cambridge, MA: The MIT Press.
Rubenstein, Jeffrey. 1994. "The Symbolism of the Sukkah." *Judaism: A Quarterly Journal of Jewish Life and Thought* 43 (4): 371–387.
———1995. *The History of Sukkot in the Second Temple and Rabbinic Periods*. Atlanta, GA: Scholars Press.
Schwarzer, Mitchell. 2001. "The Architecture of Talmud." *Journal of the Society of Architectural Historians* 60 (4): 474–487.

Sciorra, Joseph. 2015. *Built with Faith: Italian American imagination and Catholic Material Culture in New York City*. Knoxville: University of Tennessee Press.

Sered, Susan Starr. 1992. *Women as Ritual Experts: The Religious Lives of Elderly Jewish Women in Jerusalem*. New York: Oxford University Press.

Shapiro, Maya, and Matan Kaminer. 2009. "Bubbling Over: The Contestation of Urban Space and Possibilities for Joint Struggle in Tel Aviv." Re-public: Re-imagining Democracy, accessed December 15, 2010. http://www.re-public.gr/en/?p=2727.

Shohat, Ella. 1997. "The Narrative of the Nation and the Discourse of Modernization: The Case of the Mizrahim." *Critique: Critical Middle Eastern Studies* 6 (10): 3–18.

Stoeltje, Beverly J. 1992. "Festival." In *Folklore, Cultural Performances, and Popular Entertainments: A Communications-centered Handbook*, edited by Richard Bauman, 261–271. New York: Oxford University Press.

Turner, Kay. 1999. *Beautiful Necessity: The Art and Meaning of Women's Altars*. London: Thames and Hudson.

———2009. "September 11: The Burden of the Ephemeral." *Western Folklore* 68 (2–3): 155–208.

Turner, Victor. 1969. *The Ritual Process: Structure and Anti-Structure*. Chicago: Aldine.

Vlach, John Michael. 1981. *Charleston Blacksmith: The Work of Philip Simmons*. Athens: University of Georgia Press.

Vlach, John Michael and Dell Upton, eds. 1986. *Common Places: Readings in American Vernacular Architecture*. Athens: University of Georgia Press.

Von Oston, Marion. 2012. "Israeli Black Panthers," March 5. Accessed May 16, 2016. http://www.transculturalmodernism.org/article/125.

Westmacott, Richard Noble. 1992. *African-American Gardens and Yards in the Rural South*. Knoxville: University of Tennessee Press.

Williams, Michael Ann. 1991. *Homeplace: The Social Use and Meaning of the Folk Dwelling in Southwestern North Carolina*. Athens: University of Georgia Press.

Index

Due to the prevalence of the words Sukkot *(name of holiday),* sukkah *(ritual structure), and* sukkot *(plural form of* sukkah*) throughout the text, these terms cannot be practically indexed. You will find them referenced, however, in many subentries of the indexed terms below.*

Abergel, Reuven, 186–187, 190
Abraham (biblical personage), 14–15, 34, 90, 117, 124
Abrahams, Roger, 47n4, 80
Adani, Pazit, 167, 183, 194n3, 215
adonei haaretz (Rulers of the Land), 170. *See also* Other Israel; Second Israel; Second Class
aesthetics: and biblical prescription, 32; and sukkah builders, 157, 169, 177n5, 185–186
affect (as related to the body, phenomenology), 20, 48n11, 116, 123, 177n5, 183, 185, 207
Amsalem, Itzik, 184
Amsalem, Rabbi Chaim, 9, 187–191
Appadurai, Arjun, 23n2, 220n1
Arab Spring, the, 1, 9, 192
aravah (branch of a willow tree), 33–34, 187–188. *See also* Four Species; *arba'at haminim*
arba'at haminim (Four Species), 33. *See also* Four Species; *aravah*; *hadas*; *lulav*; *etrog*
arbor, 25n12, 43, 105n4
architecture, vernacular, 3, 11–14, 21, 23n5, 24n8, 24n9, 24n10
Armstrong, Robert Plant, 177n5
Ashley, Wayne, 194n2
Ashkenazim: and urban infrastructure, 51, 54, 59–60, 182; and identity, 60–61, 76n7, 170; cultural distinctiveness of, 59–65; and class struggle with Mizrahim, 69–73; and Israeli anthropology, 76n8; Orthodox 195–208.
assemblage, 39, 42, 45
asylum seekers: in South Tel Aviv, 16–17, 58–59, 65–66; statistics, 68; demonstrations against, 69–71; trafficking of, 78n17; terms for, 78n18
"at-homeness," 183, 215. *See also* *ba'al bayit*. *See also* Levinas, Emanuel
authenticity: and food, 51; and tradition, 74n1
Ayalon Highway (north-south highway in Israel), 52

Baal Shem Tov, 202–203
Baba Sali, 20
Babylonia, 29
Bachelard, Gaston, 8
Bahloul, Joëlle, 25n11, 25n17
Bamedi, Kurdistan, 169
Bar, George, 2
Bar-Itzhak, Haya, 26n22
Barashi, Kurdistan, 169
Baron, Salo, 25n18
Bat Yam (Israel), 74, 178, 179, 192. *See also* Peripheria Forum
Bauhaus, 53–54, 79
Bauman, Richard, 47n1, 74n1, 80
Beit Dani (community center in Shchunat Hatikva), 58, 60, 84, 107, 109, 118, 153, 176n2
Belcove-Shalin, Janet S., 208n2
belief: and material culture, 3, 8, 23n5, 20, 45, 210; and individual worldviews, 8, 12; and genres of folklore, 10; and Talmud, 32; in Hatikva, 50–51, 88; in God, 100, 143, 165–166, 214; at Kahalani family gatherings, 102; cultural, 61, 104; and Bnei Yehuda, 106n4; and Sukkot, 17, 110–111, 135, 152, 219; and tradition, 124; and faith, 136; in self, 144; in hope, 87–88, 166; theological, 148; and Baal Shem Tov, 203–204
belonging, social: and the sukkah, 6, 11–12, 14–17, 18, 135, 171, 202–203; and ritual and festival studies, 12; material expressions of, 15–16, 32; in Israel, 16–18, 25n14, 65–74, 77n15, 98; in the Midwestern United States, 37–38, 43, 210; in community spaces, 81–82; in devotional and domestic spaces, 88–98. *See also* hospitality
Ben-Ari, Michael, 70
Bendix, Regina, 74n1
Benedict, Ruth, 26n22
Bernstein, Deborah S., 53–54

243

244 | Index

Black City (in response to UNESCO's "White City" designation for Tel Aviv), 54, 66
Black Panther Movement, Israeli, 186
Blier, Susanne Preston, 23n5
Bloomington (Indiana), 5, 8, 36–48
Bnei Yehuda (soccer team of Shchunat Hatikva): 57, 83–88, 104–105, 105n4; players: Atar, Eliran, 86; Mizrahi, Sahar, 87; Shirazi, Hezi, 87; Bloomfield Stadium, 83–86
Bosi, Dudu, 194n3
Boushir, Persia, 120
Briggs, Charles, 74n1
British Mandate Period, 53
Bronner, Simon, 24n5, 24n9, 26n20, 27, 149n2
Brooklyn (New York), 5, 8, 22, 195–208
Bukharan (as Jewish identity associated with Bukhara, Uzbekistan), 15; women's social group, 62–63
Burgess, Ernst W., 75n6
Burke, Kenneth, 23n3

camps, protest, 179, 193. *See also* housing demonstrations, Israeli; protests, social
camps, refugee, 179, 215. See also *ma'abarot*
Canada, 39, 207
Carter, Thomas, 24n9
Cashman, Ray, 149n1, 218
Chabad (Jewish movement), 26n23, 48n9, 198–208, 208n1–2. *See also* Lubavitch
chag ha-asif, 3
chag ha-sukkot, 4
Chekol, Lea, 215–218
Chicago School of Sociology, 75n6
Clifford, James, 211
Cohen: Adi, 84–88; Pnina, 64, 153
community: creation of, in Shchunat Hatikva, 138; notion of, in Sukkot observance, 174. *See also* food, home, money, ritual, Shchunat Hatikva, social belonging, work
construction, sukkah. *See* material culture; roof; *schach*; work; Appendix
Crown Heights (New York), 195–208. *See also* Brooklyn

death, Jewish rituals of, 128–134
"Dear Sons," 190. *See also* Other Israel; Second Class; Second Israel, *adonei haaretz*
decoration, sukkah. *See* material culture; roof; Appendix
Deshen, Shlomo, 176n3

Desert, Sinai: biblical journey, 3, 7, 10, 16, 28, 73–74, 174, 178, 180, 189, 194; representations of (in material culture), 39; 41, 43, 48n12; as relates to asylum seekers, 17, 25n15, 68
Diamant, Anita, 45
diaspora, 6, 7, 15, 18, 25n14, 34, 77n12, 211
"domestic religion." *See* food and family
Dor HaMidbar (Generation of the Desert), 73–74
Douglas, Mary, 25n13
Durkheim, Émile, 25n13, 176n4
dwell, to, 16, 28, 29, 115, 168, 193
dwelling, 3, 13, 25n12, 28, 116, 124, 144, 152, 184, 192, 213–214

Educational Institute Oholei Torah, 203
Egypt, 4, 17, 25n15, 28, 51, 68, 78n18, 179, 189, 193
Egyptian (as Jewish identity associated with Egypt), 109, 176
El-Shamy, Hasan, 150n11
Elijah's Chair (a Sukkot custom), 35, 117–118
Emanuel, Marx, 57–59
emigration: from, Russia, 8; Yemen, 91, 106n8, 129; Iraq, 98, 106n8; Persia, 120; Morocco, 157, 163; Kurdistan, 170; French Algeria, 187; Poland, 196; Israel, 198; Ethiopia, 215
Emunah, Dina and Yitzhak, 19–20
ephemerality: and the sukkah, 20, 123–124, 163–164, 190, 193, 210; and social belonging, 171; and folklore studies, 212–213
equality: and the sukkah, 166–176, 189–190, 211–212, 215, 219; and architecture, 168–169; and the Israeli social protests, 189–190, 192–193, 194n1. *See also* inequality
Eritrean. *See* asylum seekers; migration; refugee
eruv (ritual enclosure that expands the private domain to public spaces), 7
Ethiopian (as Jewish identity associated with Ethiopia), 215–219
etrog (fruit of the citron tree), 32–34, 92, 118, 121, 188, 206–207. *See also* Four Species; *arba'at haminim*
Exodus (biblical), 4, 25n15, 28, 192

faith: and Sukkot, 9, 148, 152, 165–166, 195, 212–214; and the built environment, 24n9; Jewish, 27; 30, 74, 114–115; expressions of, in Shchunat Hatikva, 88–105; in God, 124, 136, 165–166, 204
farbrengen (Yiddish: Hasidic gathering), 197
Feigenbaum, Anna, 193

Festival of Ingathering. See *chag ha-asif*
Festival of Tabernacles. See *chag ha-sukkot*
fieldwork, 16, 22, 35–36, 49, 52, 60–61, 109–110, 152, 219
Fishkoff, Sue, 208n2
food: and identity, 61–62, 64; and hospitality, 62, 64, 76n10; and health, 63, 92; and politics, 64; and the notion of authenticity, 51, 74n1, 76n8; and community, 79–83, 133, 167; and nostalgia, 63–64, 92, 144, 218; and family, 100; and religion, 100–101; and belief, 102; Persian, 120; and Sukkot, 14, 123; and mourning, 129, 133, 149n6
foods, specific: *amba* (pickled mango condiment of Iraqi origin), 79; *café shachor* (Turkish-style, black coffee), 1, 96; *café lavan* (white coffee, a Yemenite herbal tea), 96; hummus, 62, 64; *hummus ful* (hummus with fava beans), 94; *jachnun* (Yemenite dish of slow-baked, rolled dough), 101; lentils, 129, 149n6; *malawach* (Yemenite dish of layered fried dough), 64; sautéed okra in tomato sauce, 61; Persian food (roast chicken, white rice with golden raisins, stewed okra in tomato sauce, spiced chickpeas, pickled peppers), 120; *resek* (grated tomato), 64; *sahlab* (milky pudding), 79; *skhug* (spicy condiment of Yemenite origin), 62, 64, 76n9; Yemenite beef soup, 93; *zalabiyah* (fried round pieces of dough), 98, 101
folklore, Jewish, 12, 18–19, 24n7
Four Species, 33–34, 188–189. See also *arba'at haminim; aravah; hadas; lulav; etrog*
French Algeria, 187
Frenzel, Fabian, 193

Gan Hatikva (Garden of Hope, community park in South Tel Aviv), 1–2, 9, 49, 111, 178–194
Gaster, Moses, 25n18
Geller, Bakol, 39–43, 210
Gemara, 28–29. See also *Mishnah; Talmud*
Germany, 54, 60
Ginsburg, Rebecca, 24n6, 24n9
Glassie, Henry, 13, 22, 23n2, 23n6–7, 37, 24n9, 24n9, 24n10, 47n1, 47n4, 148, 149n1, 150n8, 193, 220n1
God: and hospitality, 15, 124; and holy text, 30; and Sukkot, 31, 33–35, 115, 207; and aesthetics, 32, 117; and faith, 74, 99; and Bnei Yehuda, 87; and protection, 100, 114–115; and gratitude,
137; and belief, 143; and obedience, 150n11; and family, 165; and hope, 165; and love, 166; in Lubavitch Jewish thought, 206
Goffman, Erving, 26n21, 57, 75n4
Golan, Tzion, 138
Goldschmidt, Henry, 208n2
Goodovitch, Israel M., 55–57
Gould, Jillian, 207
Graeber, David, 150n13

hadas (branch of the myrtle tree), 33–34, 188. See also Four Species; *arba'at haminim*
halakha (Jewish religious law), 31, 184
Halamish (Israeli public housing company), 99
Halberstam, Rabbi Chaim, 198–201
hamsa (hand-shaped amulet believed to ward off the evil eye), 92, 102
happiness: Iraqi marriage custom for, 19; as Iraqi name, 98; and wealth, 102; 129, 142, 162–163; and Sukkot 118, 124, 139
Hasan-Rokem, Galit, 7, 25n14, 26n20, 29–30, 34, 47n3
HaShem (God), 99, 206–207. See also God
Haza, Ofra, 86–87, 105n2
Heath, Kingston, 25n11
Heilman, Samuel, 106n5
heritage, 14–16, 19, 211
Hesed L'Avraham (synagogue in Shchunat Hatikva), 90, 94–97
hiddur mitzvah (the aesthetic enhancement of a *mitzvah*), 32, 117
Hirsch, Dafna, 64
Hobsbawn, Eric, 74n1
Holon (Israel), 152, 178–179, 192
home: search for, 4–5, 22, 31, 190, 193–194; symbolic, 3, 11, 15, 171, 219; as ephemeral ritual architecture, 6–7, 123–124, 181; as transient shelter, 6, 7–8, 164, 193; as permanent place, 6, 9–10, 74, 123–124, 182–184 (see also *ba'al bayit*; Levinas, Emanuel), 190–191, 193, 209–211; as devotional space, 90, 97–105, 171, 214; and material culture, 19–20, 24n10, 32, 38–39, 44, 48n11, 171, 207; and hospitality, 14–16, 61–64, 76n10, 124, 173–175, 214; and social protests, 1–3, 22, 178–194, 215; and asylum seekers, 25n15, 70; and Shchunat Hatikva, 59; and foreign workers, 67; and Bnei Yehuda, 84–85; and Sukkot ritual, 118, 182, 218; and community, 132, 135–136, 214; social space within, 148, 214; and Lubavitcher Jews, 196, 198

homelessness, 1–3, 17, 22, 49, 56, 71–73, 179–180
hope: and Sukkot observance 5, 8, 152, 159, 163–165, 219; and Shchunat Hatikva, 51, 79, 90, 106n5; and Bnei Yehuda, 87–88; and Kahalani, Suad, 100; and living conditions, 183
hospitality (as a ritual of Sukkot), 13–18, 35, 98, 118, 124, 138, 173, 175, 207, 214
housing demonstrations, Israeli, 1–3, 9–10, 59, 72–73, 178–194. *See also* protests, social
Huldai, Ron, 64, 84
Hungary, 60, 205

Idelsohn, A. Z., 25n18
identity: Jewish, 18, 37, 38–43, 46, 48n1, 67, 101, 211; and performance, 26n21; and ritual and festival studies, 14–16, 26n20; and folklore studies, 47n1, 47n4; of Shchunat Hatikva, 17–18, 51–60, 69, 96; Ashkenazi/Mizrahi cultural, 60–61; and food, 64, 100; of Israel, 67, 75n2; Yemenite, 76n9; Kurdish-Iraqi, 170–171; and material culture, 48n11, 26n21, 171, 211–212, 215
immanence (Lubavitch Jewish thought), 204–205
immigration policy, Israeli, 70
inequality: in Israeli society, 1, 4, 22, 60, 72, 180, 187, 192–193; and the notion of authenticity, 74n1; and the sukkah, 166–176. *See also* equality
Iran, 9, 19–20, 51
Iranian (as Jewish identity associated with Iran or Persia), 16, 19–20, 35, 51, 109, 111, 149n3, 176n1
Iraq, 20, 29, 51, 99, 120
Iraqi (as Jewish identity associated with Iraq), 16, 22, 51, 61, 79, 91, 99, 106n8, 109, 111, 153, 157, 170, 176n2, 194n3
Israelites, 3–4, 10, 16–17, 25n15, 28, 30–31, 49, 73, 138, 170, 174, 178, 180, 194, 201

Jackson, Jason Baird, 15, 25n12, 74n1, 105n4, 124, 150n11, 220n1
Jaffa, 22, 50–53, 72–73, 83, 152–166
Jerusalem, 6, 15, 22, 28–29, 32, 36, 100, 120, 139, 152, 166–176, 181–182, 186, 211, 214
Jesse Cohen (neighborhood in Holon, Israel), 73, 179. *See also* Peripheria Forum
Jewish Agency for Israel, 54
Joselit, Jenna Weissman, 25n17
Judaism: Conservative, 39, 43; Renewal, 39, 43; *Masortit* (traditional), 114, 148; *Datiya* (religious), 114; Classical, 206–207; Orthodox, 5, 8, 15, 22, 47n2, 187, 195–207

Kabbalah (Jewish school of thought), 34. See also *Zohar*
kaddish (Jewish prayer for the dead), 133–134
Kahalani: Dror, 17, 71, 91, 96–97, 111, 139–149, 212; Sharona, 61–62, 98, 101–104, 145; Suad, 62, 98–102, 145; family as representative, 106n8
Kaminer, Matan, 65–66
kapparot (Yom Kippur purification ritual), 87
Kfar Shalem (neighborhood in South Tel Aviv), 73, 167, 183. *See also* Peripheria Forum
Khazzoom, Aziza, 75n2
Kirshenblatt-Gimblett, Barbara, 18–19, 25n17, 26n22, 74n1
Kitchener, Amy, 24n9
Knesset (Israeli Parliament), 181, 187
Kodish, Deborah, 74n1
Koran, 150n11
Kosovske, Yonit, 43–47, 210
Kurdish (as Jewish identity associated with Kurdistan), 22, 100, 152, 166–176, 211–212
Kurdistan, 120, 169–171

labor: and Mizrahi social history in Israel, 60; and international migrant class in Israel, 77n12; gendered division of, 114; the value of, 138–144, 148, 212. *See also* work
Lachmann, Robert, 25n18
Lapid, Yair, 70
Leef, Daphni, 1, 180
Lehman, Marjorie, 23n4
Lévi-Strauss, Claude, 25n13
Levinas, Emanuel, 183, 215
Levinsky Park (South Tel Aviv), 25n15, 72–73
Libya, 16, 51
Libyan (as Jewish identity associated with Libya), 35, 109
liminality, 6–7, 15, 69
Lipis, Miriam, 6, 28, 30
Long Island (New York), 202
Lubavitch (Jewish movement): 195–207; headquarters of (768 Eastern Parkway), 196, 198–199, 203. *See also* Chabad
lulav (palm tree frond), 33–34, 188. *See also* Four Species; *arba'at haminim*

ma'abarot (transit camp for immigrants and refugees), 99, 164
Mann, Barbara, 6–7
Marom, Nathan, 52–53
Marrakesh, Morocco, 156

Marzel, Baruch, 70
Massad, Joseph, 75n2
Masuot Yitzhak, 152
material culture: folkloristic approach to the study of, 5, 12, 23n2, 110; Jewish, 18–19; and religion, 24n9, 25n17, 26n20; 209–210; of the sukkah, 19–20, 24n10, 32, 38–39, 44, 48n11, 112, 116, 117, 121, 134, 137, 153, 154, 161, 162, 169, 171, 184–186, 199, 205, 207, 211, 213, Appendix. *See also* belief; home; identity
materialism. *See* money
McCurdy, Patrick, 193
Mea Shearim (neighborhood in Jerusalem), 36
Mead, Margaret, 26n22
mellah (Jewish quarter in Morocco), 156
Memizrach Shemesh, 167, 177n6
memory: and diasporic experience, 6; and vernacular architecture, 37; of Shchunat Hatikva, 114, 135, 140, 144; of social inequality in Israel, 60–61, 75n2; of Sukkot in Canada, 39; of Sukkot in Shchunat Hatikva, 126, 138; of Sukkot in Morocco, 154, 157; of Sukkot in Persia, 123; of Sukkot in Crown Heights, 195–197, 202; of Sukkot in Ethiopia, 215–218; of house and home, 8, 214; and longing, 218; and tradition, 41, 171, 219
Meshumar: Mordechai, 124–139; Yoram, 111, 124–139, 150n12, 214, 218; Gila, 128, 134–135; Yonah, 128, 131–135
Midwestern United States, 5, 8, 15, 36–47. *See also* Bloomington
migration: and the concept of home, 6; Eritrean and Sudanese, 58–59, 65–74, 77n12, 77n14; into Shchunat Hatikva, 91, 114, 178; and Sukkot, 6, 8, 10, 34, 209, 213, 219
Miller, Daniel, 105n1, 220n1
Mintz, Jerome, R. 208n2
Mishnah, 18, 28–30, 147, 168–169. See also *Talmud*; *Gemara*
mitzvah (commandment), 32, 100, 107, 115–116, 123, 135, 191, 199, 204, 206–207
Mizrahim: and Sukkot customs, 35; and social inequality, 51, 182–184, 186, 194, 194n3, 211; and social history of Tel Aviv, 54, 65–66, 69, 72; cultural distinctiveness of, 59–65; and food, 59–65, 105, 76n8, 167; and folklore, 74n1, 75n2, 76n8; term for, 76n7; class struggle with Ashkenazim, 186–187, 194
modernity, 74n1, 76n8, 148, 150n8, 162, 165, 215–218

money: lack of, 2, 63–64, 96, 164, 189; and Sukkot observance, 32, 205; and food, 62, 63, 64; and community relations, 83, 93; and happiness, 96, 102, 136–137, 142–144, 162; and immigration, 121; and government, 102, 181. *See also* poverty
Moroccan (as Jewish identity associated with Morocco), 22, 35, 62, 102, 109, 153–166
Morocco, 16, 20, 51, 159, 164, 176n3, 210, 218
Moses (Biblical personage), 28, 34, 48n12, 117, 147, 179, 215
Moshe (Gan Hatikva protester), 185–186
Moyal: Shaul, 153–159, 168, 218, 210; Sivan, 153, 159–166, 168
Myerhoff, Barbara, 25n17, 26n22, 219

Netanyahu, Benjamin (Israeli Prime Minister), 59, 179
New Central Bus Station, 67
New York, 5, 8, 22, 24n9, 47n2, 54–55, 60, 192, 195–207, 212. *See also* Brooklyn
North Tel Aviv, 52–58, 63, 66, 78n17, 96, 101, 179, 182
nostalgia: and Shchunat Hatikva, 91, 142; and tradition, 218; and material culture, 218. *See also* food, tradition
Noyes, Dorothy, 74n1, 150n9

obedience: and God, 143; and the Torah, 150n11
Occupy Judaism, 192–193
Occupy Movement, 1, 4, 10, 192, 215. *See also* housing demonstrations, Israeli; protests, social
Occupy Sukkot, 192, 195
Occupy Wall Street, 192–193, 194n5, 195
Ochs, Vanessa, 25n17, 48n11
Other Israel, 56. *See also* Second Class; Second Israel; "Dear Ones"; *adonei haaretz*

Patai, Raphael, 26n22
Palestine, 29, 30, 60, 91, 149n5
parachot (ornamental curtains that cover the Holy Ark in a synagogue), 169–171, 177n7
Park, Robert E., 75n6
Passover, 25n15, 28, 134, 142, 190
performance: festival, 5; collective, 138, 150n9; social, 7, 12, 14, 18, 19, 144, 152, 212; Jewish ritual, 7, 10, 16, 18–19, 149n2, 175, 212, 214, 218; as an approach to folklore study, 10–14, 150n13; of self, 19, 26n21, 212

Peripheria Forum, 73, 178–194
Persia, 114, 120–121, 123, 149n3, 184, 213. *See also* Iran
Persian (as Jewish identity associated with Iran or Persia), 91, 149n3, 170. *See also* Iranian
Piekarski: Joseph, 195–198; Rabbi Ephraim, 203–207
pilgrimage, 27–29, 173, 181, 198. *See also* Desert, Sinai
Pocius, Gerald, 24n6, 24n9
poverty: and asylum seekers, 17, 69–71, 77n16; and South Tel Aviv-Jaffa, 54, 55, 64, 137, 144, 164, 185, 187, 218; and the notion of authenticity, 74n1; and Judaism, 100, 147–148; and immigration, 120–121, 157, 166, 170, 210–211; and happiness, 137, 148; and Sukkot, 189, 187. *See also* money
Preger, Mayer, 201–203
Primiano, Leonard, 8
Project Renewal, 54–58; 75n3
Promised Land, the, 3, 4, 7, 16, 18, 28, 49, 74, 174, 178, 180–181, 195, 211, 220
protests, social, 1–5, 9–10, 49, 59, 70–73, 166–167, 178–194, 215. *See also* housing demonstrations, Israeli
purity, 117, 147, 173, 207

Rada, Baruch and Meital, 215–218
Rafi (representative from Jesse Cohen), 179–180
Rambam, 20
Ranger, Terrance, 74n1
Rebbe: Yoseph Yitzchak Schneerson, 196, 198; Menachem Mendel, 20, 195, 196, 198–199, 203–204
refugee: Jewish, 77n15, 99, 164, 179, 183, 215; as the term relates to Eritrean and Sudanese migrants to Israel, 25n15, 68–69, 77n13, 77n16, 78n17, 78n18. *See also* asylum seekers
Rehovot (Israel), 152, 157, 164, 215–218
relativism (as related to Jewish expression), 139–149, 219
religion, vernacular, 8
ritual: and Sukkot, 3–6, 11, 43, 50, 107, 110, 136, 139, 143, 197, 210–219; and architecture, 6–7, 13–14, 23n1, 28–32, 123–124, 144, 160–161, 193, 197, 201, 209, 212–213; and space, 44, 104, 105n4, 111, 116, 118, 123, 128–132, 144, 173, 190; and performance, 33–36, 46, 130, 149n2, 175, 177n5, 202; and festival studies: 12, 14–18; theories of, 25n13, 25n17; and community,

22, 90, 133, 150n9; and women, 100–101; Jewish, 105n4, 131, 149n2, 166, 176n4; and sports, 87, 105n4; and material culture, 112, 118, 138, 142, 154, 158, 177n5, 188, 207; and politics, 179–194; Lubavitch Jewish, 202, 205–207
roof: and sukkah construction, 4, 8, 11, 14, 19–20, 25n12, 29, 31, 32, 39–40, 43, 108, 123, 126, 134–135, 139, 160, 182, 191, 199, 201, 205–207, 209, Appendix; and Sukkot decoration, 35, 38, 121, 153, 186; as site of social connection, 98, 101, 103, 104, 150n8, 160; and lighting, 117, 121, 145, 153, 199; and happiness, 137; and equality, 168, 173; and lack of housing, 182, 183. *See also schach*; Appendix
Romania, 60
Rosh Hashanah (Jewish New Year), 28, 43, 94–98, 142
Rotbard, Sharon, 53–54, 66
Rubenstein, Jeffrey L., 25n19, 31, 201
Russia, 8, 20, 63, 114, 196, 205

schach (roofing material for a sukkah): legal requirements of, 31–32, 117, 190, 207; construction of, 116; 139; symbolic meaning of, 160, 201; holiness of, 201, 204–205, 207. *See also* roof, Appendix
Schwarzer, Mitchell, 27, 28
Sciorra, Joseph, 24n6, 24n9
Second Class, 72, 187. *See also* Other Israel, Second Israel, Dear Ones, *adonei haaretz*
Second Israel, 55, 190. *See also* Other Israel, Second Class, Dear Ones, *adonei haaretz*
Sered, Susan, 100–101
Seven Species, 15
Western Wall, 15
Shabbat (Sabbath), 48n11, 76n10, 81, 85, 93, 96, 101–104, 134, 145, 156
Shabbos (Yiddish: Sabbath), 41. *See also* Shabbat
Shapira (neighborhood in South Tel Aviv), 73. *See also* Peripheria Forum
Shapiro, Maya, 65–66
Shas (Ultra-Orthodox religious political party in Israel), 26n23, 187
Shavuot, 28, 134
Shchunat Hatikva (Neighborhood of Hope): social history of, 16, 50–60, 114, 135, 218; and asylum seekers, 17, 65–74, 78n18; Sukkot in, 19–20, 107–149, 184–192; stigma associated with, 51, 55–56, 75n6; urban planning and,

52–53, 55–57; housing history of, 55–57, 178; and food, 60–65, 76n8; demographics of, 69, 106n8; community spaces of, 80–105; synagogues of, 88–90, 94–97; and notion of authenticity, 74n1; social protests in, 178–192. *See also* Beit Dani, Bnei Yehuda; Shuk Hatikva; *Hesed L'Avraham,* Simon's Restaurant; Haza, Ofra; Tasa, Dudu; Bosi, Dudu; Peripheria Forum

Shmuel (juice vendor), 81–82

Shohat, Ella, 75n1, 75n2, 76n8

Shulchan Aruch (compilation of Jewish law), 24n8, 107

Shuk Hatikva (outdoor market in Shchunat Hatikva), 58, 70, 79–83, 88, 104–105, 105n1, 109, 140

simhat beit ha-sho'eva (Water Drawing Ceremony), 33, 35–36, 139

Simon's Restaurant (in Shchunat Hatikva), 90–94

sitting *shiva* (mourning ritual), 130–133

sleep (as part of Sukkot observance), 20, 30, 115, 117, 123, 205

South Tel Aviv: social protests in, 1–3, 9, 178–194; religious expression in, 4, 26n23, 107–149; asylum seekers in, 16–18, 25n15, 59; urban and social history of, 49–74; social life of, 79–105. See also *Shchunat Hatikva*

Spanish "Indignant" Protest Movement, 9, 192

stigma: and the image of Shchunat Hatikva, 16, 51–58, 63, 194n3; and the social history of Mizrahim in Israel, 75n2, 76n8; sociological perspectives on, 75n4, 75n6

Stolow, Jeremy, 47n2

Stoeltje, Beverly, 14

Sudanese. *See* asylum seekers; migration; refugee

synagogue: in Bloomington, Indiana, 37, 39, 43, 48n9; in Shchunat Hatikva, 79, 88–105, 106n5, 106n7, 107, 109, 148, 186; as related to Sukkot observance, 33, 36, 112, 115–116, 169–171, 197

Syria, 16, 51, 164, 170

Syrian (as Jewish identity associated with Syria), 22, 35, 109, 152

Talmud, 9, 18–19, 28–29, 31–32, 36, 78n20, 116, 124, 145, 148, 151n14, 168–169, 197, 201, 213. See also *Mishnah; Gemara*

Tasa, Dudu, 194n3

Tel Aviv Municipal Archives, 60

Temple, Second, 15, 25n19, 27–28, 30, 32, 35, 115, 139, 151, 173, 181

Tobi, Simon, 91–95; 139

Torah (Hebrew Bible), 18–19, 27–30, 33–34, 81, 91, 93–94, 102, 104, 106n6, 115–116, 118, 124, 143, 147–148, 150n11, 163, 177n7, 186–189, 197, 206

tradition: a folkloristic approach to, 10–12, 47n1, 110, 124, 149n1; and Sukkot, 5, 16, 31, 110, 152, 160, 165, 209–220; and building, 23n5, 26n20; and Jewish holy texts, 27–31; and identity, 38–43, 46–47, 47n4; and food, 61, 64, 149n6; and Jewish women, 100; and the notion of authenticity, 74n1; and the folklore of Mizrahi Jews in Israel, 76n8; and politics, 190–191–194; and nostalgia, 218. *See also* belief; memory

transcendence (Lubavitch Jewish thought), 136, 204–205

Turner, Kay, 42, 45, 212–213

Turner, Victor, 15, 25n13

tzadik (righteous person), 147

tzedek chevrati (social justice), 192

UN Refugee Convention, 69

UNESCO, 54, 74n1

Upton, Dell, 24n10

ushpizin (male Biblical guests who are invited into the sukkah each night of Sukkot), 33–35, 117–118, 124, 136, 173, 180, 198

ushpizot (female Biblical guests who are invited into the sukkah each night of Sukkot), 35, 45–46

Uzbekistan, 15, 16, 51, 63. *See also* Bukharan.

value, economic, 137–138, 142–144, 148, 150n13, 152, 193, 207, 210, 212. *See also* money; poverty; relativism

Van Gennep, Arnold, 25n13

Vlach, John Michael, 24n9, 25n10

wealth. *See* money; poverty

Westmacott, Richard Noble, 24n11

White City (UNESCO designation for Tel Aviv), 54

Williams, Michael Ann, 24n6, 24n9, 24n11, 214

work: daily schedules, in Shchunat Hatikva, 76n10, 101; and community, 96–97, 129, 215–216; and women, 100, 150n10; and Judaism, 116, 186–187; and immigration, 121, 156–157,

170; and sukkah construction, 123, 126, 135, 150n10; the value of, 137–138, 142–144, 149. *See also* labor; value, economic

workers, foreign, in Israel: 66–69, 77n12, 77n14

World Wide Lubavitch Communication Center, 198

Yaakov (protester in Gan Hatikva), 185–186
Yaffa, 62–63
Yehoshua, Drori, 166–176, 211–212, 219–220
Yemen, 16, 20, 31, 51, 60, 91, 125, 129
Yemenite (as Jewish identity associated with Yemen), 19–20, 22, 61–62, 64, 73, 76n9, 83, 90–93, 96, 99–102, 105n2, 106n8, 109, 111, 138–139, 176n2, 190, 194n3
Yom Kippur (Day of Atonement), 12, 28, 87, 96, 107, 134, 180, 184, 198
Yom Kipper War, 170, 187

Zada: Uriel, 111–118, 150n12; David and Edna, 114, 118–124, 184, 213
Zohar, 34. See also *Kabbalah*

GABRIELLE ANNA BERLINGER is Assistant Professor of American Studies and Folklore and the Babette S. and Bernard J. Tanenbaum Fellow in Jewish History and Culture at the University of North Carolina at Chapel Hill.